BUSINESS SKILLS
for *creative souls*

THE
ESSENTIAL ARTIST'S HANDBOOK

Tips, Strategies and **Resources** for
Fashion Designers
Filmmakers
Musicians
New Media Artists
Performers
Photographers
Visual Artists
Writers

BUSINESS SKILLS
for creative souls

THE
ESSENTIAL ARTIST'S HANDBOOK

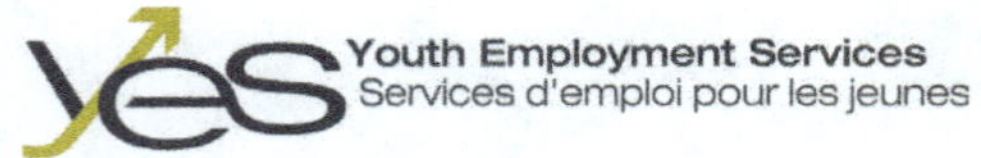

As a not-for-profit organization, YES (Youth Employment Services) enriches the community by providing English-language support services to help Quebecers find employment and start and grow businesses. It offers a broad range of employment-related programs, including an Entrepreneurship Program for those looking to start or grow their own business and an Artists' Program, which is designed to help artists find work or create their own employment opportunities.

YES (Youth Employment Services)
666 Sherbrooke St. West, Suite 700
Montreal, QC H3A 1E7

Tel.: 514-878-9788
Fax: 514-878-9950

www.yesmontreal.ca
info@yesmontreal.ca

BUSINESS SKILLS

for creative souls

THE
ESSENTIAL ARTIST'S HANDBOOK

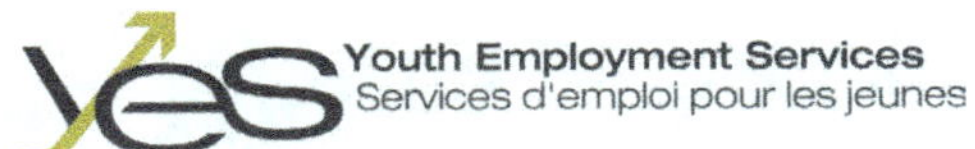

Business Skills for Creative Souls
The Essential Artist's Handbook

Published by YES (Youth Employment Services)
666 Sherbrooke St. West, Suite 700
Montreal, QC H3A 1E7
Telephone: 514-878-9788
E-mail: info@yesmontreal.ca

Business Skills for Creative Souls: The Essential Artist's Handbook seeks to assist artists by providing information which may help them establish their artistic careers and businesses. The opinions contained herein are those of the individuals expressing them only and consequently, neither the contributors nor YES (Youth Employment Services) shall be held liable for any error therein or damages resulting from the use or transmission of said information.

Library and Archives Canada Cataloguing in Publication

Business skills for creative souls : the essential artist's handbook
/ YES. -- Updated edition.

Includes bibliographical references.
Issued in print and electronic formats.
ISBN 978-0-9681946-4-5 (pbk.).--ISBN 978-0-9681946-5-2 (epub)

1. Art--Vocational guidance--Québec (Province). 2. Art--Québec
(Province)--Marketing. 3. Art--Economic aspects--Québec (Province).
4. Artists--Québec (Province)--Montréal--Interviews. I. YES Montréal,
author, issuing body

N8353.B88 2015   706.8   C2015-901816-1
                                                 C2015-901817-X

Printed in Canada.
Book design and typesetting by YES (Youth Employment Services)

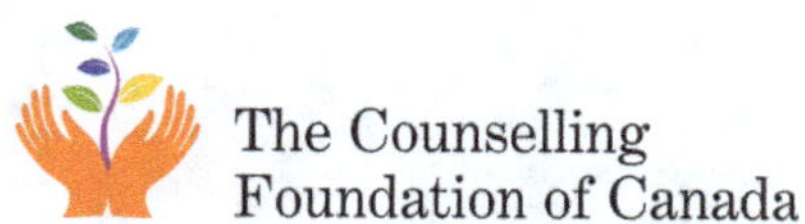

YES acknowledges the generous support of The Counselling Foundation of Canada in the production of this book.

TABLE OF CONTENTS

Being an artist is one thing. Supporting yourself through your art is quite another. Helping close the gap between the two is what the YES Artists' Program is all about. For more than fifteen years, the program has been working with artists to help them understand and apply business principles in working towards financial sustainability.

Our programming for artists includes specialized workshops, one-on-one coaching as well as group artists' and business coaching, mentorship services, a yearly art expo and sale, and our annual Business Skills for Creative Souls Artists' Conference, which has become a signature event for artists in and around Montreal since it was initiated in 2000.

This handbook is yet another important component of our extensive range of services and support for artists, arts-entrepreneurs, and creative professionals.

Business Skills for Creative Souls: The Essential Artist's Handbook, first published in 2004 and revised in 2015, is brimming with practical, down-to-earth information for emerging and established artists alike, covering a variety of topics from how to apply for grants and market your work, to accounting and legal considerations.

The advice and tips found here come from working business people, visual and performing artists, designers, photographers, and other individuals who have built success and know what it takes to make it in the arts.

The arts and creativity are recognized pillars of the Montreal and Quebec economy. Our creative industries depend on the ability of artists to make their living here and contribute to what is one of the world's most creative cities, as exemplified by the international performing arts industry located here, our thriving music, film, design, and gaming industries, and many more.

I invite you to make this book a prominent part of your library, whether as a printed book, or e-book. And I urge you to use it well!

Sincerely,
John Aylen
President of the Board of Directors
YES (Youth Employment Services)

As one who was, and as one who did, Apple's Steve Jobs once famously said that "Real Artists Ship."

With all due respect, let me point out that he missed a step.

A valuable one.

Because before Real Artists Ship, Real Artists Sell.

Many self-professed "real" artists may have gagged a bit reading the previous sentence, as authenticity in the space once meant a Berlin Wall-like separation of Church and State between art and "the art of the deal."

No more.

Selling is not about the cash, it's about the distribution. For without being sold, art is merely the silent tree falling in the forest. Art is only fully completed when seen outside the solitary confines of an artist's studio or desk.

Art becomes art through others' eyes and/or ears and/or fingers. Art comes alive in homes, galleries, museums, or concert halls; on brick walls, T-shirts, billboards, or biceps; on iPods, stages, books, or computer screens.

To get there, art needs to be sold. And ultimately, the job falls on the artist. He may not be everyone's cup of tea, but the late Steve Kaufman—a disciple and former Factory assistant of Andy Warhol—was an artist who understood, and mastered, the job of selling. At every one of his exhibitions, it was as if Santa Claus had come to town. A giant of a man, he'd parade about in an unmissable, custom-painted jacket, hands adorned by thick, glittering rings. He'd insist that parents bring their kids with them to galleries and made sure that each would go home with an original, signed 8" x 8" Kaufman canvas. And if their parents actually bought something, they would get surprise gifts ranging from hand-painted Coke bottles to guitars, all built into the purchase price, of course.

Ahh, Warhol, Kaufman's mentor, would've been proud, as he himself said: "Making money is art and working is art and good business is the best art."

And that said, welcome to this book, no matter what type of artist you may be. Yes, consider this guide a tool box, where timeless business basics are supplemented with today's timely cutting-edge equipment like Facebook, Twitter, Instagram, Pinterest, Etsy, YouTube, and all things digital.

But tools unto themselves are worthless. A hammer can bluntly crush a skull, or deftly ping the finish of a brass sculpture. It's how you use tools that counts. So if you want to make this book count, I urge you to use it to create.

But not to create art. That you already know how to do.

No, I urge you to create something way more important to an artist.

Use this book to create demand.

Andy Nulman is an avid art collector, a successful tech entrepreneur, and yes, that guy from Just For Laughs.

BOOK ADVISORY COMMITTEE

Dave Cool
Jeanette Kelly
Victoria LeBlanc
Monika Majewski
Guy Rodgers
Linda Rutenberg
Clare Schapiro
Lori Schubert
Ezra Soiferman
Iris Unger

PRODUCTION TEAM

Head Writer, Editor, and Interviewer
Liz Ulin

Writer (2004 Edition)
Caralee Salomon

Copy Editor
May Antaki

Director, Creative Design, and Digital Production
Catherine Brisindi

Graphic Design and Typesetting
Marc Wrobel

Yes would like to express its gratitude to the many people who have given generously of their time and expertise to help make this book and the original edition possible. They agreed to be interviewed or provided articles that inspired elements of this book.

CONTRIBUTORS

Ev Adad
Norma Andreu
Tony Asimakopoulos
Mila Aung-Thwin
John Aylen
Amy Blackmore
Misstress Barbara Bonfiglio
Patricia Chica
Karen Cho
Nancy Cleman
Chuck Comeau
Dave Cool
Simon Dardick
Nathalie Dion
Joey Elias
Bettina Forget
Steve Galluccio
Jennifer Gasoi
Manika Gaudet
Holly Gauthier-Frankel
Tali Goldstein
Adad Hannah
Mitch Joel
Elaine Kalman Naves
Morgan Kennedy
Andrea Kenyon
Lorraine Klaasen
Sam Lackman

Tristan D. Lalla
Roger Lemoyne
Paul Litherland
G. Scott MacLeod
Anissa Marcanio
Monika Majewski
Marisa Minicucci
Susan Molnar
Katie Moore
Elise Moser
Marcel Mueller
Jill Murray
Andy Nulman
Heather O'Neill
Monique Polak
Hilary Radley
Rommel Romero
Linda Rutenberg
Sugar Sammy
Damian Siqueiros
Ezra Soiferman
Rachel Stephan
Jacob Tierney
Kevin Tierney
David Usher
Kerry Williams
Nikki Yanofsky

SPECIAL THANKS TO:

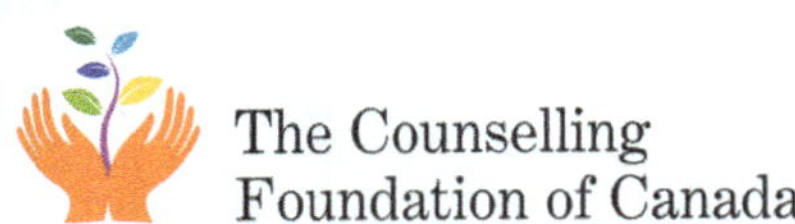

The Counselling
Foundation of Canada

We have attempted to acknowledge all those involved and regret any accidental omissions.

YES STAFF

Iris Unger, Executive Director, YES
Fernanda Amaro
Elizabeth Araujo
Catherine Brisindi
Leann Brown
Mario Clarke
Dana Cotnareanu
Ellen Englert
Alexander Gordon
Nadja Grabovari
Sherry Hollinger
Coby Ingham

Annalise Iten
Daniel Légaré
Monika Majewski
Maria Pereira
Jamie Robinson
Gerald Silverberg
Augusto Sotelo
Robert Therriault
Anna Viegas
Kelsey White
Marc Wrobel
Stephanie Zacharkiw

ADVISORY COUNCIL

Lionel Blanshay
Rob Braide
Scott Conrod
Charles B. Crawford
Peter R. Johnson
Guy Laframboise
Timothy Leyne

Peter McAuslan
Andy Nulman
Philip O'Brien
Hilary Radley
Herschel Segal
Robert Walsh

LESSONS FROM A CAREER COUNSELLOR

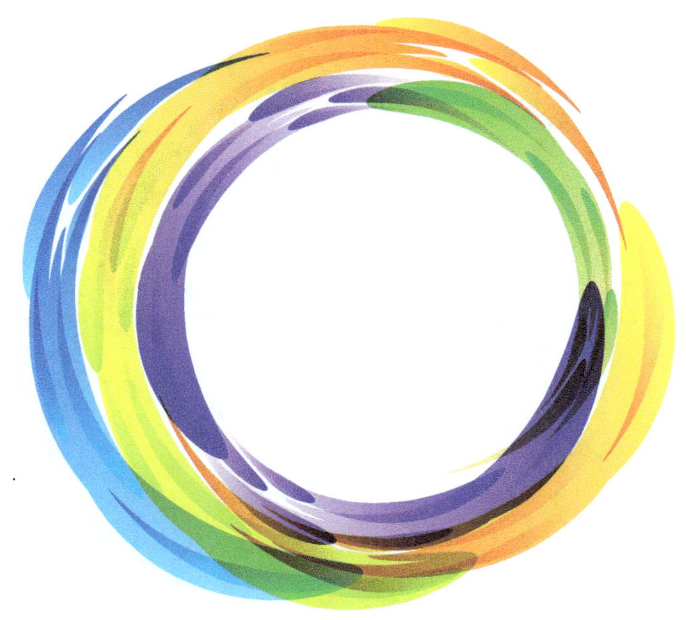

By Susan Molnar, past Career Counsellor at YES

It needs to be said from the beginning: being an artist isn't like being an accountant or an auto mechanic or even a CEO; those are professions. Auto mechanics may love nothing better than the feel of stripping down an engine and accountants may sometimes dream in Excel spreadsheets, but artists are called to a way of life.

However, art is also a job, and it's entirely possible to earn a living creating the art you love as long as you are willing to be both an artist and a businessperson.

ART IS SUBJECTIVE

A good accountant saves you money at tax time and a bad accountant gets you audited. Unfortunately, artists have no such benchmarks. Subjectivity leads to doubt and thoughts like: "Am I a good artist? Is my art worthwhile? Will the critics love me or hate me?" On top of this aesthetic stress, artists must also contend with the instability and insecurity that comes with the self-employed lifestyle. Their career choices are often not validated by parents, peers, and guidance counsellors. Moreover, artists are often poorly remunerated by employers and freelance clients. As a result, many artists approach the nuts and bolts, selling, and invoicing sides of their careers half-heartedly: they give it a shot and hope for the best.

However, it takes a lot more than a shot to make in the arts; it takes a lifetime of dedication and passion. Becoming a professional artist is not for the fainthearted.

THE FLIP SIDE OF FREEDOM

Freedom may be a blessing or a curse. On the one hand, you need to think unconventionally in order to create something out of the ordinary; being a free thinker is vital to your craft. But what happens if a client wants to limit your freedom and self-expression by imposing deadlines and requesting content changes? What will you do then?

Perhaps one of the most appealing aspects of self-employment is being your own boss and single-handedly making decisions about every aspect of your business: product design, marketing and distribution strategy, which clients to approach, what time to start and finish your day, what your office space will look like. Great! So far so good!

The flip side of not having a boss is that you need to be the boss. You need to impose structure on yourself, create a plan, and follow through with it. Self-discipline is at the heart of any successful venture, because if you don't do it, it won't get done. If you don't follow through, chances are you won't be able to make a living from your artistic endeavours.

BEING CREATIVE ISN'T ENOUGH

Before you give up your day job, you need to figure out if you have what it takes to support yourself financially with your art. If talent was the primary predictor of success, you wouldn't need this book. We've all heard of extremely talented artists who were unable to turn their talent into cash.

Being creative is not enough. You need to know how to price, market, and sell your work, negotiate contracts, finance your project, keep track of your expenses, and learn how to protect your legal rights. Unfortunately, most schools' arts programs generally do a very poor job of preparing writers, illustrators, actors, sculptors, musicians, and other creators for the hard-boiled realities of making a living as an artist.

It can't be repeated enough: a career in the arts takes more than talent, it takes business know-how. But fear not! Those skills can be learned just like a piano concerto or a pirouette. Are you up for the challenge?

WELCOME TO THE REAL WORLD

This handbook is designed to address the challenges emerging artists face as they enter the work world. It is our hope that as you read the sections about marketing, business basics, accounting, and law, you will be in a better position to decide where you want to take your artistic aptitude.

We have also gathered nuggets of wisdom from professional working artists that they learned over many decades of living the struggle you now face. If success is possible for them, it is possible for you. Make them proud; stake your claim to fame and fortune.

Susan Molnar was a Career Counsellor at YES from 1998 to 2004, and developed the "Business Skills for Creative Souls" program in 2000 to equip artists for self-employment. She currently provides career advice to PhD's at McGill's Career Planning Service.

HAVING A GAME PLAN – THE NUTS AND BOLTS

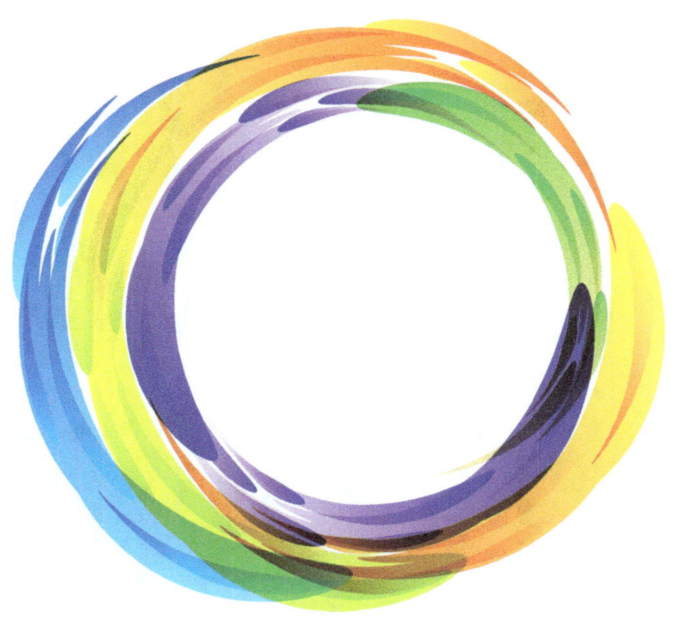

By Monika Majewski, Artists' Program Coordinator and Coach at YES

Every artist—no matter their creative discipline—can improve their chances of success by understanding the fundamental building blocks that underpin all flourishing careers in arts and culture. These nuts and bolts, taken together, cover most of the important things to consider in growing a creative practice. Moreover, bringing these components together and mapping them into a cohesive action plan will give you the added advantage of being organized and purposeful right from the start. So let's talk nuts and bolts.

TALENT AND VISION

It all starts and ends with talent, the most fundamental of an artist's many gifts. Yet even brilliant natural talent must be cultivated and given focus over time if it is to bear fruit. Most artists hone their craft by maintaining an active production of new work and through ongoing learning. However, in order to develop a consistent creative identity, artists must also be clear about their values and motivations, and must learn to translate them into a cohesive artistic vision. It's important to note that vision is not a "static" thing; as you evolve personally and professionally, so will your creative vision and the products or services you create.

CLEAR GOALS AND OBJECTIVES

As you learn to turn your talent into a body of work, it will be critical to develop a set of thoughtful long-term goals. For example, most artists hope to earn their living through their art or have an extensive fan base. Such goals represent what you would like to achieve, but these achievements will not happen overnight. They'll require many steps along the way. This is why a more concrete set of short- and medium-term goals or an action plan will be needed as you build up your creative practice. A sample action plan is provided at the end of this section.

Questions you may wish to ask yourself when developing your own set of goals and objectives are:

> What kind of work would you like to produce and be known for?

> How would you like to earn your living or monetize your work?

> How can you show and sell your work in the marketplace?

> How will you garner and maintain visibility?

> What kind of industry recognition do you want, if any?

> How will you cultivate and expand your fan base and/or professional networks?

QUALITY PRODUCT/SERVICE

In order to be even modestly successful in today's fast-moving cultural marketplace, most artists need to maintain a prolific production of new work. Not only that, but it must be their best work, which means constantly improving and refining. To be authentic, this body of work must reflect the artist's vision. And to be commercially viable, it must also find its niche in the marketplace.

Ideally, your work should be available in a range of formats and price points. If part of your practice involves offering services (like teaching or contract work), it is important that the offer of service be clearly stated and appropriately priced. Keep in mind that the marketplace is bursting with a great many offerings. How can your work stand out from the rest? Research and observe your peers to learn from their successes and failures. This can help you map your own path to be competitive in your creative milieu.

COHESIVE BRAND

An artist's brand is an ephemeral combination of the artist, the art, and the value they bring to the marketplace. In order to be successful a brand must embody and deliver a product, service, or experience that is desirable. In today's oversaturated marketplace, it is more important than ever for professional artists to capitalize on their brand power. Generally, in order to garner attention, a brand must deliver value, uniqueness, and innovation. And in order to maintain customer loyalty it must deliver consistently over time. No easy feat.

Examples of successful Quebec creative brands include: Arcade Fire, Cirque du Soleil, Margie Gillis, Moment Factory, POP Montreal, Rawi Hage, Patrick Watson, Steve Galluccio—and many, many more.

In presenting your brand to the world, it is important that you develop a "visual identity" that clearly reflects your brand, and integrate this aesthetic into all promotional materials and communications.

SKILLS, KNOWLEDGE, AND INFORMATION

In order to make your way as an artist you will need to develop skills and knowledge in many different areas. This means that you will need to embark on a life-long learning process. Luckily, we live in the "information age," which means that learning has never been easier.

But first, you must determine just what it is you need to know in order to succeed. A few examples are:

> Your craft (creative and technical, trends, new technologies).

> Your industry (norms, best practices, how to present your work, key decision makers, resources).

> Marketing and promotion (target market, pricing, distribution, visibility strategies).

> Branding (cohesiveness, brand loyalty).

> Communications and public relations (media contacts, audience development).

> Pitching and selling (writing proposals, cold-calling, presenting).

> Good governance (operations, finances, legalities).

TIME

Time is a precious commodity for everyone, and since artists must often take care of all aspects of their career—especially in the early days—it is all the more important for them to use their time wisely. You must be clear about your priorities each day, week, and month. Some find it helpful to work with a daily or weekly to-do list, while others employ a time-blocking system, mapping their week into chunks to prioritize areas like creation/production, marketing/promotion, administration, research, and communications. But keep in mind that any system will work better if you develop good time management habits in your day-to-day life. Consider employing the following strategies:

> Make time to work on a number of priorities in tandem (focusing on one at a time sequentially).

> Don't let tasks and projects linger unattended. Chip away at them several times a week—momentum is key.

> Use time-saving tools like electronic agendas, contact and task lists, reusable templates, and reminder systems.

> Practise good records management!

SPACE

Having access to functional, conveniently located, and affordable workspace is very important. To make the most of your resources, try to create a workspace that can serve a number of purposes (e.g. office, atelier, event space, meeting room, etc.). Try to maximize your productive time by eliminating the need for long commutes. If your financial means are limited, maximize your resources by sharing your workspace or combining your living and working space in some way. Take the time to make your workspace appealing. Keep it clean and tidy, maintaining and upgrading along the way.

VISIBILITY

Many artists don't devote enough time and energy to becoming "visible" and as a result have a hard time gaining momentum. Visibility, simply put, means that people know about you and have ample access to your work on a consistent basis. In order for your promotion to be effective, you need to have an up-to-date promotional tool kit, which should include most of the following items:

> Business cards

> Promotional flyers, brochures, posters

> Artist or company mission statement and bio

> Professional CV

> Quality work samples

> Web presence (website or online portfolio/portal/store)

> Social media presence (Facebook, Pinterest, Twitter, LinkedIn, etc.)

> Newsletter

> Press kit

> Media list

> Contact list

All promotional materials and platforms should be nicely designed, well written, informative, and user friendly. But these items in and of themselves do not make for visibility. They are simply tools to help you spread the news about your work. There's much more on visibility in the "Creating a Buzz" chapter of this book and within each artist section.

CREDIBILITY

Credibility is that ephemeral thing that tells the world you are trustworthy, experienced, and respected by others. It means you have "paid your dues" and are worthy of attention. In an artist's context, credibility can be built through a variety of ways, including but not limited to:

> Producing great work consistently.

> Participating in industry showcases, festivals, exhibitions, and publications.

> Collaborating with interesting artists or organizations.

> Selling your work (including digital downloads).

> Getting media attention, coverage, or critiques.

> Winning awards, residencies, and grants.

> Having an extensive following/fan base.

> Having a dynamic promotional presence and traffic to your web platforms.

> Participating in industry events, conferences and workshops.

> Volunteering in your industry or in the philanthropic sector.

> Cultivating strong and mutually beneficial relationships over time.

PEOPLE

No person is an island; we all need people to help us build success. In fact most successful people I've met have vast professional networks that they cultivate and maintain. And although many creative people may be introverts, this should not preclude developing skills in this area. It's about "playing the long game." Meeting lots of people is one thing, but cultivating friendly professional relationships takes time. Here you will find some of my best practices for building up your networks:

> Identify the types of people, organizations, and allies you will need in your professional life. Some excellent examples are fans, funders, media personnel, curators, booking agents, mentors, experts in your field, etc.

> Target these stakeholders by determining how you can reach them in person or via social media.

> Join professional associations and groups where you will meet the peers, mentors, and decision makers who can help you access opportunities.

> Make time in your life on a regular basis for strategic networking and follow-up activities.

> Take time to cultivate relationships. This means keeping in touch, following up, sharing, inviting, "liking" or "re-posting" social media content.

> Build a contact list as you go and develop an organised system for accessing certain types of contacts when needed.

Keep in mind that the people and organizations in your network may or may not be able to help you exactly when you need it. Cultivating a network is a delicate long-term project and will yield results when managed with due respect and patience. Try to base your approach on the "you reap what you sow" principle. Keep on giving and cultivating and you'll get what you need.

MONEY

Last, but certainly not least, on our list of nuts and bolts is money. We all need money to get by in our lives—that much is obvious—but what is less obvious is how to generate enough of it consistently to become financially sustainable as an artist. And while it is possible for artists to support themselves financially through their art, it will require a great deal of work and may take more time than you'd like. In my experience, most artists earning their living through their craft tend to do so by diversifying the number of ways their work can generate revenues. Limiting yourself to one sole revenue source is risky business.

One of your first steps should be to develop a financial plan to help you understand just how much money you will need annually to cover your overhead and live the lifestyle you want. Identify how much product and/or service you will need to sell to reach this target. Does it make sense?

Be honest with yourself. If your practice can't support you (especially in the beginning), you will need to develop other sources of income while you build up your creative practice. This may involve working part-time for someone else until you are established enough to go it alone. If this is the case, try to find work in and around your industry, ideally in a context that will allow you to learn more about doing business in your field.

Here are a few ways you might consider monetizing your work or services to help make ends meet:

> Artists' fees (for shows, appearances, and/or services)

> Business/start-up loans

> Commissioned work

> Crowdfunding

> Donations/in-kind donations

> Grants

> Licensing

> Part-time work

> Professional services or contracts

> Royalties

> Sales of your product

> Sponsorships

> Teaching

And don't forget to keep good track of your money along the way. All revenues and expenses should have some sort of associated documentation, such as receipts or invoices. Ideally, to make life easier for yourself at tax time, keep an organised filing system. Many business-savvy artists keep an active spreadsheet or simple accounting system going year-round and track revenues and expenditures "live" as they go. This is a very healthy practice that allows you to have a clear snapshot of your finances at any time, but don't fret if you're not quite there yet. The most important thing is to be able to substantiate your revenues and expenses at tax time, as this can have an enormous impact on your income tax balance.

ACTION PLAN

Now that you're familiar with the nuts and bolts of a healthy creative practice, let's put them together into an action plan. Do bear in mind that in some cases—especially if you are starting a business and are hoping to obtain start-up funding—you will need a more sophisticated planning document, namely a business plan (and our business coaches at YES can certainly help you with that). But for most artists an action plan is just the ticket.

An action plan is your very own set of steps to help you turn your goals into tangible and achievable actions that you can chip away at throughout your career. Here is a sample action plan that you can use to help build your own, personalized one:

Step 1: Identify your long-term goals:

> Earn a living as a visual artist

> Have an extensive body of work

> Show my work on an international scale

> Receive industry recognition and awards

> Gain media attention and critiques

> Create a large professional network

> Develop a loyal fan/client base

Step 2: Flesh out your long-term goals into action-oriented tasks:

Earn a living as a visual artist

> Ideal Cash-Flow:

> Sales of artwork: online, galleries, directly to clients, etc.

> Artist fees

> Licensing images to corporate sector

> Artistic grants

> Teaching

> Back-Up Cash-Flow:

> Part-time studio assistant and/or admin work

Have an extensive body of work

> Produce work on a regular basis

> Spend more time in studio; regular/frequent intervals

> Research and development—inspiration, trends, techniques (web, reading, shows, etc.)

Show my work on an international scale

> Prolific submitting for exhibitions, grants, residency, contests, etc.

> Direct outreach to galleries and curators

> Keep up-to-date promotional tool kit

> Have well-written project pitches and proposals

> Research and development—who, what, when, how (industry organizations and other stakeholders, portals, mailing lists, etc.)

Receive industry recognition and awards

> Industry presence

> In-person attendance at events; networking

> Memberships and participation

> Volunteer in organizations

> Get on mailing lists and join groups

> Volunteer on juries

> Be active/engage in social media

Gain media attention and critiques

> Keep up-to-date promotional tool kit and press kit

> Research and compile comprehensive media list

> Write well-written and compelling press releases

> Develop media outreach campaigns

Create a large professional network

> Have well-catalogued contact list

> Cultivate relationships over time

Develop a loyal fan/client base

> Keep up-to-date promotional tool kit

> Have well-catalogued contact list

> Use strategic promotional outreach via social media, in person, by email, etc.

Step 3: Go for it! Work hard and work smart:

Do keep in mind that in order to be truly effective, any plan needs to be actualized through purposeful and consistent action—that is why it is called an action plan. Progress tends to multiply exponentially with continued effort. Slowing down is okay but stopping and starting is not recommended. Momentum is the name of the game here, so keep that in mind as you work towards your goals. Will it be easy? Probably not. Can you do it? I say YES!

Monika Majewski is the YES Artists' Program Coordinator and Coach.

TAKING STOCK – SELF-ASSESSMENT EXERCISE

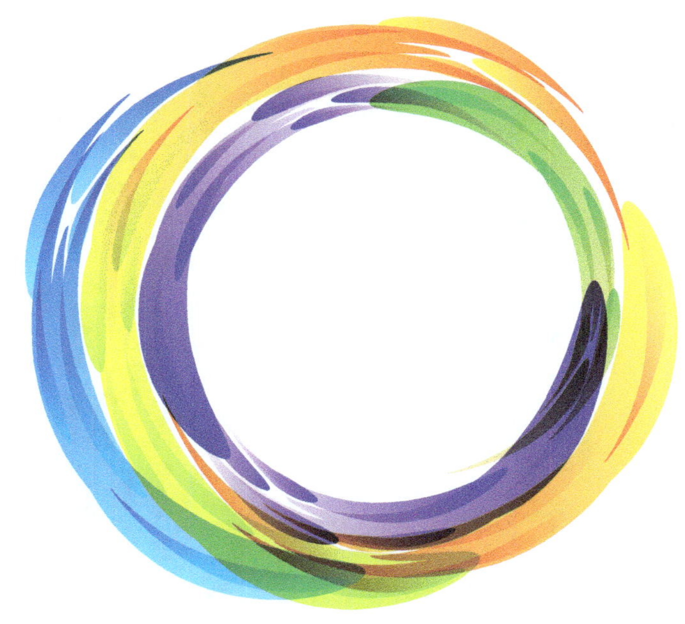

It is obvious that you are passionate about your art; why else would you have chosen an artistic career considering some of the drawbacks everyone keeps reminding you of? This is an excellent start because your career choice is based on doing what you love.

Next, you'll need to figure out if you are willing to turn your passion into a commercial endeavour. Do you want to express yourself to please yourself or your clients? Can you conceive of doing both? Are you willing to spend a sizable portion of your time promoting your work? Are you comfortable with the idea that you will have to collect and organize receipts, count pennies, and stick to budgets?

It is a challenge for many artists to get comfortable with the concept of the bottom line. Before you become a self-employed artist, you need to carefully consider your relationship with money. If you see it as the "root of all evil," odds are you won't succeed at making a profit. If you have an inherent difficulty with the notion of becoming a capitalist and you equate it with being a con-artist, your business venture probably won't succeed.

Be honest with yourself as you complete the following self-assessment exercise to see if you are ready to be a full-time self-employed artist. Perhaps working for someone else is better suited to your personality. You can always operate your self-employment activity part-time and still claim your expenses. And if you want no part of the business side of being an artist, there is always creating art for its own sake, and pleasing yourself.

ARTISTIC BUSINESS START-UP QUIZ

Are you ready for self-employment? Take this quiz to find out! Answer the questions honestly, and then add your totals. To get the most accurate assessment, first rate yourself, then have someone who knows you well rate you, and compare.

1. You want to control how much money you make, i.e. the harder you work, the more you make.
   ☐ Yes   ☐ No

2. You want independence, to be your own boss, and to have no one to answer to but yourself and your customers.
   ☐ Yes   ☐ No

3. You want to have flexible working hours, i.e. you don't mind working day and night or weekends, as long as you are the one who chooses to do so.
   ☐ Yes   ☐ No

4. You are good at making decisions.
☐ Yes   ☐ No

5. You are willing to volunteer for exposure and to build contacts.
☐ Yes   ☐ No

6. You are confident in selling and promoting yourself and your art.
☐ Yes   ☐ No

7. Are you the type of person who is always finding or creating opportunities?

☐ Yes   ☐ No

8. When you have a good idea or notice an opportunity, do you do something about it
—that is, do you seize opportunities?
☐ Yes   ☐ No

9. Do you like change and look forward to it?
☐ Yes   ☐ No

10. Do you like to constantly improve things?
☐ Yes   ☐ No

11. Do you have expertise, a skill, a product, or a service that is worth buying on the
competitive market?
☐ Yes   ☐ No

12. Have you ever worked in a business like the one you want to start? Do you have
previous experience in this industry?
☐ Yes   ☐ No

13. Do you have a base of contacts and potential future clients who might require your
services or products? (Enough to keep your business afloat in year one?)
☐ Yes   ☐ No

14. Do you have trustworthy contacts in the legal and accounting professions to assist you?
☐ Yes   ☐ No

15. Do you enjoy contract-chasing, selling, negotiating, wheeling and dealing?
☐ Yes   ☐ No

16. Do you have savings or someone to financially support you through the rough spots —for at least the first six months in business?

☐ Yes   ☐ No

17. Do you have the moral support of your family or significant other?

☐ Yes   ☐ No

18. Are you in good physical health?

☐ Yes   ☐ No

19. Are you emotionally strong and resilient? Are you able to stay enthusiastic even when the going gets tough?

☐ Yes   ☐ No

20. Are you willing and/or able to give up many hours of your personal life to ensure the smooth running of your business?

☐ Yes   ☐ No

21. Do you like to work alone most of the time? Are you self-reliant?

☐ Yes   ☐ No

22. Are you organized enough to manage your tasks and prioritize your time? (Remember, no one is watching!)

☐ Yes   ☐ No

23. Are you disciplined? Do you finish what you start?

☐ Yes   ☐ No

24. Are you willing to adapt your work to suit your clients' wishes/needs?

☐ Yes   ☐ No

25. Can you live without the certainty of a regular paycheck?

☐ Yes   ☐ No

SCORING SYSTEM

Score four points for every "YES" and zero points for every "NO." Add up the totals, and read on to see which of the following categories pertains to you based on your score: 0–49, 50–69, 70–84, or 85–100.

ARTISTIC BUSINESS START-UP QUIZ RESULTS

0–49: It doesn't sound like you are cut out to work on your own at this point in your life. You might be better off working for someone else for now. You can always reconsider this when circumstances are more favourable. Please refer to the Lessons from a Career Counsellor section of this book to help you get started.

50–69: You seem to be lacking some of the qualities, attitudes, or proper support. Don't get discouraged. With some work, skill development, or a partner who complements your skills you can still do it.

70–84: You are capable of making a business succeed. You might want to speak to several people (i.e. counsellors or coaches) and review some of the issues raised in the questionnaire—especially where you answered "NO"—before you begin the process of going out on your own.

85–100: Go for it! You will most likely be successful in business. It sounds like you've got the basic attitudes and characteristics required for successful beginnings and long-term survival.

Quiz created by Peter Johnson and Johanne Larouche, revised by Susan Molnar. © 2004 and 2015. All rights reserved.

DEVELOPING A JOB SEARCH STRATEGY

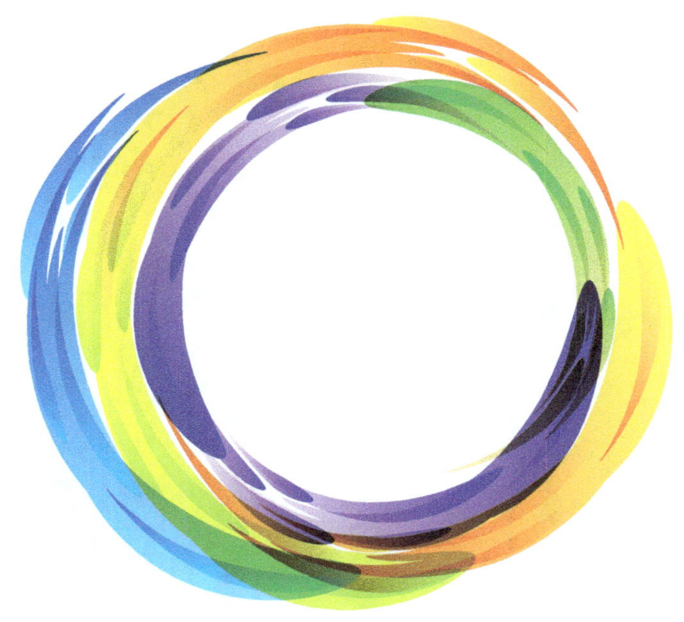

The financial instability and contract-based nature of self-employment in the arts leaves many wondering how to balance career security with their creative pursuits. If your creative practice or business is not currently or in the near future likely to yield you at least a basic living, you may need to consider finding a "pay the bills job" or other part-time employment to finance your living expenses. This can take the pressure off, help you feel financially "safe," and hopefully still leave you with adequate time to build up your creative practice along the way on a part-time basis.

Artists often have multiple income streams, not all of them in the arts. As an artist, you may prefer to find work in the cultural sector, but depending on your financial constraints, you may not have the time it takes to land that perfect job with your ideal "Work Tribe." Many artists support their career by working at jobs unrelated to their fields. When you are just getting started as a professional artist, sometimes this reality is unavoidable.

If you find yourself accepting work outside your field, never lose sight of your long-term goals and your true identity: you are a writer working as an administrative assistant or a painter working as childcare worker. Do your job well, but never let yourself forget that your art is your number one priority.

If you decide to accept an offer outside your field, remember that any job can be injected with your creativity. Think of ways you can contribute to the organization once you master the task at hand. Make your mark, add value to the position, and make it something better than it was before it found you. Propose to revamp their forms if you are graphically inclined for example. This is one way to honour your creative spirit and find satisfaction and meaning in your work. People will value your initiative, especially when it makes the workplace a more positive, productive environment. Most importantly, you will enjoy the time you spend there and possibly create a position you will genuinely love.

FINDING YOUR WORK TRIBE

If you've looked for work the last few years, you've probably discovered that many job openings are advertised through social media or online job boards, but the truth is that many are not advertised at all. Many people find employment through the so-called "hidden job market," which basically translates as personal connections and word-of-mouth referrals. The only way to tap this unofficial treasure trove of employment information is to develop a strategy: how are you going to create a network and meet people already working in your field or in closely related fields?

NETWORKING AT ITS BEST

The first step of an efficient job search is to find your Work Tribe. This group is made up of fellow artists, arts administrators, and all manner of other professionals who you admire and respect, and who share your values and interests. Seeking out your Work Tribe is networking in its purest form, and there's nothing phony or fake about it. Meaningful relationships are based on giving, not receiving. Focus on getting to know people and building relationships. Job referrals will come in time, but searching for your tribe is about more than just that.

HOW DO YOU FIND YOUR PEOPLE?

Aside from the obvious social networking approach to getting introductions and referrals through your existing networks, there are a number of ways you can connect. Get in touch with your alumni association and see what past graduates are up to. Attend events, audit classes, ask everyone you know for potential contacts (teachers, neighbours, distant relatives, bank tellers, depanneur owners, doctors, dentists, etc.). Someone will know someone you can speak to and, eventually, this type of networking could lead to your next job offer.

INFORMATIONAL INTERVIEW

Find people whose work you admire and ask them if they would be willing to meet with you for a half hour to discuss their career paths and their take on the industry and the local market. Ask them for their secrets to success, how they got their first break, any tips they have for someone entering the field, which events to go to, books to read, associations to join, people to talk to, etc. In employment speak, this is known as an informational interview.

VOLUNTEER YOUR WAY TO A JOB

Volunteering is an excellent way to meet people in your field and build a reputation as someone who is reliable, fun to be around, and competent. You want to become an indispensable volunteer. Eventually, when an opening does arise, the company will want to hire you because they will know you and like you.

> Be strategic about where you volunteer. Look for volunteer opportunities that give you access to a network of artistic or other professionals that can serve as potential employers, mentors, or referees.

> To maximize your network, consider volunteering in several places rather than at one organization only.

> Consider the role you will play as a volunteer. Make sure your position allows you to practise your craft to some extent or to acquire new skills that you can use in the future. Strive to be a proactive volunteer: help organize an event, write the newsletter, or update the company's database.

> If you cannot find a volunteer opportunity that suits your purpose, become an independent volunteer. Start a research project of your own that will give you a reason to approach people in your field, a project artists in your community will be interested in. Artists are often isolated; you could start a networking group. Artists often don't know where to find alternative sources of funding; consider compiling a list of corporations that sponsor the arts. Artists need cheap supplies; perhaps you could put together a list of resources. Use your creativity to meet people, to get your foot in the door, and to make a great impression.

FIRST STEPS FIRST

> ### Broad Strokes

Before you are ready to set realistic employment objectives, you need to assess your strengths, your needs, and your expectations. Explore your preferences: what you like to do, what motivates you, and what you have to offer a potential employer. If you don't know what kind of position you want or which organization to approach, start by penciling in the broad strokes. Figure out some basics: Would you prefer to work during the day or at night? Behind the scenes or dealing with the public? In the corporate or non-profit sector? Be clear about what you hope to get out of your next employment opportunity before you start applying for jobs.

> ### Be Realistic

Everyone has to start somewhere, usually at the very bottom. If you are applying for internships or entry-level positions, don't expect your job description to be the same as a company's CEO. Young people often have unrealistic expectations; avoid voicing these as much as possible. If you accept your role and responsibilities and you do your job well, you will advance.

> ### Get Organized

Get yourself an agenda and some sort of system to organize your leads, applications, and the business cards you collect. Keep tabs on who you spoke to, the date, and their response. Keep a copy of job postings you respond to and the CVs and cover letters you send to potential employers. Prepare questions you would ask should they call back and catch you off guard, and keep them near the phone.

> Research

Before you embark on your intensive quest for employment, gather as much information as possible about your chosen field.

The best way to get information about the local market is to talk to people in your field. Find out what typical entry-level positions are available. Ask about peak hiring periods so you can apply intensively during these times. Know what local salary ranges are so that you can negotiate an offer without under- or overpricing yourself.

Walk into organizations or companies for which you might like to work and pick up promotional literature, ask about volunteer opportunities, and snoop around the office to find out who the best person to contact is. Start building a relationship with the receptionist. Ask for a business card and follow up with a phone call or email.

> Set a Goal and Take Action

A plan is a goal with a timeline. As you consider where you would like to end up, work backwards, and try to figure out what steps you have to take to get there. Plan out how long it will take to accomplish your goals. Sometimes, your carefully laid plans unravel and you have to go with the flow. Many great careers just happen, especially in the arts. However, deciding on a plan of action is a great way to jump-start your job hunt.

The most important thing to remember when you embark on your job search is to take action. You will create more opportunities for yourself by doing something rather than contemplating vague, intangible goals from the comfort of your living room couch.

> Create a List of Potential Employers

Once you have decided what role you want to play in an organization or a company (grant writer, administrative assistant, curator, etc.), you need to identify potential employers. You can use directories, web searches, LinkedIn and other social media, online job boards, and word-of-mouth referrals. Draft a list of potential employers, and update your list as your search progresses.

> Research Some More

Research each organization or company you're interested in working for. If you're interested in a specific department or project, find the name of the person in charge. Drop off your application in person if possible. You are in a relationship business. Take every opportunity to help them make the connection between your name, your voice, your great personality, and your qualifications.

> ### Make Contact

Begin the application process with a phone call. Introduce yourself and briefly describe your training and experience. Ask key questions about volunteer opportunities, job openings, who to send your CV to, and when they recruit. Start building a relationship. If you get someone's voicemail, leave a message. Peak some interest before you send any documentation.

> ### Personalize Your Application

Tailor your application to fit the position or organization you are interested in applying for. Your CV and cover letter should reflect the research you have done. Emphasize the particular skills, competencies, and work experience required for the position at hand—especially if specifically mentioned in the job description.

STRATEGIC CVs

A well-written resume is a key component of any job search. Make sure yours includes:

> ### Personal Information

Make sure you provide up-to-date contact information. Getting in touch with you has to be easy. If you mention your email address, make sure you check your emails regularly. If you are living with people who may be taking messages for you, make sure you have a reliable system for relaying those messages. If you have an online portfolio or website, include that as well.

> ### Highlights of Qualifications or Summary

This section summarizes the key points you want employers to consider. Its content should peak their interest and make them hungry for more. It is your job to know what they are looking for; again, it's crucial that you do your research. List your most relevant work or volunteer experience, the training you received, knowledge (languages, computer skills, other), and personal qualities you may have. Include any accomplishments you are particularly proud of that may not be directly relevant to the position but demonstrate your ability to succeed. If you won an award or excelled in a sport, mention it. Let them know what you are capable of.

> ### Relevant Experience

List all relevant experience in chronological order, starting with your most recent experience. Include past employment and freelance and volunteer experiences. For each entry, mention your title on the far left, followed by the company's name and the city where it is located. Include the date on the far right. Describe your relevant tasks in detail using point form. Each description should start with a verb. Organize the job descriptions in an order that reflects the priorities of the position you are applying for.

> Other Experience

In this section, list all your other work experiences in chronological order. The main purpose of this section is to show that there are no gaps in your work history. For each entry, include your title, the company, city, and date. Don't describe what you did there. Going on about waiting tables for example will detract from the idea that you are a graphic designer and dilute the overall impression you want to make on the reader.

> Community Involvement

Never describe yourself as a volunteer; instead, give yourself a title that is relevant to your duties as a volunteer. If you helped organize an event, call yourself an "Assistant Event Coordinator." If the volunteer experience is relevant, describe your duties. If not, it is sufficient to mention your title, the name of the organization, the city, and the date.

> Education

List all relevant training you received in chronological order. Usually, your formal degrees appear in this section. You can also include workshops, conferences, and classes that are related to the position you are applying for. Start with each degree's title; don't abbreviate. Mention majors and minors if helpful, then the school, city, and date. You may want to add a few bullets to highlight a high GPA, awards won, or a thesis title if you think the information is pertinent.

> Additional Training

List any training you may have that is not directly relevant to the position you are applying for the same way you did in the "Education" portion of your resume. This may include incomplete programs or other forms of study, such as interest courses or first aid certification.

> Extracurricular Activities (optional)

This section is reserved for activities you were a part of in school, such as team sports, band, or yearbook committee. For each entry, mention your title, the name of the team or club, school, city, and year.

> **Interests (optional)**

This mentions your other interests, and can be included at your discretion. Employers often look here for the different ways you manage stress and for what else you may bring to your work. If you mention an interest in sports, be specific; list the sports you practice. If you like to read, specify which genre or author you like best. Don't mention the obvious; if you are a painter, you don't need to list "painting" as one of your interests.

> **References**

At the end of your CV, indicate that your "references are available upon request." Have three references prepared and listed on a separate sheet of paper. Each entry should include the name of your referee, his or her title, their company name, and contact information (city, telephone number, email). Referees can be past professors, employers, or volunteer supervisors—you may wish to indicate what your relationship to each person is, for clarity's sake. Let your referees know ahead of time when a potential employer will be checking your references. Your referee will do a much better job of selling you when they know what position you have applied for and for which company.

When you wrap up a contract, it's always a good idea to ask for a letter of reference. This way, in three years when you apply for a similar contract, if your referee has moved away, you will still have a record of your stellar performance.

CV WRITING TIPS

As you put together your own resume, here are a few other considerations you should keep in mind:

> Make sure you do not make any grammatical or spelling mistakes; have several people proofread your CV for you.

> One page CVs are acceptable; if your CV exceeds the two page mark, it is usually too long.

> Information you provide in a resume should go back no more than ten years.

> Always use point form in order to be as clear and concise as possible.

> Do not use a font size below 11 picas—it is too small and difficult to read at a glance.

> Since you are a creative person, strive to put together a CV that really stands out. This doesn't necessarily mean using fancy graphics or cheesy clip-art, but certainly put time and effort into your resume to demonstrate your creative talent.

> It's tempting—and easy—to just blitz dozens of potential employers with the same generic resume, but don't do it! Make sure you understand the specific requirements of each job you apply for, and fine-tune your resume for each employment opportunity.

> Never send your resume to a general "info" email address or to the Human Resources department. Find out who runs the department you're interested in and send your resume directly to this person.

COVER LETTER WRITING TIPS

Basically, your CV and cover letter should both summarize relevant information. The cover letter is different from the CV in that it allows you to personalize your application and demonstrate your writing style.

Always address it to a specific person and avoid using cold, generic phrases such as "please find attached" or "Dear Sir/Madam."

In your first paragraph, mention the position you are applying for, where, and when you saw the ad, and, if you are applying cold, which department you are interested in working in.

The next paragraph should include a summary of your qualifications. You can use the highlights on your CV and simply turn them into a paragraph. You may want to elaborate on your personality, demonstrating key traits with examples.

Finally, you want to thank them for their time and request that they get in touch with you at any time to set up an interview, or promise to follow up within a week and do so!

POST-APPLICATION FOLLOW-UP

Follow-up is critical, especially when applying cold. From an employer's point of view, follow-up shows interest. Most companies hold your CV for six months. Let's assume that at the time of your application, there is no job opening and that one becomes available five months later. If you have not followed up since you sent in your CV five months ago, your CV will have crept to the bottom of the pile and there is little chance they will remember you.

A follow-up plan can be co-created with the person you sent your application to. Let them know you have applied and that you wouldn't want to miss out on any opportunity that may come up. Ask them if it is okay if you touch base about every four to six weeks. Ask if they prefer an email or a phone call. Let them buy into the idea. When an opening does arise five months down the road, you will have made several calls or contacts and, because of this, you will most likely be considered, assuming you have been pleasant and appropriate.

PREPARING FOR AN INTERVIEW

Bring several copies of your updated CV and look the part by dressing appropriately. Keep the mood positive and talk about your strengths. Prepare an agenda of what it is you want to let them know about you, as well as questions you would like to ask about the company, its corporate culture, the position itself, etc. At the end of the interview, let them know that you are very interested in the position and ask for a business card for easy follow-up. Ask about the next step in the recruitment process, estimated timelines, and how they would like you to proceed. It is likely that you will need to wait to hear back for a week or more.

POST-INTERVIEW PROTOCOLS

> **Send a Thank You Note**

The day following your interview, or even later the same day, send a note thanking them for their time and restating your interest in the position. This shows good time-management skills and professionalism. It also reminds them of you and sets you apart from other candidates.

> **Follow Up**

If you have not heard back following your interview, after an appropriate amount of time (one week +), call to inquire as to whether the position has been filled. If you were not selected, ask for feedback and suggestions on how you can improve your chances in the future. Be polite and professional. Keep in mind that they may hire you for another position or refer you to someone they know.

KEEP ON KEEPING ON

It may take time for you to land the right professional opportunity—be it a "pay the bills" job or something that is more meaningful and career-specific. It is important that you DO NOT let time and rejection throw you off your game. Job hunting is not easy, and can be both a lonely and discouraging process. Keeping your spirits up and staying focused over the long haul is key. This is why you may consider working with an employment counsellor who can help you not only stay motivated but also to be strategic and proactive in your efforts.

CREATING
BUZZ WITH
TRADITIONAL
MEDIA

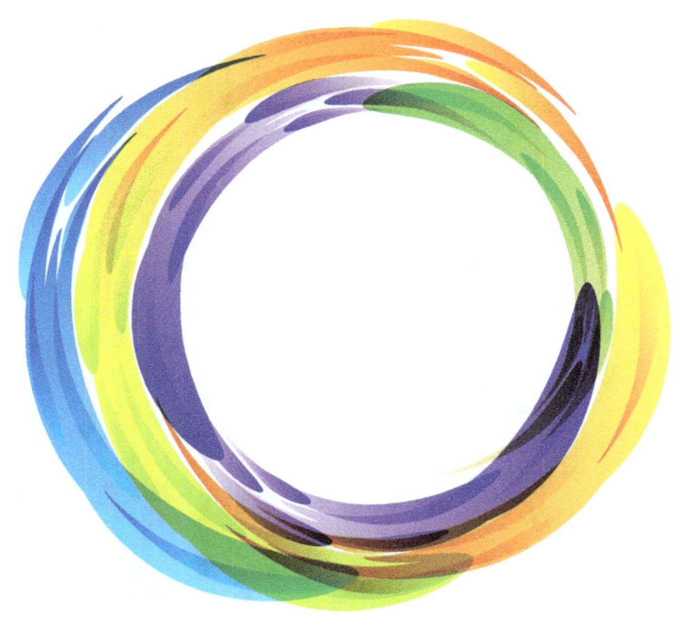

Although you are undoubtedly very talented, you are not the only artist around looking to produce a play or design a line of funky jewellery. Unfortunately, talent alone probably won't be sufficient to separate you and your art from the masses. As a self-employed artist, one of the key skills that you must master is the art of effectively marketing yourself and your work.

Let's be honest, until you become red hot on the market, you probably won't have a budget for advertising or a big-name agent to peddle your wares. That'll all come with time, strategy, and good networking.

Until then, you do have unlimited access to the most powerful tool in a businessperson's arsenal: creativity. This section features tips on getting your name out there, your story talked about, and your voice heard.

Nowadays, when people think about getting attention, they're generally thinking virtual attention—getting noticed on the web. But let's not forget about good old-fashioned TV, print, and radio. They've still got the ears and eyes of millions of people, in your city, and beyond. And they can help sell your art. Here's how you can harness the power of traditional media to make a name for yourself.

DEVELOP A PRESS KIT

A press kit is a dossier containing essential promotional and practical information about you and your work. You will need to have both a print and an electronic version of your press kit.

Use your innate creativity to develop a design that reflects your personality, your artistic sense, and the product or service you wish to sell. If you are not graphically inclined, consider consulting a graphic artist. Although you should thoroughly research the most cost-effective mode of production, your press kit may be one of the few things you need to invest in to present yourself in the best light possible.

A basic press kit includes:

> A one-page (max) artist or company bio (and that of your partners, if applicable).

> An artist statement: a simple introduction to your work and/or creative practice. It should answer the following questions: Why and how you make your art. What it's made out of. What your art means to you. What are the main themes behind your work.

> An arts-focused CV detailing your education, shows, collaborations, awards, grants, or publications.

> A company background (if appropriate): a briefing for reporters that includes information about how long you have been in business, who your biggest clients have been, where the reader might have seen your work, or awards you have received.

> Samples of your work—be they images, videos, music files, etc. (on CD for the hard copy of your press kit)

> High resolution promotional images of yourself, your collaborators, or past shows.

> Prior press clippings or extracts of media coverage relating to you and your artwork. This can include any format including print, TV/video, radio, and web.

> Up-to-date contact information, including phone, email, web, and social media.

Your press kit is always a work in progress. Add to it as you build up your portfolio and stage successful media events. Always keep it fresh and current with updated material as you go along.

DEVELOP A MEDIA CONTACT LIST

As an emerging artist, you may be most familiar with artsy magazines, journals, and 'zines, but it is in your best interest to develop relationships with other types of media outlets—be they mainstream or niche, local or not. That way, you can introduce your work to a much wider audience.

Go online and search for relevant publications or visit a well-stocked magazine store and be ready to take notes. Identify the publications in which you'd like to be featured. Take down the name of the publication, the names and titles of the editors, and any contact information you can find (email, phone number, web). If you can't find contact coordinates in the magazine itself, you should still be able to find these online later.

For newspapers and television, find out the name of the editor or reporter most likely to be interested in you and your work. Most large newspapers have editors, reporters, and writers assigned to each of the following and other "beats":

> Arts and Culture

> Business

> City Life

> Entertainment

> Fashion

> Finance

> Lifestyle

> Technology

> World

If you're planning an event, submit a listing to local calendar-of-events editors. It's usually free, but don't be insulted if your event doesn't make it; space is often limited.

For television and radio stations, in addition to contacting specialized reporters, you should develop a relationship with assignment editors. These are the folks who decide which stories will be covered on a daily basis.

Remember: not every story and event tip is appropriate for all news sources, so choose wisely. If a news editor receives too many useless media releases from you, she will eventually stop reading them altogether.

GET THE MEDIA'S ATTENTION

How do you get anyone's attention? By making noise!

A common misconception exists that media types are hostile towards PR people. In fact, that's rarely the case. By sending in a well-written press release with a ready-to-go story, you'll be making a reporter's life a lot easier. If you have a high-resolution photo or a good audio or video clip to go along with that story, you're saving the news organization a lot more time and money.

Keep in mind that if you want to make the six o'clock news or the morning paper, you will need to issue a press release pitching a "story" and your story should be some, if not all, of the following things:

> **New:** Do you have a big show coming up? Did you recently open a gallery or studio? Are you launching a new magazine? Are you about to publish a book of poetry?

> **Relevant:** News editors look for stories that touch their audience or readership; they want a story that will sell. Tailor your release to the viewing or reading population of the news outlet you are targeting. For instance, readers of the *Financial Post* will be interested in reading about big name foreign buyers that your first collection of women's wear is attracting; *Flare* magazine readers will want to know why it's cool to wear your clothes; and consumers of the *Canadian Retailer Magazine* will want to know what you are bringing to the industry.

> **Entertaining:** Okay, so you aren't bringing the story of the century to the media, but that's no reason to shy away from them. Is there something funny, quirky, or compelling about the piece of work you have produced or the way your business is run? Think about what makes your work entertaining and try to play this angle up both in your press release and in the pitches you deliver to reporters or news editors.

> **Important:** As an artist, you likely feel that you exist to deliver a message to the world. Make sure your passion comes through when you let the media know why you do what you do.

> **Happening:** Time your press release with an event, such as a product launch, book signing, or fashion show, and send it along with a personalized invitation to your media contacts the day before and again the morning of the event.

Remember, a press release is not an advertisement. A press release is written in the public's interest, while an advertisement is written in the company's commercial interest. Decide why the public would benefit from knowing your story and build your press release around that.

WRITE A GREAT PRESS RELEASE

If you want to grab the media's attention with your press release, it needs to be crisp, sharp, and to the point.

Editors usually assume a news story takes the form of an inverted triangle: the most important information goes at the top, while the least important information ends up at the bottom of the text. They always cut for length from the bottom up.

For strongest impact, your first paragraph should include as many of the five Ws and one H as possible. **Who? What? Why? Where? When? How?**

Example: "(WHO?) Jane Doe and John Smith (WHAT?) announce the launch of the first-ever Graphic Design Expo for AIDS Awareness (WHY?) in honour of the late Keith Taylor, former partner at Taylor, Doe and Smith Designs. (WHEN?) The Expo takes place on March 10, 2015 (WHERE?) at Parc Lafontaine and will begin at 2:00 p.m. (HOW?) with a digital retrospective of Taylor's work as an artist and AIDS activist."

Any other information about your story or event should follow the lead paragraph. This includes:

> A brief quote from the CEO, event organizer, or other key stakeholder involved in the project (yes, you can quote yourself but refer to yourself in the third person).

> Additional information about the artist(s) involved, the business (what the company does, what industries it serves, who else is on the team), or about the event (what kinds of activities are planned, anyone of note who will be in attendance, photo and video opportunities).

> Contact information, including phone, email, website, and social media accounts.

You should use simple words and short phrases, and write in the active voice to keep it interesting and to the point. Remember to put the most important facts near the top of the release.

CREATING BUZZ WITH TRADITIONAL MEDIA

PRESS RELEASE SAMPLE

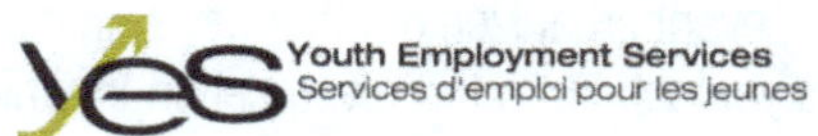

FOR IMMEDIATE RELEASE

TAP INTO THE ARTS: TWO EVENTS OVER TWO DAYS FOR LOCAL ARTISTS AND ART ENTHUSIASTS

Montreal, May 28, 2012 – Youth Employment Services (YES) invites all art enthusiasts to appreciate, encourage and support young up-and-coming Quebec artists at the YES Art Expo, a two-day event taking place at the Montreal Science Centre on June 3rd and 4th, 2012.

With support from the Forum jeunesse de l'île de Montréal (FJÎM) and Canadian Heritage, 60 young and talented emerging Quebec artists under the age of 30 were selected by a panel of experts from more than 115 applications to showcase their unique artworks to the public for free.

The event features one-of-a-kind paintings, drawings and prints; ceramics and sculptures; photography; mixed and digital media; fashion, jewelry and crafts. With hundreds of unique pieces, from a wide spectrum of disciplines, and showcasing live musical performances from local talent, YES' annual art exhibition and sale has something to offer every level of art enthusiast and collector.

The Art Expo is free and open to the public on Sunday June 3rd from 2:00 PM to 7:00 PM and on Monday June 4th from 10:00 AM to 5:30 PM.

On Monday June 4th, the Art Expo will run simultaneously with the 12th Annual Business Skills for Creative Souls Artists' Conference, a full-day event for both novice and seasoned artists looking for insight, inspiration, networking opportunities and essential business skills.

The Artists' Conference will be hosted by Jeanette Kelly, host of CBC Radio's show Daybreak Montreal, and features a keynote from award-winning singer/songwriter Coral Egan. Eighteen other accomplished Quebec artists and industry experts from Pop Montreal, the Quebec Drama Federation, the Conseil des Arts de Montréal, the Ballet Ouest de Montréal and more will also be on hand to share their stories of making it in their respective professions and provide valuable tips and guidance on marketing, finance and funding for artists. Tickets are $30.

The YES Artists' Conference is sponsored by The Counselling Foundation of Canada and Canadian Heritage.

For more information about these events or to register for the Artists Conference, interested participants can contact YES at 514-878-9788 or visit www.yesmontreal.ca

ABOUT YES
As a not-for-profit organization, Youth Employment Services (YES) enriches the community by providing English-language support services to help Quebecers find employment and start businesses.

-30-

For further information, interviews or photos, media representatives may contact:

Catherine Brisindi
Director of Marketing and Special Events
514-878-9788 ext. 322
cbrisindi@yesmontreal.ca

Iris Unger
Executive Director
Tel: 514.878.9788 ext. 301
iu@yesmontreal.ca

LEARN TO PIGGYBACK

Have you ever noticed how protest groups come out of the woodwork and dominate news coverage whenever a controversial figure visits the city? These people have mastered the "piggyback": timing their appearance to coincide with a story that's guaranteed media coverage.

Here's a great example: A foundation that raises money for elderly residents of Montreal invited a klezmer band to play for residents and staff of a retirement home. The concert was free and was simply meant to raise awareness for the home.

While the concert would have been a success with the residents at any time of the year, its organizers sought to capitalize on the frenzy that envelops the city each summer during the Montreal International Jazz Festival. They planned the concert during the Jazz Fest and sent out media releases inviting reporters to the resident's first annual jazz fest.

The story had all the elements mentioned above: it was local (perfect for local newscasts and community papers), different (no other old folks' home had done anything like that), relevant (the jazz fest is the biggest story in the city during its run), important (it was about an issue close to the hearts of many Montrealers: helping the elderly), and it was happening (reporters were invited to broadcast live from the show).

All in all, the concert was a success and the event garnered a huge amount of media coverage for the foundation.

When you organize your own event, think about how you can time it wisely to create your own "piggyback" opportunity. Keep track of any dignitaries or high-profile leaders who might be visiting the city and think about how your message can fit in with the atmosphere the visit generates. As well, keep a list of national holidays and other days of significance. There are a multitude of obscure "Hallmark holidays" that you might be able to use to your advantage.

GO WHERE THE CAMERAS ARE

Let's go back to our previous example of the protesters. For 364 days of the year, nobody hears from them. But leaders of the G8 show up and suddenly, the activists are splashed all over every newspaper and TV newscast in town.

Instead of creating their own unique event, they piggyback on a story they know the media will be following closely. They may send an alert to the media advising them of their presence, but they don't usually have to work very hard to get in front of the cameras.

The point is this: don't try to move heaven and earth to bring the media to you. Instead, bring your story to them.

Twist Image digital marketing guru, Mitch Joel, recalls one of his earliest days at the helm of a now-defunct magazine that he started up with a friend. After printing up the first edition, the two partners sat in Joel's basement with boxes and boxes of the magazine, idly flipping the channels on the television, wondering how they were going to get all the magazines distributed.

Suddenly, they came upon MusiquePlus, the French-language music station. MusiquePlus was expecting a big name musician at their studios and the cameras were fixed on the throngs of Montrealers lined up outside in the pouring rain, awaiting the star's arrival.

Then, they hit on a bright idea. They grabbed some boxes, got in Joel's car, and raced down to the TV station. They gave out the magazine to all the poor souls waiting in the rain. The partners returned home and switched on the TV to MusiquePlus. Splashed across the screen were hundreds of copies of the new magazine, as some fans read it while they waited and others used it as protection from the rain.

Without paying an extra cent for advertising, Joel got a few hours of TV coverage on a station targeting his market, and picked up some new readers along the way.

As you organize your own event, think of ways that you can take advantage of other big festivals and media events happening in and around your city, like:

> Blue Metropolis Literary Festival

> International conferences, symposia, etc.

> Just For Laughs Festival

> Montreal International Jazz Festival

> Montreal or Quebec Fashion Week

> Visits from notable media personalities

Also, don't be surprised if the media are no-shows at an event you've planned in the suburbs on the same day, at the same time, as the opening concert of the Jazz Fest by Celine Dion. Camera resources and reporters are limited so don't try to compete. Research upcoming events in advance and work around them if you can't work with them.

INVITE A PUBLIC FIGURE

One of the best ways to ensure media coverage is to bring in a big-name guest. You can almost guarantee a photo in the newspaper or a few seconds of TV coverage if an important artist, a member of parliament, a city mayor, or the president of an important company is in attendance. Think of who might raise the profile of your event. Phone their assistant and find out the best way to send them an invitation.

If you manage to land an important guest, consider asking them to make a few remarks at your event as this is a sure draw for photographers, TV cameras, and radio reporters searching for a sound bite. While many people fear their message will get lost if the focus of their event becomes a high-profile personality, consider it as a worthy sacrifice in your ascent towards notoriety.

VOLUNTEER OR MAKE DONATIONS OF YOUR WORK

Even though she has sung for world leaders like Nelson Mandela, won a Juno, and played alongside the likes of Ray Charles and Patti LaBelle, Montreal jazz singer Lorraine Klaasen still makes a point of volunteering with local community groups. She says that working at a grassroots level allows her to develop an enormous support network.

Volunteering your time is a great networking opportunity as well as an easy way to build a name and reputation for yourself. Moreover, it is perfectly acceptable to let the media know that you'll be performing at a charity event or that you have recently donated your work for a good cause.

MASTER MEDIA ADVISORIES AND INVITATIONS

If you are going to plan an event, it's wise to send along a media advisory the day before and the morning of the event, along with your press release. The advisory should be much shorter than your press release and is often most effective when written in summary or point form.

It should include:

> The five Ws and one H (in point form)

> A list of photo/video opportunities

> Names of notable individuals who will be attending the event

> Key people who can be interviewed

> Suggested interview topics

> Contact information

MEDIA ADVISORY SAMPLE

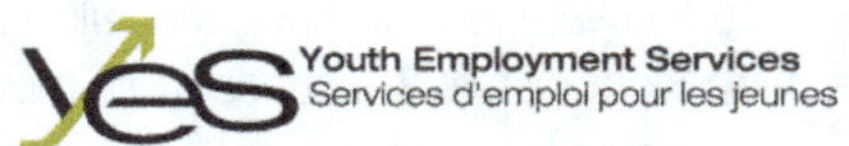

MEDIA ADVISORY

WHO: YES Montreal (Youth Employment Services) enriches the community by providing English-language support services to help Quebecers find employment and start businesses.

WHAT: Youth Employment Services (YES) is hosting a 2-day Art Expo to encourage young artists and artisans under the age of 30 to turn their artistic passion into profit. With support from the Forum jeunesse de L'île de Montréal (FJÎM) and Canadian Heritage, the community-inspired event will provide an opportunity for young, talented emerging artists to showcase their work to the public, for free.

Over 60 young and talented Quebec artists will be exhibiting and selling one-of-a-kind paintings, photographs, sculptures, fashion, crafts, jewellery, and more. Admission to the Art Expo is free to the public and will also feature live musical and dance performances by local talent.

WHEN: **Thursday, December 1st**
VIP Cocktail: 5:00 PM – 7:00 PM
Open to the Public: 7:00 – 9:00 PM
Friday, December 2nd
Open to the Public: 10:00 AM – 4:00 PM

WHERE: **Marché Bonsecours**
350, St-Paul St. East
Montreal, Quebec

GUEST SPEAKERS: **Bill Brownstein** from the **Montreal Gazette** and **Andy Nulman** of **Just For Laughs,** are among the confirmed guests who will be giving presentations about why they support the arts.

For interviews or additional information, please contact:

CONTACT: **Catherine Brisindi**
Director of Marketing & Events, YES Montreal
514-878-9788 ext. 322
cbrisindi@yesmontreal.ca

Iris Unger
Executive Director, YES Montreal
514-878-9788 ext 301
iu@yesmontreal.ca

OFFER ALTERNATIVES WHEN THE MEDIA CAN'T MAKE IT

Sometimes, if you have a well-packaged story, the media will cover your event even if they are not able to attend.

> Have a photographer on hand to take high-resolution digital photos that you can later email to newspapers.

> Have a professionally recorded or otherwise high-quality video made at your event.

> Call target reporters and offer an interview. They'll want to know why they should interview you, what is important or interesting about your story, and what kinds of things you plan to talk about. Prepare answers for each of these questions before you start contacting them.

> Offer to provide a list of questions for the interviewer and write up good background notes for them to make their job easier, and to increase your chances of getting coverage.

BECOME A SPOKESPERSON

Research groups that are active in your industry or areas of special interest to you. Find out what their mission is and read up on the issues that concern them. If you find one with which you can identify, become a member, get involved, and offer to be a spokesperson for them. As a well-spoken media go-to person, you will bring credibility to yourself, your organization, and your art. And you'll get your name in the media an awful lot!

CREATING
BUZZ ONLINE

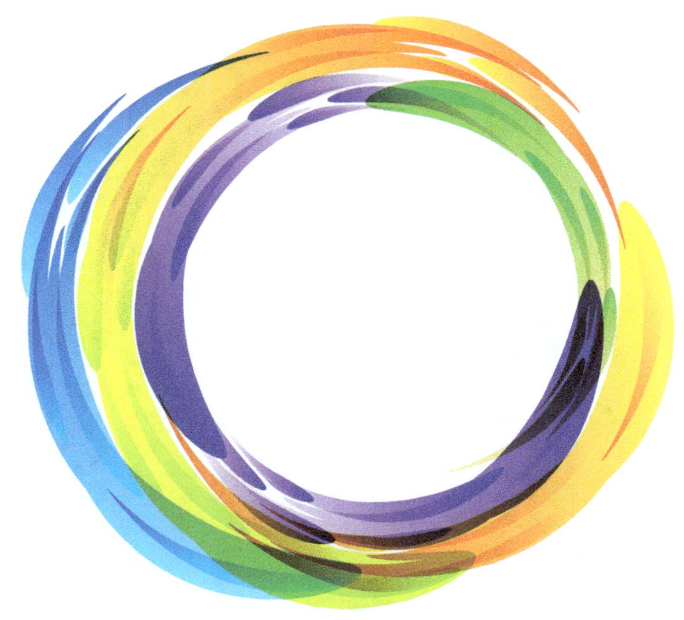

by Dave Cool, Director of Artist Relations for Bandzoogle

PART 1. WHY YOU NEED A WEBSITE

Do you really need a website for your career in the arts? With Facebook, Twitter, YouTube, blogs, and other free platforms, you might think that owning your own .COM website isn't necessary. However, having a proper website is still important, and it should be seen as the central hub of your online presence.

Here's why:

> ### You Own the Address

> First and foremost, you own your .COM address. As long as you renew it, it will always point to your website. This is powerful, as you are guaranteed to own that little slice of the Internet. Even if you switch companies that host your website, your .COM can be transferred, so people will always be able to find you.

> ### You Own the Experience

> With your website you also own the experience. You can control what people see, and the messaging that you send to them. You can present your story and your art however you want, with no sudden changes, no ads and distractions, and no design limits.

> ### Professionals Expect to Find You There

> If you're serious about your art, having a well designed website with great content will make you appear professional and dedicated. When people search for you online, they'll expect to find you at yourname.com.

PART 2. BUILDING A GREAT WEBSITE

When building your website, there are a few important things to keep in mind to ensure you're making the most impact and giving a great impression to visitors.

> ### Use Professional Photos

> The importance of using professional photos for your website cannot be overstated. Great photos can create a positive first impression, but if the images on your website look unprofessional, people might not take you or your art seriously.

> Make a Strong Home Page

Your home page is usually the first page visitors to your website will see, so it's important to make sure that you have the right elements in place to grab their attention, make a strong first impression, and keep them on your site.

Include a strong visual for your header or background image, a short bio, some latest news, and a strong call-to-action. A call-to-action is designed to direct people's attention to something specific that you want them to do while on your website. It could be to sign up to your mailing list, check out your portfolio, buy your new album, or watch your latest video.

> Include the Best of the Basics

In addition to a strong home page, you should include tabs navigating people to samples of your best work, a selection of articles you've been featured in or events you've been part of, an updated calendar of where your work can be seen or heard, and a way to contact you.

> Keep Navigation Simple

Make navigating your website easy for everyone who visits your site. People have very short attention spans, and not a lot of time. If they have to think about what content *might* be in a certain section of your site because the name is fancy/cute/artsy, chances are, they're going to skip it. Save the creativity for your art; your website is your business.

> Keep It Updated

Your website shouldn't be a static flyer online. If a returning visitor doesn't find anything new on your website, the chances of them coming back are pretty slim. Add new content on a regular basis, which can be a blog post, photos, an update to your portfolio, new music, or a new video.

If your site isn't easy to update yourself, consider changing to a service that is. There are lots of options that make updating websites painless.

PART 3. THE IMPORTANCE OF FAN ENGAGEMENT

Once you've built your .COM real-estate, you'll want to show it off. It's not enough to depend on live shows and public readings to keep you in the public eye. That's where social media comes in.

Artists are busy people. Often they're involved in several projects, have day jobs, families, or all of the above. So whenever there is talk about social media, and marketing in general, it's understandable that it can be a little overwhelming.

It takes a lot of work just for the artistic side of things, but the reality is that it's no longer enough to write, rehearse, create, and perform to develop a sustainable career. Fan interaction has become part of the job description for today's artists. Here are three reasons why it's important to interact with your fans:

> ### Interaction Keeps Fans Aware of You

The biggest reason to interact with your fans is to keep them aware of you and your art. With countless other artists out there, you can easily get lost in the noise if you aren't interacting with your fans regularly.

> ### Engagement Solidifies Relationships

More and more, fans want to feel a direct connection to the artists themselves. Every time a fan makes a comment or asks a question on your blog or through social media, you have the chance to respond and make them feel like they're an active part of your career.

> ### Communication Creates "Super Fans"

As you solidify your relationship with fans, some of them will become "super fans." These are the fans who will buy almost everything you release. More importantly, these are the fans who are going to talk about you and promote you.

Whereas marketing used to focus on finding ways to communicate the value of your art to potential fans and buyers, now the key is getting fans themselves to communicate the value of your art to other people.

People are tuning out ads and giving more weight to the recommendations of their friends for what movies to watch, which books to read, and what music to listen to.

Developing a relationship with your fans by interacting with them on a regular basis is one of the best ways to create that kind of word-of-mouth marketing.

PART 4. DEVELOPING AN ENGAGEMENT STRATEGY

But how often should this be done? Can managers, agents, or interns handle fan engagement for you? Here are a few things to keep in mind when developing a strategy for fan engagement:

> Be Authentic

First and foremost, communication with your fans must come from you, the artist, in your voice. People aren't interested in hearing generic updates from your manager, an intern, or your sister-in-law. They want to get to know your personality, hear about your experiences. Essentially, fans want to feel like they're on the journey of your career along with you.

> Be Consistent

Consistency is key when it comes to engaging with your fans. You can't post an update on Facebook and then disappear for several weeks. People will likely stop paying attention if you don't have a consistent presence.

There are tons of distractions out there, so to truly break through the clutter, you have to be consistent. Take some time every day to check your social media profiles, respond to fans, ask questions, and start conversations.

> Sustain It!

Finally, when it comes to fan engagement, you have to sustain it over the long- term. Don't expect immediate results. It might take months of being consistent to start seeing more quality interactions with your fans, which in turn could lead to new fans.

If you engage with your fans in some way every day, and you sustain that over months and years, you will no doubt develop a solid fan base.

> Never Leave Your Fans Hanging

One last important thing to keep in mind when it comes to fan engagement: never leave a fan hanging. If they email you, email back. If they leave a comment on Facebook, respond, or at least "Like" it.

If they reply or ask a question on Twitter, reply back. A short answer or a quick thank you can go a long way in making that fan feel special.

PART 5. USE A FACEBOOK PAGE NOT A PROFILE

Facebook is the biggest social media site out there. We love to hate it, but the reality is that Facebook is an essential marketing tool for artists, as it's likely where you'll find most of your fans. But before you start planning a Facebook strategy, make sure you're using a Facebook Page, not a personal profile. Here's why:

> ### No "Friend" Limit

Facebook Pages don't have a limit on the amount of fans you can have. Personal profiles have a limit of 5000 "friends."

> ### Separates Personal and Professional

Having a page is a great way to keep your personal and professional lives separate. As you become successful this will become more important.

> ### Analytics and Insights Offered

Page Insights can be a powerful tool to let you know where your fans are from, who are the most engaged, and what kind of content is working best (photos, videos, text, etc).

> ### Promoted Posts

With Pages, you can "promote" a post so that it reaches more people.

> ### Ads Available

Having a Page allows you to use Facebook Ads. You can use ads to promote your page and increase "likes," as well as promote products and events. You can even target specific geographic regions, demographics, and interests.

PART 6. FIVE THINGS YOUR FACEBOOK PAGE SHOULD HAVE

When setting up your Facebook page, there are a few things you'll want to have in place before inviting people to "Like" the page:

> ### A Custom URL

The first thing you should do is customize the URL for your page: www.facebook.com/ username/.

> **Your Branding**

Your cover photo and profile photo should have a consistent look that matches your other social media profiles.

> **Your Bio**

Include a short bio in the main "About" box that people see right away when landing on your page. Then add a full bio in the "Biography" section.

> **Link(s) to Your Website**

Make sure to include a link to your website after your bio in the About box, in your Bio, and in the Contact Info section.

> **Career Highlights**

Use the Timeline feature to tell the story of your career. Add significant highlights and events from when you first started until the present.

PART 7. FACEBOOK POSTING QUICK TIPS

Another reason Facebook is great for fan engagement is because it's free. But as we all know, free is rarely ever truly free, and Facebook is no different. There are lots of ads and distractions vying to grab people's attention. More importantly, due to Facebook's algorithms, only a small percent of your fans see your posts. Here are a few tips that will help increase the engagement and visibility of your posts:

> **Spread Your Posts Out**

When posting updates on your Page, be sure to spread them out. Updates don't necessarily appear right away in the newsfeed, as the Facebook algorithm needs time to measure engagement of each post. So if you post too many updates close to one another, Facebook will likely ignore the ones with less engagement. You should leave at least a few hours between posts.

> **Use Images**

Images get much more engagement (likes, comments, and shares) than simple text posts. So whenever you're posting an update, try to use some kind of image or photo along with it.

> **Highlight Important Posts**

Use Facebook's "highlight" function to give more visibility for important posts on your page.

> **Promote Big Events**

For big career highlights, you can consider promoting the post. Spending money on promoting posts can add up quickly, so save this only for really important announcements.

PART 8. TWITTER BASICS FOR ARTISTS

Twitter is a social media platform that is all about short-form communication. With a maximum of 140 characters per tweet, it's a great way to quickly promote your career and interact with your fans. Here's how you can set up your Twitter profile in four essential steps:

> **Select a Consistent Username**

Your Twitter username should be consistent with your other online profiles. If your Facebook page is Facebook.com/Artistname, then your Twitter handle should be @Artistname.

> **Upload a Profile Image**

The default profile image when you create a Twitter account is an egg. People generally don't follow accounts with the egg as the profile image. You likely won't be taken seriously, or people will think your account is spam. Upload your own profile image before starting to use Twitter.

> **Add Your Bio**

Twitter gives you 160 characters for your profile's bio. It might not seem like a lot of space, but you can make someone curious about your career and give them a real sense of your personality within those 160 characters.

> **Include a Link to Your Website**

Twitter allows you to enter a link that will appear under your bio. There is only one link you should have, which is to your own website. Send people to your site where they can sign up to your mailing list, read your blog, watch your videos, and shop at your online store.

PART 9. USING TWITTER

Twitter allows up to 140 characters per tweet, and should be used for shorter, more frequent updates. How often should you tweet? Whereas on Facebook you can get away with one update per day or every couple of days, tweeting several times a day is not only okay, it's almost expected.

Some artists tweet six to ten times throughout the day, others only once or twice. Just be sure to spread your tweets out and mix it up between personal and promotional tweets.

> **Talk the Talk**

Twitter also has its own language and etiquette. Here are some actions you'll be taking on Twitter that are important to understand:

> **Reply**

If you hit "Reply," you'll be responding directly to someone on Twitter. The tweet will start with their Twitter @username, and only people who follow both you and that other person will be able to see that tweet in their stream.

> **Mention**

If you want to mention another Twitter user and have everyone who follows you see it, make sure that your tweet doesn't start with their Twitter @username. You can simply add a "." before their username, or include their username somewhere later in the tweet.

> **Retweet (RT)**

To "Retweet" someone is similar to forwarding an email; you're sharing someone's tweet with your followers. You can simply hit Retweet so that the person's tweet appears exactly as it is to your followers.

On the mobile Twitter app, they give you the option to "Quote Tweet," which puts the original tweet in quotations and you can add your own comment after. On other Twitter applications like Tweetdeck, Hootsuite, and Echofon, you can Retweet (RT) and add your own comment before the original tweet.

> **Use #hashtags**

A hashtag is the pound # sign followed by a word or group of words. The hashtag is automatically hyperlinked, creating a new search stream if you click on it. That stream will include all tweets using that hashtag. It's a great way to be found on Twitter, start conversations, and join in other conversations with users who don't follow you.

> **Favourite**

You can click to "Favourite" a tweet, which in some applications is done by clicking a star. This has become similar to the "Like" button on Facebook. This can be a great way to quickly acknowledge a fan who compliments you on Twitter.

PART 10. USE SOCIAL MEDIA TO DIRECT TRAFFIC

Social media sites come and go (remember Myspace?), so it's important to still drive fans back to your own website. With your website, you own that slice of the Internet. You also control the experience fans have on your site (no ads or distractions), as well as the data you collect from it. Here are some ideas on how to drive traffic back to your own website:

> **Link to Your Bio**

Make sure to at least include a link to your website in the About box, in the Bio section of your Twitter profile, and in the Contact Info section of your Facebook page.

> **Direct Traffic with Photos**

Do you have a lot of great photos from your last event? Instead of uploading them all to Facebook, post one or two, and then provide a link to the full gallery on your website. And provide a link to the gallery for your Twitter followers.

> **Use Blog Post Teasers**

Whenever you have a new blog post, post a brief description to your Facebook page with a link to drive fans back to your site to read it. And tweet a link and invite your followers to read the post.

> **Entice with New Creative Content**

Have some new merchandise or a new creative work? Tweet a link to your online store. And post an image on Facebook with a link taking fans away from that noisy environment to shop in peace and quiet.

> **Don't Forget: Social Media is a Conversation Tool**

The most important thing to remember when using Twitter or Facebook (or any social media platform), is that it's a tool for conversation. Use it to show fans who you are and what you're all about, not simply to promote to them. A big part of conversation is actively interacting with fans. Answer their questions, "like" their comments, and thank them for compliments. Facebook, for instance, gives priority to updates that have a lot of engagement, so the more you do this, the more fans will see your updates. If used properly on a consistent basis, social media can help you build a following of loyal and engaged fans.

Dave Cool is Director of Artist Relations for musician website and marketing platform Bandzoogle. Find more of his writing at: www.bandzoogle.com/blog and at www.davecool.ca.

NETWORKING BASICS
FOR ARTISTS

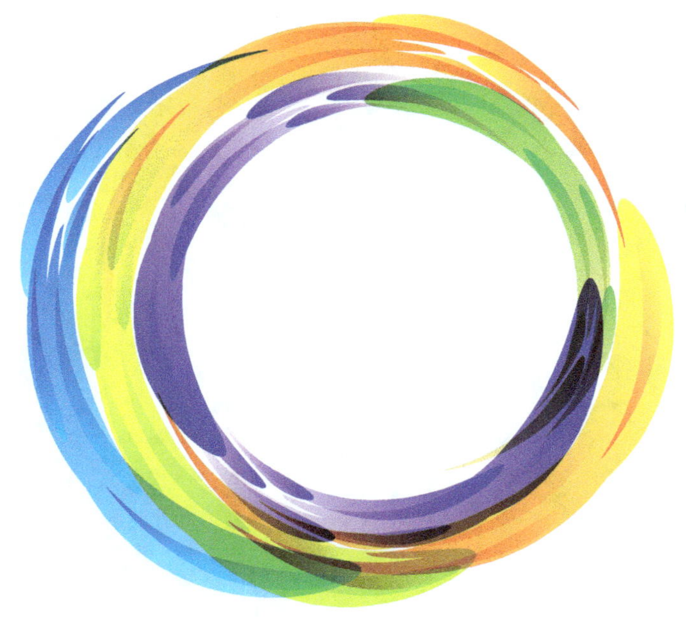

If you had it your way, we're guessing you'd spend 95% of your time creating art and 5% of your time getting it out into the world. And likely none of that 5% would have anything to do with strategic "networking." It's unfortunate that networking gets such a bum rap. After all, why should you suddenly feel manipulative and inauthentic for wanting to enrich your world with new people and share your genuine enthusiasm about your art?

The problem for most people is that they confuse networking with selling. And most artists abhor selling (for reasons that could take up a whole other book). So let's set the record straight: networking is not selling. In fact, if you expect to sell anything while you're networking, you will most likely fail (and rightly feel manipulative and inauthentic).

We're going to assume your art is important to you; it's a big part of your life and who you are. Letting people in on your art is letting people in on you; sharing yourself with the world. And there's nothing wrong with that, is there?

Networking, while definitely not selling, can and should be strategic, however. And there are ways to make it both fruitful and fun, but you need to integrate it into your artistic life the right way. Here are some tips to make the most of your networking time, regardless of how much or how little you are willing to invest in it:

IDENTIFY KEY PEOPLE IN YOUR INDUSTRY

Make it your business to know who's who in and around your industry. Research and identify organizations, individuals, and others who you'd love to meet. People who can help you move forward. Lay the groundwork for a future meeting by informing yourself about their projects and initiatives.

BE SELECTIVE AND DILIGENT

Since most of us don't have the luxury of unlimited networking time, you must be selective about which events and activities you attend. Identify and act on the "highest-value opportunities." This may sound crass, but in reality you only have so many hours in a week, right? So you'll need to focus on the events and people that are most relevant to your objectives.

JOIN GROUPS

You may choose to belong to a number of groups relating to your art, your community, certain charitable pursuits, or other interests. You never know who you'll meet out there. But remember, belonging means participating and engaging, so be prepared to do more than just "attend" events.

ALWAYS NETWORK

Consider social events—a party, a ball game, a play—as opportunities to meet new acquaintances who can become part of your network. This doesn't mean you start going to parties with an agenda; people will sniff that out in no time and avoid you like the plague! But social occasions are, by their nature, networking opportunities where people are looking to connect. Just share and share alike.

BE PURPOSEFUL YET BALANCED

Plan the events you'll attend and define your purpose for attending, but don't get so caught up in your objectives that you get stressed out. Don't force outcomes. Be willing to change your "game plan" as you go depending on how the event plays out.

PRESENT YOURSELF WELL

First impressions are important, so make sure you present yourself as well as you can. Dress well, polish how you speak, make eye contact, smile, be courteous and attentive—all the usual social graces we expect of each other.

BE YOUR BEST SELF

Don't be fake or try to be something you're not—people can see through that. Be natural, be open and friendly, and let your "best self" shine through. This gets easier with practice.

TAKE A ZEN APPROACH

To borrow a principle from Zen Buddhism, the best way to network is to be unconscious of the fact that you are networking. Remember, think "sharing." Don't let your mind dwell on the purpose or mechanics of networking. Allow yourself to enjoy the moment and to fully engage with the people you meet.

FIND THE CENTRE OF INFLUENCE

In the movie *The Pursuit of Happiness*, Will Smith plays a stockbroker who befriends an extremely important banker with dozens of clients, friends, and contacts. While the banker himself does not do business with the stockbroker, his contacts do. The lesson is that every group has a centre of influence; your networking efforts should focus on this type of individual.

DON'T BROADCAST, INTERACT

If you approach networking solely as an opportunity to talk about yourself and your art, you'll bore people. Make networking enjoyable and interactive by asking questions and engaging others in conversation. Listen carefully, contribute generously, and have fun.

HELP OTHERS

While your ultimate goal may be to find people who can help you advance your artistic career, don't forget that you may also be able to help others. Offer whatever resources you can—advice, contacts, support, or collaboration—in order to increase your value to people in your network. This kind of enlightened altruism will eventually be reciprocated.

CONSIDER FAMILY AND FRIENDS

Look to your existing social network to enhance career opportunities. Chances are that your family and friends already know plenty of people who could help you in some way. Connecting with these people can be easier than pitching your art to complete strangers.

EXPLOIT DIGITAL MEDIA

In addition to in-person networking, make sure to use social media platforms like Facebook and/or LinkedIn to expand and cultivate your networks. Make sure you are actively engaged on the platforms you do use. Don't have more accounts than you can keep actively up-to-date.

FOLLOW-UP AND FOLLOW-THROUGH

The day after a networking or social event, make it your practice to enter the contact info of your new acquaintances into your electronic address book. Tag them by category and note where and when you met them, along with any specifics you wish to remember. If appropriate, send a quick email letting them know how much you enjoyed meeting them, and suggest you connect on social media.

PLAY THE LONG GAME

Cultivate relationships with people in your network over time, understanding that it takes a while to develop trust, respect, and consideration. Keep in touch with people, send them useful information. Like, share, comment on, or repost your contacts' news and/or social media content, invite them to your events, help them when you can. Your engagement will, over time, earn you goodwill and pay off in kind—in due course.

COME PREPARED

Carrying a few business cards in your wallet is good practice. You don't need to fob them off on every new acquaintance, but when someone shows an interest in your art—and they will—that's your cue to offer them a card. Make sure it has your name, website, and coordinates so they can find you. And then, of course, you should ask for theirs.

PRICING AND PROFIT

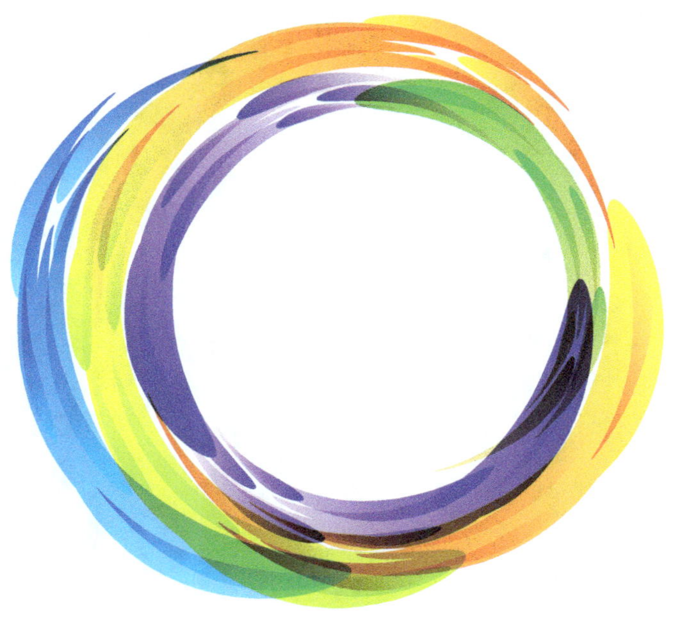

Some artists feel that the message they deliver through their work is too important to be sold for profit and have therefore had to accept the financial consequences of their convictions.

This book is for the rest of you.

Artists often struggle with how to price their work. As an emerging artist you might be tempted to sell your work at bargain basement prices just to see it move. But this strategy can backfire, as pricing your work too low makes it "appear" cheap or less valuable. In addition, many consumers understand that "you get what you pay for," and are willing to spend a little more for something of true value.

Another consequence of undervaluing your work may be that, at the end of the day, you're not even covering your own costs related to the production of your work—let alone making a living. So, as a starting point, it's important to understand how much it actually costs you to produce your art, and secondly, to determine how much you can reasonably sell it for in the marketplace.

EVALUATING YOUR COSTS

There are two types of costs you have to consider in calculating the cost of your work:

FIXED COSTS

Costs that are independent of any particular project, that is, any expense that is incurred, regardless of whether or not you produce any work, are fixed costs. Examples include:

> **Indirect labour costs:** fees, wages, and/or honorariums paid for administrative or other general services related to your business or creative practice (i.e.: your accountant).

> **Overhead costs:** costs that are not directly related to any one project, but are required in the day-to-day running of your business, including studio or office rental, utilities, advertising and promotion, professional membership fees, insurance, etc.

Your fixed costs stay the same (or "fixed") whether you make five paintings in a year or fifty of them. In order to gain a clear understanding of the true cost of your work, a portion of these costs will need to be allocated to each of your projects.

VARIABLE COSTS

Costs that are directly related to a particular project and vary depending on the level of production are variable costs. Examples include:

> **Direct labour costs:** fees, wages, and/or honorariums you pay to yourself and any other employee or contractor on a given project or production series.

> **Raw materials:** material costs incurred during the production of a particular project. These might include paint, fabric, buttons, beads, string, paper, printer toner, etc.

As an artist, your highest variable cost will likely be your own labour cost—and yes, you have to include this in your calculations! In order to make your business or practice sustainable, it is important that you be compensated for your time. The amount you "charge" for your own labour should be at least what you'd have to pay someone else to do the task(s) in question. And, ideally, at or above the minimum wage.

The next logical step, once you know how much it costs you to make your art, is to determine how much of it you have to sell to actually make money over and above these costs. The way to do this is to calculate your break-even point.

BREAK-EVEN POINT

Particularly for those who produce tangible goods, the break-even point allows you to determine how much of your art you will need to sell at a certain price point to cover your fixed and variable costs. When you "break-even," it means you've covered all costs related to making your art. Anything over and above this will be profit. (Note that this "profit" is over and above the wages you will have paid yourself as part of your variable costs.)

Here is a formula to help you determine your breakeven point:

$$\frac{\text{Fixed Costs}}{\text{Unit Price} - \text{Variable Costs}}$$

Let's look at an example for a painter. Assume each painting made during the year was about the same size and required the same amount of materials and labour.

We'll assume the painter's fixed costs (studio rent, utilities, etc.) are $3,000 per year.

We'll assume that her variable costs include paint and canvas, which cost $25 per painting. And we also have to include the number of hours she worked on each painting at a fair hourly wage. Let's say each painting takes 10 hours at $15/hour = $150. So her total variable costs per painting are $175.

She's done some market research and determined that she can sell her work for about $300 per painting. So, at that price, how many does she have to sell to break-even?

$$\frac{\text{Fixed Costs (\$3,000)}}{\text{Unit Price (\$300)} - \text{Variable Costs (\$175)}}$$

This boils down to:

$$\frac{\$3,000}{\$125} = 24 \text{ paintings}$$

This means that in order to break-even, she'll have to sell 24 paintings. At that point, she will have covered all her out-of-pocket costs (studio rent, utilities, and materials) plus her own labour costs at $15/hr.

But let's say she felt she could increase the price of her work to $350 per painting. Crunching the numbers again would reveal that her break-even point would be reached after selling only 17 paintings:

$$\frac{\text{Fixed Costs (\$3,000)}}{\text{Unit Price (\$350)} - \text{Variable Costs (\$175)}}$$

This boils down to:

$$\frac{\$3,000}{\$175} = 17 \text{ paintings}$$

That small difference in price could make a big difference in the amount she has to sell to cover her costs. By playing around with different price points, you can come up with a realistic scenario for how much work you need to sell at what price in order to at least break-even. Remember, the break-even point relates to covering your fixed and variable costs (including your own per-hour wage). Selling over and above the break-even point is when you start making a profit (over and above your own wages), and that's the goal.

EVALUATING YOUR MARKET

Regardless of the costs you incur in producing your work, the price you charge for your work must be within the acceptable price range of what the market will bear—how much people are willing to pay for it. You can nudge your prices up or down within what's acceptable in your industry, but if you're too much of an outlier—be it on the high or low end of the spectrum—your art will either collect dust on the shelf or be quickly under-valued and discarded.

So how do you decide what an acceptable price range is? Through market research. Look at what your competitors are charging for similar products and services. Contact the leading professional organizations or unions representing your artistic discipline or industry sector. Speak to more established artists for advice on pricing strategies.

Do some legwork. Visual artists and fashion designers, for instance, can visit galleries or target stores before bringing in their work to see what kind of price points they carry. If you price your work too high or too low, it will be obvious you haven't done your research and you'll likely lose credibility.

There is also plenty of information on the web. For example, freelance writers can visit www.writers.ca and check out the suggested fees table indicating industry guidelines on how much to charge based on the type of writing they'll be doing. An extensive listing of various arts service organizations is included at the end of this book.

TIPS FOR INCREASING PROFITS

Of course, pricing is only part of the profit equation. There are many other ways to ensure you're making and keeping the money from your art. Here are some tips:

> Sell more work—either by increasing your own efforts or by hiring someone on a commission basis to help you increase sales.

> Charge more for your time, if the market determines this is reasonable.

> Choose a lower rent location for your studio or office. Or, better still, further decrease your overhead (fixed) costs by working from home.

> Minimize your production (variable) costs by obtaining products, services, and work materials through co-ops or bartering programs.

> Subcontract part of the work to someone who can do it for less money than you are willing to. The painter in the example above may need and wish to pay herself at least $15/hr. for the creative work, but may be able to find someone to do the framing for $10/hr.

DON'T UNDERVALUE YOUR ART

Probably the most important piece of advice for making a living as an artist is: Don't under-value your work. Remember, this is your livelihood, your career—not a hobby. This is what you do (or are working towards doing) to put food on your table. You work at your job just as hard as any lawyer or doctor. It's fine to volunteer your time when you're just getting acquainted with your milieu, and in most cases, doing so will help launch your career. However, you have to know when to start charging what you are worth. If your writing is good enough to be published, your photos good enough to be printed, then you are good enough to be paid.

BUDGETING
BASICS

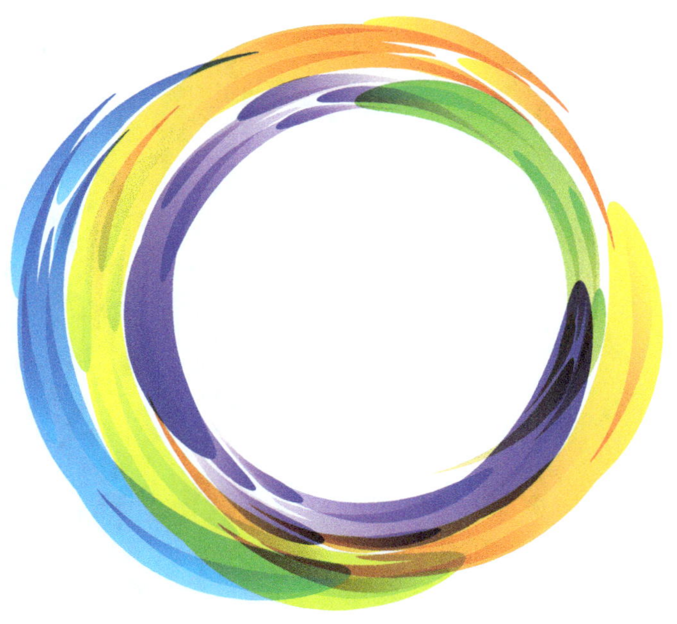

It may not be something most people want to hear, but creating a budget is one of the most critical things you can do to ensure your artistic career survives beyond the first few years. Most artistic entrepreneurs like yourself start with a load of talent and tremendous enthusiasm. But, unfortunately, that's not quite enough. You've chosen a feast-or-famine kind of income stream. There will be months when the money rolls in, and there will be dry spells that last far too long for comfort. Honing your budgeting skills will be the only way to ride this rollercoaster lifestyle without wanting to jump off. Still need convincing? Have a read below to see how a budget can help.

GOAL SETTING

Creating a budget forces you to have a clear financial goal in mind, which helps shape your work schedule for the year. How many gigs or contracts do you need to make ends meet? How much do you have to sell to afford that new equipment? Budgeting gets you to think about these questions in advance and gives you the opportunity to find appropriate and realistic solutions.

ACCESS TO FINANCING

At some point you may want to apply for a grant or take out a loan for a project or big equipment purchase. A budget will show the granting agency or lender how much you actually need. So, solid budgeting skills can increase your credibility and your chances of getting funding.

A SPENDING GUIDE

Ever check your bank balance and wonder where all your money went? Not a great feeling! Your budget will give you information about how much you really need to live on, and how much you can spend each month without going broke.

TRACKING

Making a budget forces you to track all of your income and expenses (spending). It's a pain at first—no question, but you'll be amazed at what you learn about your cash flow. And you may be pleasantly surprised at your revenue numbers. Tracking will reveal important patterns that you can use to smooth out the bumps in your financial road. Is your business income more seasonal than you expected? Are there a few persistent small expenses that add up to a huge drain on your bank account?

SELF-SUFFICIENCY

As a self-employed artist or artist-entrepreneur, it is likely that no one is looking after this part of your career for you. Financial self-sufficiency is part of the package you've bought into. It's not glamorous or exciting, but good budgeting ensures your financial freedom. And this should be no less important than your artistic freedom if you want to make it over the long haul.

HOW TO CREATE A BUDGET

> ### SET ASIDE TIME

Sitting down to create a budget for the first time can be a very daunting prospect. Do you know when your strongest revenue months are throughout the year? Conversely, when are your quiet times? If you've been a working artist for at least one or two years and you don't have a budget, now is the time to go back over your monthly revenue and start working out when the money's coming in and, just as importantly, when it's not.

> ### DETERMINE YOUR COSTS

You need to determine where each and every dollar you're spending is going. This means identifying and allocating your living expenses, labour costs (if you're paying anyone), material costs, office expenses, financing costs, and all other outgoing expenses.

It is helpful to identify the fixed costs and variable costs associated with your practice or business, as detailed in the Pricing and Profit section of this book. The next step is to allocate and tally the various expenses into a monthly spreadsheet or other tracking tool. This will help you have a clear idea of how much money is or will be going out each month. You may find that certain months will have greater financial outlays, e.g. when you are purchasing a big batch of supplies. This will help you plan ahead, and maybe put some money aside in advance.

> ### FORECAST YOUR REVENUES

Try to (realistically) forecast your monthly and annual revenues for the course of the year, and add them to your budgeting spreadsheet or other tracking tool. This will be easier if you've been working for a while. If you're just beginning, a good deal of research will be required. Ask the advice of other artists in the field what you might conservatively expect to earn.

> ### BUDGET LINE BY LINE

Contrast revenues versus expenses to determine whether you have enough money coming in to cover your expenditures. Try to determine the likely impacts on your bottom line of either reducing or increasing certain expenses and/or revenues. If marketing costs are high, but you're not getting additional clients as a result, now's the time to consider reducing the expense or changing your advertising strategy. By that same token, you may well find yourself in need of additional income in order to make ends meet. This will require some decisions and action on your part, including possibly supplementing your revenues with a part-time job.

> STAY FLEXIBLE

Finally, the real secret to any budget is its ability to be flexible. You'll need to be willing to do what it takes to make it work. This may mean scaling back your expenses, finding ways to increase revenues, or even deferring certain projects until your finances are in better shape. Of course, having some savings in the bank that you can lean on during a particularly rough month wouldn't hurt either.

BUDGET PSYCH. 101

> DON'T ASK, DON'T TELL

Why is budgeting so hard for so many people? Perhaps it's because many of us are taught not to talk about money. In social situations, we never ask how much someone earns for a living. It's easier to ask very personal health or relationship questions than money questions. Many of us grew up having no idea what our parents made or how household expenses were paid (or debt accumulated, for that matter). And for many of us budgeting isn't taught in school.

> IT'S A ROADMAP, NOT A ROPE

While budgeting is often associated with constraints—binding you to certain fixed limitations—it's actually only a roadmap to guide you. Budgeting doesn't really tie you to anything. In fact, it's the process of budgeting, sitting down and thinking out what your expenses and revenues will likely be, that is more important than the actual budget document. That document can be adjusted—and should be adjusted—as you move ahead with your artistic career.

> A DAUNTING TASK

Many people put off budgeting because it seems such a daunting, time-consuming task. When you're excited about your art, the temptation is to get started, start creating, start selling. Budgeting can seem a drag on the process. But what's certainly worse is to get going full-tilt, only to falter a year later due to an empty bank account and unexpected credit card bill. Budgeting is the biggest reality check you're likely to have. Daunting? Yes. Optional? No.

> GOOD DEBT VS. BAD DEBT

Taking on manageable debt is often the best way to jump-start your artistic career or manage cash flow shortfalls on a big project, but debt can be a dirty word to some people. Why is some debt "good" and other debt "bad"? When you use debt as a means of investment, it's generally considered "good debt." That $5,000 you borrow to invest in camera equipment for your photography business is expected to turn into (let's say) $10,000 in profit if your career plan is solid. So, in principle, the interest you will pay on that loan will be more than adequately covered by your gain. "Bad debt," on the other hand, is debt taken on to pay day-to-day living expenses or for personal items that will only decrease in value (or have no profit or investment potential). Going into debt for a $5,000 Caribbean holiday, for instance, would be considered "bad debt."

FINANCING
YOUR WORK

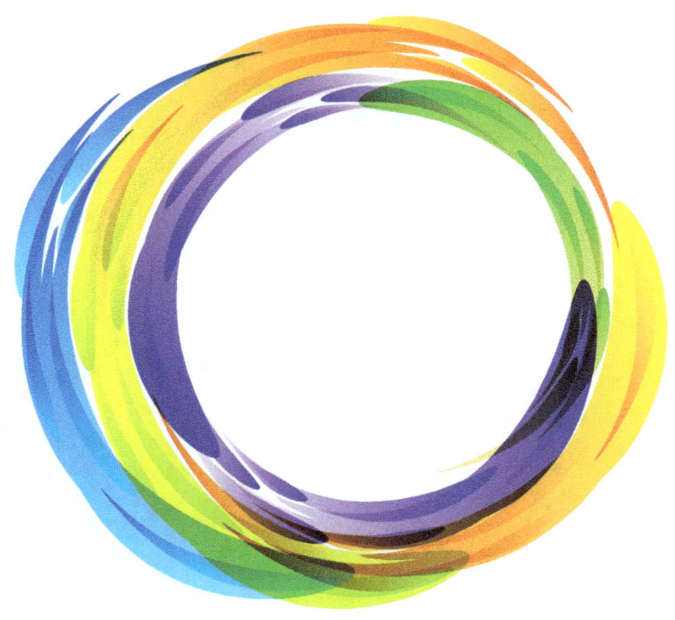

There are several places an artist-entrepreneur can look for funding. Generally, you'll start with your own resources and those closest to you and work outward as more capital is needed.

PERSONAL ASSETS

It is expected that you will invest your own savings and "sweat equity" in your business before seeking outside funding—especially in the early phases of your career. Sweat equity refers to the amount of unpaid time and labour you put into your art to get it going.

LOVE MONEY

The next place most artists look for capital to fund their projects is to friends and relatives. While these lending or investment arrangements can be made informally, it's best to treat them professionally. You should create proper written agreements. Misunderstandings are all too common and can jeopardize these relationships.

CROWDFUNDING

Crowdfunding has become a popular way for artists and entrepreneurs to raise money online through websites like Kickstarter and Indiegogo, among others. This type of fund-raising entails building a promotional campaign that offers perks related to your project in exchange for varying amounts of financial contribution. It is a great way to raise money AND engage with supporters at the same time, but requires a great deal of planning, strategy, and promotional effort, so must not be undertaken lightly. Please refer to the Crowdfunding for Fun and Profit section later in this chapter for some first-hand advice from a successful crowdfunder.

FINANCIAL INSTITUTIONS

Banks and credit unions are a common source of financing. For small business loans of under $25,000, you may not need personal collateral, but you'll need a good credit rating. For more on credit ratings, see the section on credit later in this chapter. Loans of over $25,000 will likely require some form of personal collateral. In this case, be prepared to use your home, your savings, or your investment accounts to guarantee the funding.

GOVERNMENT, NON-PROFIT FUNDERS, AND FOUNDATIONS

Depending on the artistic industry or creative discipline you're in, your age, and other criteria, you may be eligible for certain grants and loans. To find out more about this category of financing, check out the YES website at www.yesmontreal.ca for the next workshop on grants and loans. And for more on grants, in particular, have a look at our section on Arts Grants further in this chapter.

INVESTORS, PARTNERS, AND ANGELS

An investor or silent partner puts money into your business project in exchange for part ownership. He or she would likely have nothing to do with creating the art or the day-to-day operations of your company, but will take a share of the profits once they occur. An angel refers to a wealthy individual that provides capital to a business, but generally doesn't invest for the long-term. Enter these relationships with caution. Do your research.

QUALIFYING FOR A BANK LOAN

After personal resources and "love money," banks are actually the most common source of project financing, so it's worth knowing what the bank will be looking for when assessing you for a loan. According to Simon Restall, Director of Small Business for Scotiabank Canada, a bank looks for the "five Cs" in a credit application:

1. CHARACTER

This will be judged by your credit history, the length of your banking relationship, and possibly your experience in the field, among other things.

2. CAPACITY

The bank will assess whether you have the ability to handle the loan payments and day-to-day expenses of your project.

3. CAPITAL

It's not the bank's function to grant 100% of the money you need. It will want to know how much you yourself are investing, and what your net worth is. It will also want some idea of the net worth of your project.

4. CONDITIONS

The bank will want to be comfortable with the current marketplace conditions. For instance, does it make sense to be starting up a new film fest in a city that already has several?

5. COLLATERAL

If you require collateral, the bank will want to know you have enough assets in your possession to cover the loan. Some types of collateral they might ask for include: cash, GICs, bonds, real estate, and equipment.

YOUR CREDIT RATING

A credit rating is an assessment of your credit worthiness. That is to say, it's an indication of how much of a "risk" you likely are to a lender. Your credit rating is determined by private rating agencies, based upon your history of borrowing and repayment, as well as the assets and liabilities in your name. Artist-entrepreneurs looking for a business loan or line of credit are generally required to have their personal credit rating checked before accessing financing.

CHECK IT!

Before applying for any grant or loan, you should check your credit rating. Both Equifax and TransUnion will supply a detailed account for a fee ($22). You may be surprised by what you find. An old, forgotten savings account racking up small fees every year can tarnish your credit history without you even knowing it. Late cell phone bills or credit card payments can affect your score.

BUILDING A GOOD CREDIT RATING

What if your score is poor or nonexistent? You can apply for a credit card, use it, pay it off promptly several times, and then cut it up. Lenders will want to see some kind of score (preferably high), so you're best to check it before they do. But be aware that credit card payments don't count as part of your score when the card is secured by someone else (like a parent).

CREDIT SERVICES

Want more information on credit? Check out these websites:

Credit counselling: www.creditcanada.ca
Credit reports info: www.equifax.ca or www.transunion.ca
Current loan and credit card rates: www.banx.com
Interac Association: www.interac.org

SAMPLE ARTIST BUSINESS PLAN

Whether you're applying for a loan or grant, you may be required to provide some form of business plan. Here's a summary of what that should include:

Project Summary (no more than 1 page)

Write this section last; this will help you write a well-directed, concise summary.

> Provide a short description of your work or project.

> Briefly describe your marketing and financial strategy.

Artist Statement (about a paragraph)

The artist statement, or your mission statement, is a basic introduction to your work, project, and your creative practice.

> Include basic information about why you create your art, how you create it, what it means to you.

Description of the Art (1 to 3 pages)

In this section, present a detailed description of your work or project.

> Provide information about yourself, your skills, and any previous experience you have had.

> Explain what exactly makes your artwork unique (What types of materials do you use? What does your work look like? Does it serve any kind of purpose? How is it made?).

> Include your resume and high-quality images of your art at the end of this section.

Target Buyer (1 page)

This is a detailed description of your typical target buyer or consumer.

> Provide information about your buyers' demographic profile: their gender, their income, their age range, their level of education, their marital status, etc.

> You should also include information about your buyers' psychographic profile: why they buy, how often they buy, when they buy, and where they buy.

Marketing Your Art (1 to 3 pages)

> Explain what makes you different from other artists in your field, what unique advantages you have in the marketplace.

> Define your advertising and promotion strategies for reaching your target buyer (which tools you will use and how you intend to use them).

> Define your pricing strategy (how much does it cost you to produce your art, what kind of profit margin would you like to make, etc.).

> Define your distribution and sales strategies (Will you be selling through a wholesaler? Retail? Private showings?).

Financial Strategy (1 to 3 pages)

> Project your sales and expenses for at least the first year of operations (ideally more) and put them into an income statement format or spreadsheet format for easy reading.

> Include information about potential and confirmed sources of financing.

Action Plan (1 page)

> Provide a timeline of the various strategies outlined in your plan.

ARTS GRANTS: AN IMPORTANT SOURCE OF INCOME

It's sad but true: as an artist, you need money to make money. Whether you're set to make your first feature-length film, or you're intent on publishing a volume of poetry, you'll need money to finance your endeavour and pay the household bills in the meantime.

In this respect, Canadian artists are lucky. Relative to other countries, there is a great deal of money available in the form of grants for both emerging and established artists in Canada. However, it remains that not every project earns a grant. While there is no way of guaranteeing the success of an application, not applying for a grant guarantees no money granted. The following section provides basic tips and guidelines on applying for funding and answers some frequently asked questions about the process.

Note that the information presented is of a very basic nature and, in most cases, doesn't refer to specific granting agencies. Although the application process is generally similar from one granting agency to another, expect each to have its own requirements.

BEFORE YOU BEGIN

Have a clear idea of your project (concept, logistics, etc.) before you start researching and applying for grants, and identify the artistic discipline (film, music, theatre, etc.) and/or industry to which your project belongs. Know what function it aims to fulfill (community development, education, etc.) as most granting programs are structured and thus offer funding according to these considerations.

Research potential sources of funding, and take note of programs and initiatives that may be appropriate for the type of work you do, and build a list of grants and their application deadlines for which you are eligible. Keep your eyes peeled for new grants and initiatives as funding programs change regularly.

Review the agencies' eligibility criteria before investing your time and energy in applying for any grant. This includes determining the agency's funding priorities and submission deadlines. Don't start filling out the application form until you are sure that you and your project qualify. If in doubt, contact the program officer that will have been assigned by the granting agency. Contact information should be readily available on the agency's website. Do not leave this to the last minute.

Understand the overall application process, including each section, question, and guideline. Most funding agencies provide a resource guide that accompanies the application package and outlines their particular requirements.

Think about how your project fits within your career path. Does this project make sense in the grand scheme of your career and in light of your prior work? Is it a complete departure?

Know what makes your project unique, innovative and important, both to you and to the community/audiences.

Don't distort your work to fit an attractive grant. Instead, be persistent in your research for grants that do support your type of work. Do, however, consider broadening your creative horizons as you go.

Start preparing your application well ahead of the deadline. If helpful, create a timeline for completing the various pieces of the application. Remember, you are competing with many other people and projects, so the more time you have, the better and potentially more successful your application will be.

Prepare a checklist of essential information you do not want to forget to include in your application package. As you write and compile material for your proposal, check off the completed items.

Ask for letters of support far in advance. Make sure to explain the context for your needing these documents to those providing them.

Don't be shy to seek the advice of artists who have successfully obtained a similar grant. To maximize your chances of success, capitalize on the resources and services available to you online, through your professional associations, or artists' guilds, and through service organizations, like YES, that work with artists.

AS YOU WRITE YOUR PROPOSAL

Choose an interesting and evocative project title. A thoughtful and creative title is the very first thing the judging committee will read and first impressions count. Do make sure your title reflects the nature of your project.

Create a short project summary before you start seriously working on your application and project description, to help you clarify the project in your own mind. Try to answer the basic questions: what, why, how, where, when, and by who? You can recycle an upgraded version of this summary as the first paragraph of your proposal.

Create an outline for the project narrative. Once the project idea is clear, draft a basic outline detailing the key points you will need to write about in order to explain your project as thoroughly as possible. Once you have an outline built from start to finish (beginning with "project summary" all the way through to "conclusion"), you can start writing a paragraph or more under each outline heading. You may choose to keep the headings, or you can remove them later, once you've completed the writing process.

Make sure your first paragraph is clear and concise. The beginning of your proposal is crucial. It must capture the nature, context, format, and essence of your project. Think of this as a "project summary." See project summary above.

Respect the word or page limit indicated by the funding body. Since you will be working within these limits, make every word count; use powerful and descriptive language. And let your creativity shine through by writing a proposal that is unique and memorable, but not convoluted.

Emphasize what makes you and your project unique, interesting, important, and in line with your artistic mandate. In the project description section be sure to discuss the context, outcome, and themes of your work, including techniques and materials you intend to use. Include information about yourself and your artistic practice, touching upon your inspiration and motivation. Discuss past, present, and future projects. How does the current project fit in with all of this?

Mention any community support, accolades, awards, and special attention earned, including notable showings of your work and previous grants received.

Avoid using industry jargon. Not all grant applications are judged by juries of your peers. You should never assume the committee judging your grant proposal is familiar with your artistic discipline or your work. So present your project and your ideas in a way that is easy to understand, comprehensive, and accessible.

Consider getting help writing the grant. If writing is not your strongest skill, don't be shy about using reference guides for writing tips, such as E. B. White's *Elements of Style* or *Merriam-Webster's Concise Handbook for Writers*. Look into the services of a writer or ask a writer-friend who may be willing to work for free or through a bartering arrangement. Whatever you do, edit and re-edit your proposal. It is not unusual to go through several drafts before arriving at a well-thought-out, impeccably written submission. Time permitting, let your proposal sit for a while, and then work on it again.

Have friends, family, and mentors review your proposal for grammar, orthography, and content. Choose people who can bring different perspectives to your project.

Present a high quality, up-to-date portfolio with your best work. Don't inundate the jurors with everything you've ever produced. Any slides, images, or demos that you include should be top-notch and well catalogued. Make sure to respect the funding agency's guidelines as to what formats are acceptable.

Read through your proposal one last time right before you package and send your application and accompanying documentation. Pay attention to details. Did you spell the name of the granting organization correctly? Are all supporting documents and visuals there? Are all the pages in order? Remember, this package will speak for you, let it express itself eloquently and favourably on your behalf.

Send the application on time. Latecomers are not permitted under any circumstances, so save yourself the heartbreak of rejection by respecting application deadlines.

Have several grant applications on the go simultaneously to increase your chances of getting a grant. Since there are no guarantees of having a particular proposal accepted, funders assume that you are looking for more than one funding source at a time.

Keep everything up to date as you go. Your first grant application will likely be the most difficult, as subsequent applications will involve some previously created and compiled elements, such as your artistic statement, portfolio, CV, and reference letters.

CREATING YOUR GRANT PROPOSAL BUDGET

Depending on the type of grant for which you are applying, in addition to a project description or "pitch" you will likely be required to submit a project budget. There's not one way to do a budget, as this document will vary a great deal depending on artistic discipline, nature, and scope of a given project, and funding agency protocols.

Seek advice from senior artists, the granting agencies themselves, or your professional association. Creating a budget can be challenging at first. Some funding agencies, along with a project application form, will provide a budget template for you to use, others do not.

Fill in all appropriate sections if you are using a funding agency's budget templates. If you are creating your own budget document, ensure it's simple, clear, easy to understand, and complete. Excel is an excellent software platform to use.

Provide information that is comprehensive, well sourced, and well thought through. Your budget should be realistic, clear, and feasible in relation to the project. Remember, these documents seek to demonstrate the feasibility and cohesiveness of a project.

Start working on your budget well in advance of the grant deadline, especially if you need to research various costs or other information related to your project.

Make sure you understand what expenses and revenues are eligible for the particular grant for which you are applying. If in doubt, double-check with the funding agency. Often a list of what is and isn't eligible is included in the grant application guidelines. Most funding agencies do not fund infrastructure expenses, such as the purchase of equipment or other items considered assets.

It's perfectly acceptable to request the maximum amount allowed by a funding agency, but only if the scope and projected costs of the project truly merit the amount. Be mindful that some funding agencies will fund only a certain percentage of a given project, in which case you will be expected to demonstrate the sources of the remaining funding.

Be prepared to contribute to the project funding. It is acceptable (and even desirable) in some cases for the artist to contribute a certain portion of a project's costs out of their own pocket. It shows that the artist is invested in their own work.

Don't fudge the numbers. In putting together a cohesive and comprehensive budget, you must determine all pertinent projected expenses and then research and source them carefully so that the budget reflects a realistic financial portrait of your project. Don't limit your research to the Internet. Call, connect, and interface with people, especially if you will be contracting services and incurring costs that may be variable and difficult to predetermine. In trying to determine projected revenues related to a project, especially where revenues are linked to ticket sales or are yet to be confirmed, you will need to rely on projections based on your own knowledge and research.

For larger-scale projects (films, performing arts tours, etc.) you may be required to further itemize your budget by allocating costs/revenues to appropriate project phases such as pre-production, production, post-production.

Typical expense categories include: subsistence pay (your living expenses); studio fees and rentals; art and other supplies; equipment and other rentals; artists', technicians' and other labour-related fees; reproduction rights; transportation and travel costs; promotional materials; costumes; etc. (See also in-kind donations below).

Typical revenue categories include: projected ticket sales; in-kind donations; anticipated funding sources; artist's own contribution to project; etc.

In-kind donations are goods and services with a financial value that are donated to your project by a person or company, but for which you will not be paying. The value of these items must be accounted for in your budget in both the expense and revenue sections to: a) reflect the true monetary value of the project, and b) to cancel each other out, and thus reflect the project's real cash value.

Be prepared to provide details. A budget should itemize all pertinent expenses and revenues, including descriptions, amounts, quantities, and category subtotals, as well as the overall budget totals. Follow the funder's lead by providing the cost and revenue subtotals and totals as required.

You may be able include sales taxes in your budget unless you have a GST/QST number (and receive GST/QST rebates from the government). If in doubt, verify this with the funding agency.

A 5 to 10% contingency fund may be prudent to include in your budget for any unforeseen project costs. This will depend, of course, on the nature and scope of your project.

Make sure your budget adds up! Double-check all calculations to avoid potential embarrassment or, worse, rejection of your project.

Keep track of your expenses and revenues if you are successful in obtaining a grant, as you will be required to report on your project's financial outcomes. Keep all receipts and invoices; they are indispensable proof of your project expenses and revenues (for both the funder and Revenue Quebec/Canada) and will be used to track where you are in your budget as you go along.

CREATING YOUR GRANT PROPOSAL TIMELINE

Many grants require you to provide a project timeline. This timeline must explain, in a brief yet comprehensive manner, how a project will be realized over its duration, answering the question "What will get done when?" A timeline demonstrates your capacity to conceive and plan a project from start to finish, and will be used by the funding agency, at least in part, to determine your project's feasibility.

When creating a timeline, it is helpful to start by breaking the project down into key phases, and then identifying main activities that will need to be undertaken to complete each phase. Start with a brainstorm and build your timeline or "action plan" from there.

Sample key phases can include: pre-production, research, experimentation, production, post-production, promotion, distribution, and post-completion reporting.

A timeline is not a to-do list, but should include details that elaborate the main processes you must undertake to complete the project and its various phases from start to finish. For instance, "promotion" might be broken down into: media list research, graphic design, printing, poster distribution, press releases, and media outreach.

Use your timeline as a guide to keep you moving through your project in a timely fashion. Keep in mind that in any given week or month, you may work on items belonging to various key phases simultaneously. And do understand that timelines can and often do change. If your timeline changes dramatically due to unforeseen circumstances during the course of your project, you may need to communicate that with your funding agency.

FOLLOWING UP ON YOUR GRANT PROPOSAL

Once your proposal is in the mail or sent online, don't just forget about it.

Call the agency a week or so after you send in your proposal to make sure they have received your application package, and take the opportunity to find out when the decisions will be announced.

If you don't get the grant you applied for, ask the program officer for feedback as to how you can improve your chances in the future. Sometimes, it is a question of fine-tuning, be it your ideas and your work, or simply your application itself. So don't be shy to find out.

If you do get the grant, CONGRATULATIONS!!! You will likely be contacted by your program officer, and will be required to sign a contract regarding the various obligations and deliverables each party will undertake.

Roll up your sleeves and get to work. Remember, there are timelines, budgets, deliverables, and other contractual obligations for you to consider. Your credibility and reputation with your granting agency depends not only on producing high-quality creative work, but also on your ability to deliver on and respect your obligations, so make sure you do.

Send a thank you letter to your program officer, regardless of whether you were successful in getting a grant or not. Good manners are never out of style, and can go a long way in making a good and lasting impression. While you're at it, add the program officer to your mailing list, so that you can keep the connection alive by later inviting him/her to your shows or including him/her on your newsletter list.

ARTIST GRANT APPLICATION CHECKLIST
By Monika Majewski, YES Artists' Program Coordinator and Coach

Before submitting your grant application, ensure you have everything you need to maximize your chances of getting a YES.

☐ **APPLICATION FORM**

☐ **PROJECT DESCRIPTION:**
Between one and four pages depending on the organization and the grant.
Verify in each case.

> **PROJECT TITLE**
Ensure the project title is well thought out and reflective of the project itself.

> **INTRO PARAGRAPH/PROJECT SUMMARY** (1 to 2 paragraphs)
This should address the following questions: What is your project? What is its scope/purpose? What does it consist of? How much of it is there? What is it about? What is its significance? How does it relate to you and the public?

> **DETAILED PROJECT NARRATIVE**

>> Describe the project/product, the concept behind it, and its components. Describe the nature of the project. What is it? What is it made of? How much of it is there? What is its aesthetic? Think finished product and process (if appropriate).

>> What is the project about? (Purpose, theme, relevance, etc.).

>> Why is this project significant for you in relation to your artistic practice? (Personal motivation, inspiration, relevance vis-à-vis past work, positive impacts on your practice, etc.)

>> What techniques, processes, and materials will you use to create this work? How is this relevant to what you've done before? How is this new and innovative?

>> How will this project be realized? (Methodology, approach, rough time frame/phases, who will do what, and when, etc.)

>> Who are you? Provide a brief version of your artist statement and bio to give some context to the project in light of your artistic practice. Include highlights like your artistic education, past projects, and career trajectory in a way that shows how you have gotten to your current project—think growth/development. Mention any major distinctions you and/or your work have garnered along the way.

>> Who are your collaborators (if any) and what are their roles? How/why are they important in this work? What significant contributions are they bringing to the table?

> Does this work references others' work? Is it influenced by an ideology? A movement? A particular form of artistic or other expression in your own discipline and/or other fields?

> How or what does this project (and your work) contribute to your artistic practice and discipline? the community? the wider society? (What are you trying to achieve? What are you offering?)

> How will the public experience this work and/or how will they benefit?

> What is the future of this project (if appropriate)? Will you be exhibiting, presenting, or touring the work? Will there be a part two?

> **CONCLUSION** (1 to 2 paragraphs)
Summarize/reiterate the project in brief and explain how it and the grant money will contribute to your development/progress as an artist. Also include what impact the project will have on the public/community. Don't forget to thank the funding agency for their time and attention.

☐ **ACCOMPANYING DOCUMENTATION:**

> **TIMELINE**
Duration and key phases of the project in a simple chronological work plan format broken down by month or week. (What will get done when?)

> **BUDGET**
The total costs and revenues related to the project, itemized by expense categories. Expenses may include subsistence pay (if any), studio expenses, art supplies, rentals, artists' fees, rights, promotional materials, etc. Revenue categories may include grants, in-kind donations, artist's own contribution, etc.

> **ARTISTS STATEMENT AND BIO** (only if requested)

> **ARTISTIC CV**

> **CVs OF COLLABORATORS**

> **SAMPLES OF PAST/RECENT WORK** (with a list of what you're submitting)

> **PRESS KIT OR CLIPPINGS** (if available)

> **LETTERS OF INTENT** (if any public showings of the work are booked)

> **LETTERS OF SUPPORT** (if allowed)

Monika Majewski is the Artists' Program Coordinator and Coach at YES and works closely with artists, artist-entrepreneurs, and cultural workers to support them in the development of skills, tools, and strategies needed to build sustainable careers.

FREQUENTLY ASKED FINANCING QUESTIONS

Who decides who gets a grant?

Although the selection process varies from one granting agency to another, usually a jury comprised of individuals familiar with the specific milieu of the grant is chosen to evaluate applications.

Where do I find organizations that might fund my project?

There is ample information on the Internet about granting agencies and there are also a number of books and other resource materials written on the topic. Research both.

Pay attention to press releases and publicity material from other artists or arts groups. See who they list as sponsors or who they are presenting "in association with." That will give you a great indication of both specific companies engaged in funding the arts as well as the types of companies that you might consider approaching for funding.

How do I approach organizations or corporations to see what kind of art they might fund?

Start by researching the organization's website. If you can't find specific information, there are a few people you can call.

> If you're dealing with an organization that you already know awards grants to artists, call a program officer and discuss your work with them.

> Many large Canadian and multinational corporations have art collections, usually run by professional in-house curators. They are frequently inundated with calls and letters from artists hoping to sell their work to corporate collectors. It may be difficult to get in touch with them, but it's worth it as they are invaluable industry resources.

> If you're unsure about an organization's arts grant and collecting policies, contact the person in charge of their public relations department.

> If a corporation or organization has funded art programs in the past, these will be listed in their annual reports. These reports are often public documents and can be obtained simply by requesting them from a receptionist or administrative assistant.

I can't find a granting agency that's right for my project. Where else can I look for funding?

Depending on your planned project, it may be wise to approach organizations that aren't strictly limited to arts funding. For instance, if you are looking to open an interactive art gallery, you could qualify for a business entrepreneurship grant. If you are looking to photograph Canadian national parks and package them as a keepsake calendar, you might qualify for funding from a tourism agency.

Some of my portfolio samples are very risqué, others are more commercial. Is it better to include all these varieties in the portfolio I send?

If your intended project doesn't involve anything risqué or if the agency from which you seek money isn't specifically geared towards non-commercial artists, don't risk putting off the jury with something that might offend them.

Do I eventually have to pay back the grant money I receive?

No. Grant money is given free and clear but is considered a part of your annual taxable income, and will need to be declared (along with your expenses) on your income tax return for the year in which it was received.

Do I have to pay taxes on the money I've been awarded?

Yes, you do, but do keep in mind that you will be paying taxes on the grant amount received MINUS project expenses incurred in the execution of the project for which the grant was given. If you are in any doubt about how to report your grant-related income and expenses, please take the time to speak with an accountant or a representative of the Canada or Quebec Revenue Agency.

I've received a grant based on a proposal I submitted, but now I have an even better idea. Can I keep the grant money to finance the new idea or do I have to follow through with the original proposal?

Some agencies may be open to allowing this kind of change, but it is best not to start your new project before setting up a meeting with a program officer to discuss the detour. You may also be taking a risk in requesting this change.

I have received a grant and things are going really well. I think I'm going to have a surplus of grant money. Do I have to give what's leftover back?

The grant money is yours, as long as you fulfill the terms of your application. However, if you have not used the grant money as intended, you may have to return it. If in doubt, check with the granting agency's program officer.

Should I acknowledge the grant I've received?

Definitely. Thank-you notes go a long way. Send one to the program officer associated with the grant, and do so for all of the contacts you develop along the way to show your appreciation and to keep the lines of communication open.

Many granting organizations will require you use their name and logo on any promotional material you produce. Also, indicate their support on your website and in any press releases you send out about your work.

Why was I denied a grant?

Being told you are ineligible for a grant does not mean your project is not worthwhile. Don't get discouraged. Successful grant applicants usually have been refused several times before they receive a grant.

There are several reasons why applications are turned down. The application process is very stringent; there are exacting guidelines to follow and very precise criteria to be met. You might have erred in a portion of the application, or the jury might have decided that you didn't quite meet the organization's criteria. In the end, quite simply, there may not have been enough money in the pot for everyone.

Regardless, DO ask for feedback from your program officer, and take notes as this will help you fine-tune your proposal or project for next time.

Where else can I look for sources of funding?

Financial support doesn't only come in the form of cold, hard cash. Consider creating your own funding opportunities. For instance, offer to give free publicity to a print shop in exchange for free posters. Or include a restaurant logo on your launch invitations in exchange for platters of food to be served at the event. There is also the brave new world of crowdfunding through platforms like Indiegogo and Kickstarter. Check out the Crowdfunding for Fun and Profit article by filmmaker Tony Asimakopoulos on how it worked for him, later in this chapter.

Do I need to include a business plan in my grant application?

Only include a business plan if the granting agency requires one. Before you write your own, we highly recommend that you check out the numerous online or hardcopy resources on the topic. Or, better yet, consult with one of the YES Artists' and/or Business Coaches.

CROWDFUNDING

FOR FUN
AND PROFIT

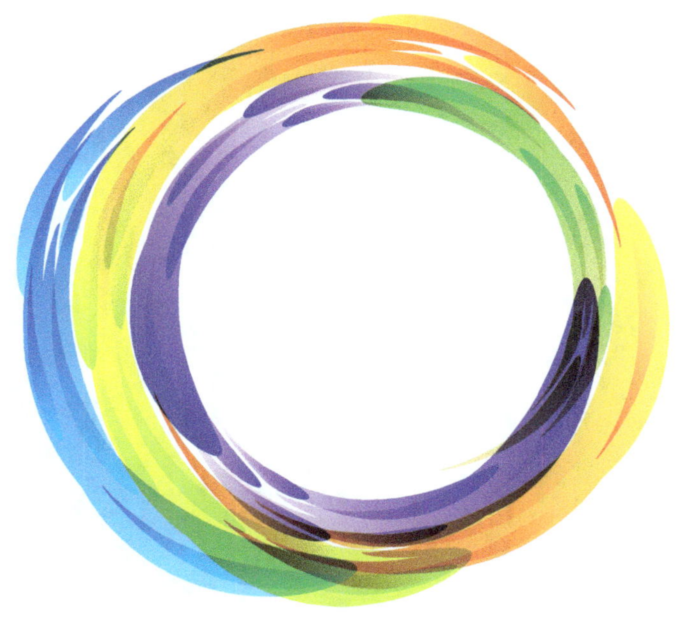

An interview with Tony Asimakopoulos, Montreal Filmmaker

Crowdfunding is the practice of funding a project or venture by raising money though various levels of financial contributions made by many people, typically via the Internet. Many artistic entrepreneurs have used this model successfully. In artistic endeavours, the funders are generally repaid with pledge gifts in exchange for their contribution. There are dozens of crowdfunding platforms out there. Popular ones include Kickstarter and Indiegogo. Each platform is different and should be thoroughly researched before committing to a campaign. Here's what Tony had to say about his experience:

What project did you crowdfund for?

I launched a campaign to fund my film, *A Walk in Park Ex*, a documentary about Montreal's Park Extension, the immigrant neighbourhood where I live. Crowdfunding seemed like the best choice because I had a limited timeline and no other options! I needed to shoot at Easter time; I had less than two months and many people to hire for that shoot. And I got a wonderful show of support from a grateful community, who was happy to have a film made about their home, and gave generously.

What were the downsides of your experience?

None! Other than this: know that you will learn things about people you "thought were your friends" and were sure would give/help in some way, but don't. Do your best to gently remind people, to keep the thing afloat in their consciousness, but, for some reason, some people just won't give—or even post about your campaign. Maybe they've got another friend's campaign they're favouring, or they are crowdfunding-fatigued (everyone's doing it), or your project isn't cool enough, or whatever. Know that it might change the way you feel about people. It definitely caused me to push some people to the edges of my circle, but also brought others closer. This is not a bad thing, but expect it.

How do you set a funding goal that makes sense?

Research, and have faith in what you're doing. Think hard and honestly about what you'll really need, and ask for it, or ask for part of it, and be clear that you are asking for funding for a specific phase of a project if you think the whole thing cannot be funded via crowdfunding donations.

If I had done more research, I would have set our goal much, much higher! If I had asked people on Facebook who would fund such a project, if I had put out feelers, the response would have surprised me and emboldened me, as it did during the campaign. And I wish I'd given the campaign a bit more time. I set the goal at $12,000, we got $22,000+, and I believe we could have set it at $35,000 and met that, if not even surpassed it.

How do you choose and price pledge gifts that make sense?

Work backwards from what you can realistically offer. I over-offered; a mistake. For example, many of my perks involved giving out DVDs of the finished film, but I could have started with downloadable versions of the movie, then in larger perks, a DVD, then a DVD plus something, etc. Budget your perks in terms of time and money; you don't want to spend the next year working off this money; that's not the point!

What likely "hiccups" should the novice be made aware of before embarking on a crowdfunding campaign?

As mentioned above, you'll be surprised and hurt by those who don't give.

And Indiegogo has issues with American donations to Canadian projects, when people want to pay with PayPal, for instance. And there were some banking issues with credit cards. There were many people who couldn't give, and eventually gave up. A few sent cheques, but I feel that we lost a lot due to that issue. I used Indiegogo, but it's worth looking into Kickstarter. Kickstarter may not cover all the same types of projects, but might be more stable.

How do you get over any awkwardness/shyness about asking people for money?

Think about not having any money at all.

Do you have any opinions on the crowdfunding platforms out there?

Besides the payment issues mentioned above, the benefit to Indiegogo is you can choose an option to collect even if you don't reach your goal. With Kickstarter, it's all or nothing. With Indiegogo, know that you will pay 9% of what you get to Indiegogo, even though they say it's 5%, there are hidden costs, "payment processors," they call them. So set your fundraising goal at 9% higher than what you think you'll need.

Do you have to have a certain type of personality to be successful at crowdfunding?

Good ideas are all you need, and a bit of a sense of entitlement.

Which types of projects lend themselves to crowdfunding and which don't?

Expansive projects that address and empower communities, any community, a real neighbourhood like mine, or an online community of D&D'ers (Dungeons & Dragons), or whatever. Anything that is good for many, not just yourself.

Most of the appeals for self-centered projects (horror films, calling card films, "career" advancement type projects) don't do well at all. If you have a great film idea, it better be something a lot of people can relate to. Experimental art projects won't do well—unless you're famous. And even then…

What's the biggest misconception regarding crowdfunding?

That it's a scam, a money grab. In some cases this might be true, I don't know. But you will have to deal with that, so it helps to take the time to build your community well before your campaign.

Tony Asimakopoulos is a Montreal-based filmmaker. He released his first documentary feature, *Fortunate Son*, in 2012 (produced by EyeSteelFilm, www.eyesteelfilm.com/distribution/fortunate+son). He has directed online comedy shorts for CBC Radio's syndicated *Wiretap* with Jonathan Goldstein, and is currently developing the documentary, *A Walk in Park Ex*, partly funded through Indiegogo.

ARTISTS AND THE LAW

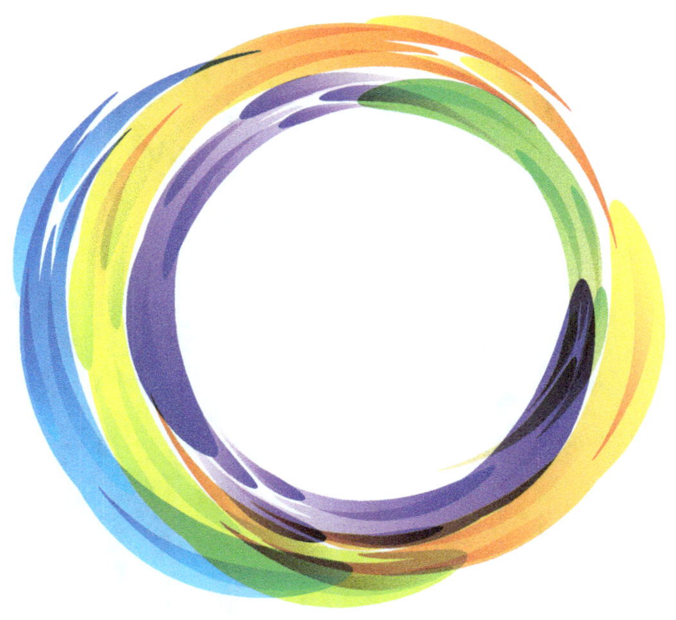

ARTISTS AND THE LAW

**By Me. Nancy Cleman, Sternthal Katznelson Montigny LLP
and Me. Kerry Williams, Creative Legal**

The purpose of this chapter is to provide artistic entrepreneurs with some basic legal information and relevant sources, which will be helpful to them in the conduct of their businesses. Artistic entrepreneurs include a large group of people, including musicians, filmmakers, performers, designers, software and web developers, writers, and painters. While the ways of doing business (e.g. as a company, partnership, or sole proprietorship) are the same as for other types of entrepreneurs, the nature of the business may require special types of protection.

The challenge that presents itself for artists is that much of what they try to protect is based on things we cannot see, i.e. "intellectual property" (IP), as opposed to tangible property such as tables and chairs. The world of information technology adds countless ways to duplicate material and transmit it in a manner and to places that would have been unthinkable in earlier times.

This chapter will provide high-level advice of a very general nature. It is focused on artists doing business in Quebec. It does not constitute legal advice. It should be used as a reference only, and does not replace the need to contact a lawyer or other professional. The goal here is to provide you with some basic guidelines and tips on how to carry out your business and protect yourself and your work.

One thing you should know about Canadian law is that there are two legal systems. One is federal and one is provincial. Within the provinces there are differences. Quebec is a civil law jurisdiction and has a Civil Code. The rest of Canada is a common-law jurisdiction and is based on Common Law. Federal laws apply in all provinces. Federal laws are laws that are created by the government of Canada, as opposed to provincial laws, which are enacted in each province. Intellectual property (copyright, trademark, patents, etc.) is governed by federal law for the most part. Doing business, entering into contracts, and employment matters are for the most part governed by provincial law. Some areas of law which may be of interest such as the Canadian anti-spam legislation are not covered here. The resource section at the back of the book provides a list of resources to address these topics.

PART I: LAWS OF IMPORTANCE FOR ENTREPRENUERS

For most artists a key concern is how to protect their work. In this section we will briefly touch on some of the laws that have relevance for artists. In the resource section of this book you will find a bibliography of websites and other references that provide some helpful information. A large part of the discussion will focus on copyright law because this has a large impact on all artists. We also draw your attention to two laws in Quebec that are specifically enacted to protect artists in their dealings with promoters and producers. In addition, we will discuss trademarks and trade secrets. For more information on intellectual property see the Canadian Intellectual Property Office (CIPO) website at www.cipo.ic.gc.ca.

COPYRIGHT (COPYRIGHT ACT CANADA)

As the name implies, copyright is the legal right to copy or reproduce a work protected by copyright law. This right belongs to the copyright holder to the exclusion of anyone else, except for very limited exceptions.

WHAT DOES COPYRIGHT PROTECT?

Copyright protects the *expression* of an idea but not the *idea* itself; this includes books, works of art, dramatic works, musical works, sound recordings, performances, broadcast signals, literary works, and software programs.

What is the difference between expression and idea? For example, let's think of a story about a little girl who goes to sleep and wakes up transformed into a cat because her stepbrother put a spell on her, etc. This is the idea. One person can write a story, another may write a screenplay, and a third a stage play. These three works are expressions of the idea. If the first thing to be published is the book and from the book someone decides to make a movie or stage a play, the movie and stage play would be derivative works that follow from the book. Likewise, each work could conceivably be created independently in which case the authors would want to be able to prove that they created their work without copying other works.

Under the *Copyright Act*, a "work" can take many forms. It may be a design, music, a play, a painting, a literary work, a sculpture, or an animated film, but it must be the direct result of the author's labour. It sounds simple, but it can get a little complicated, especially when more than one person is working on an artistic project. Joint authors of a novel would share copyright, but their editor would not, even if his input had an impact on the final product.

Copyright is vital to artists because the copyright holder has the exclusive right to copy, reproduce, translate, dramatize, or adapt the work. If you're an author, a publisher must enter into an agreement with you before publishing your book. If you're a filmmaker, a film distributor needs to sign a contract with you to have the right to put your film in the theatre. Digital technologies make it extremely easy to copy and distribute your work, so it is important to understand both the legal and technical realities of digital and electronic rights to protect your work and make sure you are fairly compensated for it.

A key element that must be present in order for copyright protection to arise is that the expression (be it a song, story, film, or other creation) must exist in a *fixed* and *tangible* format.

Copyright protection arises automatically in such a case.

A copyright holder has exclusive rights for the length of the copyright protection. These include derivative rights such as translation of the work and making other versions of the work; the copyright holder determines who can use the material and for what purpose(s).

The nature of copyright can vary depending on the field in which you work. For example musical works can include a number of types of copyright depending on how the work is being used, including performing rights, publication and reproduction rights, mechanical rights, and synchronization rights.

HOW IS COPYRIGHT OBTAINED?

Copyright arises automatically the moment you create an artistic work in a fixed and tangible format. You can register your copyright with the federal government through the Canadian Intellectual Property Office, but the law does not require it. It is useful to have some proof that you came up with the idea since it is possible for two people to own copyrights on similar creations (say, a story idea), provided they can prove they independently came up with their ideas. If not, there is a risk that one party will sue the other for infringement or unauthorized use. It's also not a bad idea to mail a copy of a creative work in which you claim copyright to a trusted advisor with a note to leave it unopened. In the event there is a problem, the sealed and dated letter may help prove when the work was created, and therefore help determine who created the work first.

Copyright gives the holder control over how their work is used. For instance, this means they have the sole right to produce, reproduce, perform, publish, or translate the work or any substantial part of it. See Section 3.1 of the Copyright Act for more details.

Copyright owners in Canada can add a notice to their work to confirm copyright protection: © NAME OF OWNER, 2015. ALL RIGHTS RESERVED.

HOW LONG DOES COPYRIGHT PROTECTION LAST?

The term of copyright protection is generally the lifetime of the author (the person who created the work) plus fifty years from the end of the calendar year in which the author died (though there are some exceptions to this rule). Registration provides additional protection in Canada and other countries throughout the World Trade Organization as well as signatories to international copyright treaties like the Berne Convention, the Universal Copyright Convention, and the Rome Convention. Citizens of countries that are members of these conventions enjoy the benefits of Canadian copyright law in Canada.

Sound recordings are also protected in Canada under the Copyright Act, but the protection accorded to sound recordings under international treaties varies considerably from country to country.

WHO OWNS COPYRIGHT?

Copyright usually belongs to the author of a work, although there are exceptions. If you create an artistic work on commission, you keep control of the copyright unless you sign a contract explicitly transferring the copyright to the person who commissioned you. It is important to check the rules for your area. For instance, the rules for photographers generally provide that they retain the copyright in their photos even if they are hired by someone else to take photos. An artist can sell their painting and still retain the rights to reproduce the work. They cannot stop the buyer from re-selling the work but they can stop the buyer from having the work reproduced on coffee mugs or posters.

However, if you're a full-time employee, your employer owns the copyright to any work created as part of your employment. For example, if you paint an illustration for an advertisement while working for an ad agency, it's the ad agency (or their client) that owns the copyright, not you. Similarly, if you're a staff journalist working for a daily newspaper, any stories you write will belong to the newspaper. Freelance journalists work under a different arrangement, and usually keep their copyrights, because they are independent contractors and not employees.

DO CONSULTANTS AND FREELANCERS OWN COPYRIGHT TO THEIR WORK?

As noted above, your employer owns the copyright in anything you create while working for them. However, if you're a consultant or freelancer rather than an employee, the copyright stays with you unless your consulting contract states otherwise, so read your contracts carefully before signing!

Make sure you and your employer both understand your legal status before you start work. Are you an employee or a contractor? Are you keeping your copyrights or assigning them as part of your contract? This is why people are often asked to sign complex employment contracts or letters of agreement that include an assignment of all rights to anything they develop in the course of their employment or engagement. It is very important that you read and ask questions before you sign any agreement so that you know what you are giving up and what you are keeping and at what price.

WHAT DOES ASSIGNING COPYRIGHT MEAN?

Assigning copyright means that the author legally transfers the ownership of a work to a third party, often for a specific fee. Once an assignment has been made, the author no longer owns the work, though they still usually retain their *moral rights* (see below).

WHAT DOES LICENSING COPYRIGHT MEAN?

Licensing is a less drastic step than assignment. An artist can license a third party to use their work in a specific context for a specific length of time without surrendering ownership of the work. For example, an artist may license a character to an ad agency for use in a TV commercial. The agency may only use the character for that specific purpose, for the length of time specified in the license agreement. Otherwise the artist still controls the character.

WHAT IS COPYRIGHT INFRINGEMENT?

Under the *Copyright Act*, it is infringement for any person to use a substantial part of a copyrighted property without the consent of the owner. This includes selling, renting, and making other works based on the original work. This means, for example, that you cannot stage a play based on a best-selling novel without the author's permission. Nor can you make unauthorized copies of copyrighted material (whether existing in a digital or analogue format) and download, distribute, or sell it. The determination of whether you are using a substantial part of a copyright work involves a complex legal test based on both quantitative and qualitative considerations; a lawyer specializing in intellectual property law can help you make this determination.

There are limited "fair dealing" exceptions under the Copyright Act, which allow you to make use of someone else's copyrighted work for such things as criticism, review, satire, and parody. The question of whether use of copyrighted material is fair depends on the circumstances of each case. Keep in mind, however, that the rules of fair dealing are often complex and what's permissible is limited, so it is a good idea to get permission to use someone's work or seek legal counsel.

WHEN DOES A COPYRIGHT WORK ENTER THE PUBLIC DOMAIN?

Once the copyright on an artistic work has expired, the work falls into the "public domain;" that is, it becomes everyone's property. Shakespeare's plays, Leonardo da Vinci's paintings, Beethoven's symphonies, and Sir Arthur Conan Doyle's Sherlock Holmes stories are in the public domain in Canada because the authors all died more than fifty years ago. It's perfectly legal to publish your own edition of *Hamlet* or reproductions of the Mona Lisa. Under the Copyright Act, basic facts, ideas, and news are also considered part of the public domain.

NOTE OF CAUTION: A new work based on the public domain—like a new movie based on Shakespeare's *Hamlet*, or a specific performance of a Beethoven symphony, is protected under copyright law. No one can stop you from making your own *Hamlet* movie, but you are not permitted to sell bootleg copies of someone else's *Hamlet* movie. Also keep in mind that foreign countries may have different definitions of the public domain, and a work you can legally use in Canada may still be under copyright protection in other jurisdictions.

IS PUBLIC DOMAIN WORK DIFFERENT FROM OPEN-SOURCE MATERIAL?

It is important to distinguish between works that are in the public domain and so-called "open-source" materials. Open-source licenses, including creative commons licenses, generally apply to technological information such as software code, digital content, and the like, but can also apply to other types of works that are subject to intellectual property law.

When a work is made available via an open-source license, it does not mean that copyright law does not apply. Rather, open-source licenses typically make a copyrighted work available for use by others for collaborative sharing and development purposes on certain terms and conditions. Depending upon the type of open-source license, works that are protected by copyright are generally made available subject to certain restrictions that are contained in the terms of the open-source license.

Some of the most common open-source restrictions include, **attribution**, meaning that the author must receive credit for the work; **share-alike**, meaning that derivative works must be made available via a similar open-source license; **non-commercial use**, meaning that the work can only be used for non-commercial purposes; and **no derivative works**, meaning that only the original work can be used.

Open-source software development projects such as the web browsers Mozilla Firefox and Chromium (the open-source platform behind Google Chrome) as well as the Android mobile operating system are some of the most well-known examples of projects built and maintained by volunteers that are subject to open-source licenses. The same principles of open-source collaboration apply to Wikipedia.

Accordingly, whenever you wish to make use of open-source materials it is very important to first review, understand, and abide by the terms of the open-source license since any use that is in contravention of the license will still constitute infringement of copyright. Remember to print or keep a copy of the terms of the license in force at the time of use. Also remember to respect the conditions of use.

WHAT ARE "MORAL RIGHTS" UNDER INTELLECTUAL PROPERTY LAW?

Moral rights are a separate class of intellectual property right. Unlike copyright, moral rights cannot be assigned to anyone else, though under certain circumstances the author may sign a waiver agreeing not to enforce them. Moral rights protect a work's "paternity." That means an author retains the right to have their name (or pseudonym) associated with a work even if the copyright has been sold or assigned to someone else. The author also has the right to remain anonymous.

In addition, moral rights protect artistic integrity. For instance, even if the copyright of a work has been assigned to someone else, moral rights may give the artist a certain degree of control over any action that "deforms, mutilates, or changes" their work in a way that might harm their honour or reputation. For example, several years ago a Toronto artist successfully invoked his moral rights against the owners of a shopping mall who made changes to a sculpture the artist had sold them. Though he no longer owned the sculpture, he was able to force them to restore the sculpture to its original condition.

WHAT ARE "NEIGHBOURING" RIGHTS?

Neighbouring rights are similar to copyright and protect the rights of performers who perform works copyrighted by someone else. Since 1997, the *Copyright Act* has acknowledged that, for example, a singer has certain intellectual property rights to their performances even if they are singing a song composed by someone else. Performers also receive royalties when their songs are broadcast. Under certain conditions, neighbouring rights also protect record labels and broadcasters.

Neighbouring rights impact relationships in the recording and music industries. Just as a singer needs to get permission from the composer to perform one of their songs, the composer now must also get permission from the singer to use a recording of their voice or make sound recordings available on the Internet. Filmmakers and multimedia producers must also make sure they have all the necessary neighbouring rights clearances when using recorded performances in their productions. Needless to say, this is a complex area of the law, and it's advisable to get professional legal advice if you have questions.

WHAT ARE "PERSONALITY" RIGHTS?

Personality rights are the rights of individuals to prevent unauthorized commercial use of their name, likeness, or other personal attributes. In Quebec, these are protected by the *Civil Code of Quebec* and the *Quebec Charter of Human Rights*. To summarize the articles of the Civil Code, "everyone has a right to have his reputation and privacy respected. No one may invade the privacy of the person unless authorized by law." Using a person's face and/or voice without their consent can constitute an invasion of privacy. The same applies to using the person's likeness, name, voice, or image for a purpose other "than the legitimate information of the public." This also applies to the use of their correspondence, manuscripts, or other personal documents.

WHEN DO I NEED TO USE A RELEASE?

If you are creating a project that uses a person's image, voice, or likeness in your work, you should first obtain that person's consent in writing. For example, a filmmaker must get written permission or a release to use a person in their film or video.

Personality rights need to be distinguished from privacy rights. Both federal and provincial legislation address how personal information may be used, but that is beyond the scope of this chapter. For more information, you should contact a legal professional.

HOW DO I PROTECT MY WORK?

People will often use contracts to protect confidential information and trade secrets. If you have work that you wish to protect, even if it is already protected by copyright, you may want to ensure that any potential partners, collaborators, or investors sign what is commonly referred to as a non-disclosure agreement or "NDA." While this type of contract can help in protecting your work by ensuring that the party with whom you are sharing your work agrees not to publically disclose it or make any unauthorized use of it, you still need to be careful about how much you disclose and when. For example, if you have written a screenplay and are looking for partners or investors to help bring your project to life, you will want to be sure that you have potential partners sign an NDA before you hand over your work for review. Also, regardless of whether potential partners have signed an NDA, you will still want to exercise good judgement and only share your work with people that you trust, since enforcing an NDA against an unscrupulous person who has stolen your ideas can be costly and time consuming!

Some producers or investors may not want to sign an NDA for business reasons. If they receive a similar product or script they do not want to be accused of infringement if they choose another's product or script over yours. Therefore, think about what you reveal and keep track of whom you share your work with.

SUMMARY COPYRIGHT TIPS

> The author is generally the first owner of the copyright in an original work.

> As a general rule, you may not use someone else's work, image, voice, or likeness without their permission. This applies to the entire work and even parts of it.

> Just because you can *technically* copy something does not mean that you have the legal right to do so.

> Assignment gives away your copyright but *not* your moral rights.

> Moral rights cannot be assigned to someone else, but you can waive them.

> If you use someone's work without permission, you can be sued for copyright infringement and be required to pay damages.

> Read terms of use and privacy policies on websites; put copyright notices on your work and websites (see SOCIAL MEDIA later in this chapter). Include a privacy policy as well to inform users what happens to their personal information.

> Musical rights can be complex; they include publishing or synchronization rights, recording rights, artist rights, and arrangement rights.

INTELLECTUAL PROPERTY AND SOCIAL MEDIA

Social media platforms such as YouTube, Facebook, Twitter, and Instagram (to name just a few), as well as websites such as Etsy and SoundCloud, can be a very effective means for sharing your work. However, it is important to know that your use of such websites is typically governed by the websites' terms of service, which will set out the manner in which your content will be treated and shared. You will want to carefully read the terms of service of any such websites, especially the sections dealing with intellectual property rights, before you upload your work.

In many cases, by uploading content you are granting the website rights in your work, most often including a license to use your content by publishing it on the website. For instance, on a website where you upload an image of your work for resale, if the image is not watermarked or otherwise protected, another person in another country may copy it and use it without your permission. Some licenses contained in such website terms of service can be quite broad and may include an expansive grant of rights including the right to use, reproduce, distribute, display, prepare derivative works from, perform, publish, and/or sublicense your works.
In addition to carefully reading the terms of service before you share your works, you will want to consider the relative risk of your work being misappropriated since, once it has been uploaded onto the Internet, it can become very difficult to control how your work is disseminated. You may want to consider protecting your work via digital watermark or upload lower quality versions of the work to discourage unauthorized reproduction and distribution. If there is a legal right to take action, it may not be practically possible since the appropriated image can be transmitted worldwide and may require legal action in several different jurisdictions.

TRADEMARK LAW

NOTE: Canadian Trademark laws are in the process of being modified. Canada recently passed legislation that will change the *Trade-marks Act* significantly. The law is expected to come into force with regulations in 2015. The trademark term will be reduced from fifteen to ten years. The way that applications are filed will change to comply with several international treaties. In addition, the description of wares and services will have to conform to what is known as the Nice Classification.

WHAT IS A TRADEMARK?

A trademark can be a word, shape, or symbol used to distinguish the goods and services of one seller from another. For example, Pepsi®, 7-Up®, and Sprite® are trademarks of different types of soft drinks, while Tide®, Cheer®, and Sunlight® are laundry detergent trademarks. A trademark is not the same thing as a trade name, which is the name under which a company or an individual carries on business.

HOW ARE TRADEMARKS PROTECTED?

If you can show that you have used a specific trademark for many years and that the public has come to associate your goods or services with this trademark, you can claim "prior use" if someone else tries to use a similar name or design. However, it is advisable to register your trademark with the Canadian Intellectual Property Office because registered trademarks have much greater protection under the law. A registered trademark gives the owner exclusive jurisdiction in Canada to use a name or logo in association with the goods and/or services covered by the registration. It also gives the registered owner certain rights to pre-empt others from registering trademarks that are similar or confusing.

Trademark registration can be a fairly complex process. It involves filling out an application and awaiting a lengthy review. Acceptance of the application is not guaranteed, especially if someone else objects to your application. It's advisable to seek professional legal help in the trademark registration process.

HOW LONG DOES TRADEMARK PROTECTION LAST?

For registered trademarks, generally the term of the protection is fifteen years and is renewable. Under the amended act the term will be reduced to ten years. If you are using an unregistered trademark, your rights continue as long as you use the mark properly and no one opposes you. If you stop using your trademark, however, you risk losing legal protection.

WHAT JURISDICTIONS DOES A CANADIAN TRADEMARK COVER?

Registering a trademark in Canada does *not* necessarily give you legal protection in other jurisdictions. You must register your trademark in every country where you plan to do business.

HOW IS A TRADEMARK IDENTIFIED?

In Canada, you are required to give notice to the public if you are claiming a trademark. You give notice by putting a ™ in superscript near the name. You may sometimes see ®, which is another way to note a registered trademark. You can also put an asterisk (*) next to the trademark, which refers to text elsewhere that explains that the name or logo you are using is a trademark you own or license. The trademark owner must also demonstrate some type of control over how the trademark is used and over the quality of goods and services that bear the trademark.

WHAT IS A LICENSE AGREEMENT?

If a trademark owner wants to let a third party use their trademark, they need to enter into a written contract such as a license agreement. A license agreement is also the best way for the trademark owner to ensure that their trademark is being used in an appropriate manner.

CAN I LOSE MY TRADEMARK RIGHTS?

To maintain ownership of a trademark, you must use it and police your rights. You may lose the rights to the trademark if you don't use it. You can lose your trademark rights if:

> Others start using it (or a trademark confusingly similar to yours) without your permission and you do nothing to stop them;

> You allow your trademark to become the generic, commonly accepted word for a particular product or service;

> You do not use your trademark properly or you allow others to use it improperly or without the appropriate trademark ™ or ® symbols; or

> You do not exercise control over the goods or services which the trademark represent.

Common words like cellophane, zipper, and escalator were all trademarks at one time, but their owners lost them to the public domain because they allowed their trademarks to become generic, commonly accepted words for the relevant product or service. An easy rule to remember is to use your trademarks as adjectives and not nouns. Also enforce strict guidelines on those whom you allow to use your trademark, such as colour, font, etc. This is a necessary part of legally protecting your trademark.

TIPS FOR PROTECTING YOUR TRADEMARK

> Establish guidelines for how you want your trademark to be used and make sure your guidelines are respected.

> If possible, choose trademarks that are not descriptive and have a unique element.

> Trademarks can be expensive, so do a search before you apply to register the mark. Such a search can be done on the CIPO website.

LAWS REGARDING WORKING CONDITIONS OF ARTISTS

The province of Quebec has two pieces of legislation that are designed to protect artists. *"An Act respecting the professional status and conditions of engagement of performing, recording, and film artists"* (**Producers Act**) and *"An Act respecting the Professional Status of Artists in the Visual Arts and Crafts and Literature and their Contracts with Promoters"* (**Promoters Act**).

The main purpose of these two laws is to recognize unions, guilds, and professional associations that represent artists. The laws regulate or encourage collective bargaining between the artists and the people who hire or engage their services as producers, promoters, or employers. In the Producers Act the status of the performer as independent contractor is recognized.

The main difference between the two Acts is that the Producers Act covers artists with a long history of voluntary collective bargaining. The Promoters Act deals with a different group of artists who have a different way of working. It has provisions that require the use of individual contracts between artists and their promoters and gives the government authority to set minimum terms for such contracts by way of regulation.

In addition, there is a federal piece of legislation known as the *Status of the Artist Act* under which certain collective agreements are recognized. For example, the Conseil des métiers des arts is certified under the Status of the Artist Act as is the Writers Guild of Canada.

SELLING AND LICENSING RIGHTS

ASSIGNMENT

Generally, when an artist sells their rights they are asked to sign an "assignment," which gives the buyer all rights, title, and interest in their work. The artist will sign the assignment and give up all their rights to that particular work, unless the agreement provides otherwise.

OPTIONS

Sometimes an artist will give a person an option to purchase certain rights. This is referred to as an option deal. In such a case the purchaser pays a certain amount for the right to purchase the work, exercisable for a certain period of time. Purchasing an option on an artistic work essentially puts a hold on it for a period, usually while the option holder seeks financing. For example, an author of a book may give a filmmaker the option to make a movie. The price of the option is one fee, and the right to exercise the option (i.e. purchasing the rights to make the film) is another.

LICENSING

As discussed, if you incorporate someone else's work into your own or someone wants to use your work, the two parties should enter into an agreement setting out the terms and conditions of the arrangement. In this section, we will discuss some of the basics of licensing. There are several issues to be considered in any license agreement:

> Subject matter that is being licensed

> Type of license: exclusive vs. non-exclusive

> Term (months, years)

> Territory (e.g. Canada, U.S.)

> Scope: What uses are permitted? (e.g. TV, broadcast, Internet, advertising)

> Royalties or license fees (one-time fee, per-use fee, percentage of sales)

> Audit rights

> Termination: Who keeps what? What happens when there are sales in progress?

COLLECTIVE SOCIETIES

Since it is complicated to manage and collect royalties, there are collective societies that exist to help people manage their royalties including SODRAC, ASCAP, BMI, SOCAN, and CMRRA. All of these groups are important resources for those who want to register their music rights or license the rights of others.

DEVELOP YOUR OWN LICENSING AGREEMENT

If it is your work that you are licensing, it is worthwhile for you to invest some time and money in a proper licensing agreement. Larger organizations may have standard-form agreements that they want you to sign. In that case, you should take a look at your own contract and see where your contract differs from theirs. You may not be able to successfully have all the terms of their agreement changed to mirror yours but, at the very least, you will know the difference between the terms of their agreement and your own.

PRACTICAL LEGAL SUGGESTIONS

Just because artists are involved in cultural and creative endeavours does not mean they should be creative in doing business. It is beneficial to have some rigour and discipline in entering into legal agreements, because the consequences can be very important at the end of the day.

Remember, if you want to incorporate someone else's work into your work, you need permission. You may need to sign release forms, pay royalties, and get written permission. You should have a checklist and make sure you retain a file with all the releases and other contracts connected to your project. When dealing with minors, you must get releases from their parent or legal guardian.

It is very important, whether or not you hire the services of professional advisors, to clearly understand what you sign. If you don't understand, ask questions. And remember, there are no stupid questions. If you think you have a problem, you may be right. It is better to take action sooner rather than later. Once you have given your rights away you may be unable to get them back.

Seek advice from a lawyer or through a professional association.

Another important thing to remember when seeking advice from any professional is to tell the person the whole story. This doesn't mean recounting what you thought you should have done, could have done, why the other side is wrong, etc. Just tell your advisor the facts as you remember them. It is also useful, when you think you are getting into a dispute, to keep track of events, and document facts, names, and dates. It is often difficult when things get to court or arbitration, sometimes months or years later, to clearly remember what happened.

PART II: BUSINESS MODELS

There are three main ways an artist can structure their business.

SOLE PROPRIETORSHIP

An individual can conduct business as a sole proprietorship. In this case, a person may register a business name at the ***Registraire des entreprises***. Please note, a registered business name is a trade name under which a person carries on a trade or business; it does not constitute a company. For example, Jane Doe, a graphic designer, doing business as Jane Design or Jane Communications, tells the world that this is the name Jane does business under. But Jane remains liable for the business personally. She may use her business name on a business card but she must sign contracts in her personal name. Similarly, if Frank does business with Jane, Frank needs to know her complete name and address because if there is any problem, Frank needs to go after Jane personally.

If you do business as a sole proprietor, *you* are the business, and therefore any contracts you sign in your name make you personally liable. Sole proprietorship should be registered under the ***Registraire des entreprises***. In addition, a business name can also be registered.

PARTNERSHIP

Another model is "partnership." This is when you and another person go into business together. In a general partnership, the partners share the profits and losses. They are liable personally for the acts of the partnership. It is important to know the person you get into business with and what the contribution and responsibility of each partner is. It is advisable to have an agreement that sets out some basic terms such as what each partner expects of the other, and what happens on death, disability, or dispute. Who will own the assets of the partnership, etc.? Like a sole proprietorship, a partnership in Quebec must have a name and needs to be registered with the ***Registraire des entreprises***. Be careful when you enter these relationships. You can be held personally liable for the acts of your partner and have to pay for them even if you were not at fault personally.

CORPORATION

A corporation is what's called a "moral person," and is therefore a separate person from you. Since it is a separate entity, it has separate legal obligations. An owner of a corporation is called a shareholder. A corporation is run by its directors and officers. In Quebec, the corporation must register with the ***Registraire of enterprises*** and the name of your corporation must comply with certain requirements. If your business is incorporated as a Canadian corporation or that of another provincial jurisdiction it may have filing obligations under that regime. For example, a Canadian corporation must also file annual returns with Corporations Canada.

The important thing to remember about a corporation is that, legally, it is a separate person. Therefore, you will not be personally liable for the acts of the corporation except in limited circumstances. It is also important when you sign a contract that you sign in the name of the corporation and not your own name. For example, "ABC Inc. per: Jane Doe." That way you know who you are contracting with. You may have to assign intellectual property rights to your corporation if you want the corporation to own them.

The corporation has its own legal obligations and must file its own tax returns. If more than one person owns the corporation (i.e. there is more than one shareholder), it is useful to have a shareholder agreement to set out roles and responsibilities. For example: who can sign at the bank and for what amounts; what happens if one shareholder wants to sell their share; what happens if they die or become disabled; who will be responsible for financing the business. These are just a few points that are typically addressed in a shareholder agreement.

Also remember that there are other laws that impact how you carry on business in Quebec. That discussion is beyond the scope of this chapter but there will be references to some resources on this subject in the bibliography.

PART III: CONTRACTS

SIGNING CONTRACTS

Many artists are asked to sign agreements that give others the right to use their work. It is important that you understand the documents you sign. If you have been asked to give something up that you may not be able to regain, make sure you understand what you are giving up. Be clear about what you are signing and how long the agreement will last. You should also ensure that you have a means of terminating the agreement if things do not work out. Also, make sure that you are protecting yourself and that you are not giving away rights that are not yours to give.

In addition to getting appropriate accounting advice to deal with taxes and record keeping, there are several other things to keep in mind when contracting with other people.

Often people say they have made a "handshake deal." But be careful. Although it is possible to have oral agreements, they are much more difficult to enforce. Traditionally, important agreements should be set down in writing. Even if not all terms have been negotiated or finalized, as long as there are certain key elements that have been agreed upon, there could be a binding agreement between the parties. This means the parties can legally enforce their obligations against one another.

BEFORE SIGNING, WHAT YOU NEED TO KNOW

WHO ARE YOU DEALING WITH?

You need to know who you are doing business with. Is it a company? Is it a person? Is it a partnership? Make sure you get the full name. A full name of a corporation or company should include "Inc." or "Ltd." It is not enough just to have half the name of a company because, if you need to take legal action, it may not be possible to sue.

WHAT ARE THE KEY CONTRACT TERMS?

Make sure the key elements of the contract are set down in writing, even if it is only a letter agreement. For example, why do we have a contract? Is it to sell something, to assign something, to perform something? What are the terms? What is the length of the contract? How much money do you get paid? When do you get paid? When does the contract begin and end? What happens if the contract doesn't work out or if there is a disagreement?

WHEN DO YOU HAVE A CONTRACT?

In order to have a legally binding contract, the parties must have the capacity to enter into the contract. For example, a contract entered into with a minor is probably not binding if the child's parent(s) or guardian did not enter into it.

The parties must also agree on the contract and its terms. Generally, the contract should set out its purpose and the key elements, such as time, price, obligations of the parties, deliverables, etc. The contract is formed when and where its terms are agreed upon. Until the terms have been agreed upon, the parties may just be exchanging offers and counter-offers. In order to form a legally binding agreement, there must be both an offer and an acceptance between the parties.

Contracts can be freely negotiated between parties. Sometimes one party drafts the key terms and the other party signs the contract without negotiating them. This is known as an adhesion contract. Adhesion contracts are interpreted in favour of the person who signs and against the person who drafted the agreement.

Be careful to make sure you know who you are dealing with and whether or not that person has the authority to enter into the contract. Make sure that everything that is important to you is set out in the contract before you sign it. If something is missing, you may want to include a sentence that states that it is an initial agreement to govern your relationship until such time as you enter a long-form agreement with standard terms and conditions.

CONTRACT TERMINOLOGY AND CONDITIONS

Most sophisticated contracts may include some terms and conditions that you may not understand. Some of the standard terms and conditions you will typically see in an agreement are as follows:

REPRESENTATION AND WARRANTIES

Many contracts require that you represent and warrant certain things. These are statements that indicate you have the rights and capacity to deliver what you are promising under the contract.

If the work you are licensing is a multimedia work, a film, or composite work, you will likely be asked to represent and warrant that you have the rights for any third party work that you use in your own work. For instance, a filmmaker would need to ensure they have the rights to the music used in the film. That is why it is very important, whenever you start any multimedia project, that you keep very good records, including permission to use or sell any third party work that you have incorporated in your art. All releases for location, artists, and works should be kept in one place.

Maintaining good records is also important for insurance purposes, because if you need to get coverage for errors and omissions, which is sometimes required when you broadcast a work, you will be able to help your lawyer in validating the fact that you do have all the proper releases.

INDEMNITY

If you agree to indemnify someone, you may have to compensate that person for any loss they may suffer as a result of your actions.

LIMITATION OF LIABILITY

In certain cases, the parties will seek to limit their liability to either a fixed amount or direct damages. If you agree to indemnify someone for a loss or harm, you should try to set limits on what you will be responsible for.

ARBITRATION

This is a dispute resolution mechanism. This means that instead of going before a judge or a court, you choose to go before an arbitrator, a specialist in dispute resolution to help resolve the issue.

Any technical legal questions generally should be discussed with an attorney to ensure you properly understand them. If you belong to an artist association, you may have mandatory obligations or standard form contracts you are required to sign. You can contact your association to get more information about this.

GOVERNING LAW

The law that will govern the contract will be addressed in the governing law clause. If it is a jurisdiction outside of Quebec, it means another law can apply and sometimes may lead to resolving any dispute in another province or country. This is complex and expensive, and all the more reason to understand what you are agreeing to from the beginning.

STANDARD FORM AGREEMENT RESOURCES

If you visit the websites listed in the legal resource section, you will see many references to standard form agreements that are commonly used in your industry. For example, if you are a writer, you may want to look at the Writers Guild of Canada Agreement.

TAXES AND RECORDKEEPING

CLARIFY YOUR TAX SITUATION

It is important to understand your status and reporting obligations. For example, when you negotiate your rate, you must ascertain whether the other party is withholding taxes, so you will know the amount you get in your pocket after the deal is done. You may have reporting obligations to federal and provincial tax authorities. If you sell online you may have an obligation to collect and remit sales tax. This can vary from province to province. There could be sales tax and/or withholding tax. It is important to get your financial advisors to inform you of any effect on your earnings from a tax perspective.

TAKE RECORD KEEPING SERIOUSLY

It is important to keep a record of your discussions with others (or partners, people, etc.) when you are dealing with people. Although it may sound obvious, you should create a separate file for every contract or project you enter into. Keep a copy of the contract and the drafts and notes you have made. They may not be admissible if a matter goes to court, but they will be helpful reminders as to why certain clauses were negotiated or what your intention was. They could also be useful in subsequent transactions.

Keeping track of your digital files is equally important. Unlike paper files, these often include the requirement to know login information and passwords. It is important to have a plan to keep track of this information and in case you become incapacitated and cannot access your files. When artists work within the "cloud" they are entrusting their data to third-party sites often outside of Canada. Read and understand the terms and conditions so you or your authorized representative knows how to access your information.

Generally, large organizations that deal internationally may have certain standards that they need to apply in order to protect themselves.

FINAL THOUGHTS

In these pages we have attempted to summarize some of the key points that you should be aware of working as an artist. Be organized and know the rules of your trade. Much of the value in what you do is intangible and could or should be protected so that others don't take advantage of your efforts. We cannot emphasize enough the importance of being organized and keeping good records.

The value of your creative endeavours is often in your intellectual property. The ability to prove ownership and rights largely depends on how well organized and documented you are in releases, licenses, and the like. If you go into business with a friend, organize it like a business and make sure that you have an exit strategy if things don't work out. Similarly, if you appoint an agent to represent you, understand the terms and parameters of the relationship. This is the difference between a hobby and a business. If you don't understand something, ask questions and consult professionals who can guide you.

LEGISLATION

- > Copyright Act, R.S.C. 1985, c. C-42.

- > Trade-marks Act, R.S.C. 1985, c. T-13.

- > Trade-marks Regulations, SOR/96-195.

- > Civil Code of Quebec, (CCQ) (Legal Persons: art. 298-364; Partnerships: Art. 2186-2279; Employment Contracts: art. 2085-2097; Personality Rights: art. 1-9; 35-36).

- > Business Corporations Act , (Quebec).c.S-31.1

- > Securities Act (Quebec) ; Regulation 45-106 ; CQLR ch.V-1.3

- > An Act respecting the legal publicity of enterprises ,CQLR c P-44.1

- > Canada Business Corporations Act, R.S.C. 1985, c. C-44.

- > Status of the Artist Act, SC 1992, c 33

- > Industrial Design Act, R.S.C. 1985, c.-19.

- > Charter of Human Rights and Freedoms, R.S.Q., c. C-.

- > Bankruptcy and Insolvency Act (Canada), Art 83.

- > An Act Respecting the Professional Status of Artists in the Visual Arts, Arts and Crafts and Literature, and Their Contracts with Promoters, CQLR c S-32.01

- > An Act Respecting the Professional Status and Conditions of Engagement of Performing, Recording and Film Artists CQLR c S-32.1

Additional legal and copyright-related links can be found in the Resources Section at the end of this book.

ACCOUNTING BASICS
FOR ARTISTS

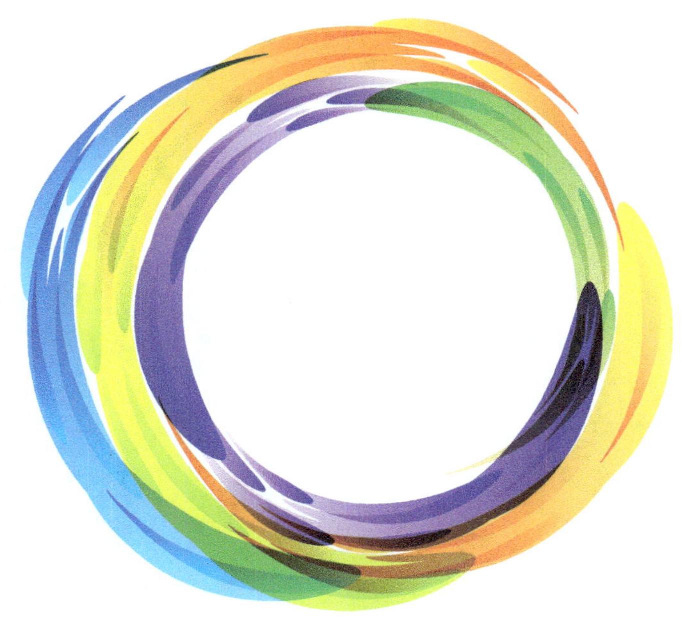

Artists and other entrepreneurs in creative fields often view accounting, taxation, and bookkeeping as foreign intrusions into their real work. After all, taxes bring angst, while art brings pleasure.

Nonetheless, if you want to be a self-sufficient, self-employed artist, you need to be aware of some accountancy issues so that you don't get in trouble with the government.

In this section, we give you some basic accounting pointers to help you get started, including several tips that can help you save money and taxes, and make even greater profits.

Here are some key words you'll come across in accounting and bookkeeping:

Deductibility: Generally, a business is allowed to deduct expenses incurred in the course of earning taxable income.

Assets: Assets are things—both tangible and intangible—that you own, and also amounts owed to you for goods sold or services rendered.

Liabilities: Debts, monies you owe.

Revenue: Money coming to you for goods sold or services rendered. Also "non-earned" money like dividends, interest payments, and arts grants.

Expenses: Money spent in the course of running a business.

KEEP TRACK OF YOUR MONEY

Be sure to keep track of all the money coming into your account. This is your revenue (whether through sales, earnings, or financial grants). And keep track of all the money going out to pay for business-related expenses and assets (see below for what counts as a business-related expense). There are two common ways to keep track:

The Monthly Filing System: If you're well organized, you'll want to develop a monthly filing system whereby you will file all receipts and invoices by month, and then tally your revenue and expenses each month and attach all related invoices and receipts.

The Shoebox Method: If you're overwhelmed at the thought of doing your own bookkeeping, start by using the shoebox method. Keep all receipts together in one envelope and all invoices in another. Store these in a box so that they are accessible at tax time. Ideally, try to at least keep all receipts and invoices grouped by month.

FILING INCOME TAX

Each April, Canadians have to file an income tax return with the federal government. Residents of Quebec must also file a separate but similar income tax return with Revenu Quebec.

Both governments want to know how much money you've earned during the past year, and other facts, including:

> Are you are married?

> Do you have children? If so, how many?

> Do you have any other dependents?

> Did you attend school over the course of the year?

> Did you make any charitable donations?

> Have you received any money other than through employment?

> Are you self-employed or do you have a business?

Based on your answers to these and other questions, the tax agencies determine whether you owe them any income tax or whether you've overpaid and are eligible for a tax refund. The latter case usually only applies to people working as employees who've had deductions already made at source.

It is very important for entrepreneurs and self-employed artists to keep track of their business-related expenses throughout the year because it can really save money at tax time.

HOW CAN YOU PAY LESS TAX?

Expenses you can claim from business or professional activities will reduce your net income. And the lower your income, the less income tax you have to pay.

For instance, say you sold four canvases last year, each for $25,000 (we can dream, can't we?). With an income for the year of $100,000, you'd find yourself owing a lot of tax.

But suppose it cost you $15,000 to pay for the materials, transportation, and advanced oil painting technique classes for each of the four canvases. That means that in order to produce the four canvases, you spent $60,000 on business-related expenses.

Add to that the hypothetical $12,000 a year you pay to rent your studio.

And don't forget to add the $3,000 spent producing marketing materials during the year, including your website, business cards, professional portfolio, and press kit, which is how you got noticed in the first place and why you've had a steady stream of sales. Now let's do the math:

Revenue: 4 canvases sold @ $25,000 each $100,000
Minus cost of materials, etc. per canvas: 4 X $15,000   ($60,000)
Minus monthly rent for studio: 12 X $1,000   ($12,000)
Minus cost of marketing materials: $3,000   ($3,000)
Your actual "taxable" income at the end of the year   = $25,000 (revenues minus expenses)

After you've factored in all your expenses, your net income is quite a bit less than what you earned in sales revenues.

By recording your work-related expenses, you'll be able to prove to the government that your real (or net) income is $25,000 for the year—not $100,000. And, consequently, your income taxes will be greatly reduced.

WHAT COUNTS AS A BUSINESS-RELATED EXPENSE?

In short, you deduct expenses that you incur while earning or trying to earn income. The rules for deductible expenses are laid out in the Tax Act, but for a far less convoluted explanation, read the booklet that comes with your tax returns.

Below are some of the types of expenses you'll likely incur as a self-employed artist. Note that credit card statements are not sufficient proof of expenses. Keep all your original receipts.

RENT, MORTGAGE INTEREST, AND UTILITIES

You can claim your workplace rent as an expense and, if you work from home, you can claim a portion of your monthly rent or interest on your mortgage payment. You can also claim utilities such as hydro and gas.

For example, imagine that you have a 1,000 square foot apartment, and you use one room measuring 150 square feet as a studio. How much of your apartment can you deduct as an allowable business expense?

Here's the formula:

150 sq. ft. / 1,000 sq. ft x 100 = 15%

The proportion is generally calculated by floor space. So, in this example, 15% of your home expenses can be claimed as business expenses. This percentage applies to the cost of home expenses such as rent, mortgage interest, electricity, heating, repairs and maintenance.

TRANSPORTATION

If you own or lease a vehicle, be sure to keep track of your mileage for business-related excursions. You're allowed to deduct a portion of your car costs as legitimate business expenses.

For example, imagine that you put 30,000 km on your odometer in a year. Of that, 10,000 km were business-related excursions (visits with clients, travel to an arts festival in the Eastern Townships, etc.). How much of your car can you deduct as an allowable business expense?

Here's the formula:
10,000 business km / 30,000 total km x 100 = 33.33%

So, in this example, 33.33% of your total car costs can be deducted as legitimate business expenses. This includes things like gas, insurance, registration, license fees, lease payments*, parking space rental, parking metres, interest paid on finance loans, repairs and maintenance, and car washes.

*Check with an accountant to discover the maximum allowable lease expense for your car payments. There is a cap on this amount.

If you don't own a car but use public transportation or taxis, these costs can be expenses too, so long as you keep your receipts.

ENTERTAINING CLIENTS

At the federal level, you are allowed to claim 50% of the cost of business lunches (or dinners or breakfasts) at which you treated a work-related colleague. The deductibility rate is lower at the provincial level. Keep your receipts and write the name of the client (or potential client) on the back of each receipt.

You can also claim some of the costs for organizing an event such as a catered vernissage, a book launch, or a business Christmas party.

FEES AND HONORARIUMS

You can deduct the cost of hiring people to work for or with you, or who perform certain functions to help you run your business. Examples include:

> Artist fees or honorariums for collaborators or other creative/technical help.

> Fees or honorariums for accounting, legal, graphic design, sales, marketing, and other services related to your creative practice or business.

MARKETING AND PROMOTION

Any money disbursed to market, promote, or advertise your products and services are allowable business expenses. These include:

> Costs of creating and maintaining a Facebook page or website (including domain name registration, web hosting, and hiring a professional web designer to create the site).

> Costs to design and print business cards, press kits and folders, and other promotional materials.

> Costs associated with throwing promotional events, like a comedy night, piano recital, poetry reading, etc.

> Any advertising costs incurred throughout the year.

OFFICE SUPPLIES

You can also deduct the cost of office-related supplies and other expenses, like:

> Office supplies (pens, staplers, etc.)

> Office equipment (phones, scanner, printer, etc.)

> Land line and long-distance charges, Internet connection, cell phone, etc.

TOOLS, MATERIALS, AND ART SUPPLIES

Here you can deduct all the specialized tools and materials you need to practise your trade. These might include:

> Canvases

> Clay

> Computer software

> Costumes

> Fabric

> Makeup

> Paint

> Paintbrushes

> Sheet music

> Wardrobe

NOTE: The purchase of items that last significantly longer than a year cannot be claimed as business expenses in the same way. But they can be written off against your income over their useful lifetime. This is known as depreciation, which is defined as "the allocation of the cost of the asset over the useful life of the asset."

For example, if you go through several pairs of ballet shoes, paintbrushes, or knitting needles in a year, you can legitimately claim these as expenses. However, if you buy a computer, or car, or an expensive drawing table for your business that will last longer than a year, you have to spread out that initial cost over time and claim the depreciation (loss of value) on the purchase over the next several years. An accountant will let you know how to handle these larger, long-term purchases.

TRAVEL

In general, if you have to travel for work-related purposes, then you can claim transportation costs, hotels, and meals. For instance:

> If you are a comic headed to the comedy festival in Angoulême, France, to research the industry, your travel costs would probably be considered legitimate expenses.

> If your band is heading to Victoriaville, Quebec, to perform at the Festival International de Musique Actuelle, your travel costs would probably be considered legitimate expenses.

> If you take an "inspirational" trip to Bora Bora in advance of the launch of your fall fashion collection, there's a good chance you will not be permitted to claim these costs as legitimate business expenses.

PROFESSIONAL ASSOCIATION FEES AND DUES

You can usually deduct the fees paid to belong to a professional association, guild, or trade union.

TRAINING AND DEVELOPMENT

You can deduct the cost of courses or classes taken during the year if they are related to updating and improving your skills. You cannot claim courses or classes if they are unrelated to your declared trade or are preparing you for another career.

You can also claim the costs of relevant book purchases and magazine or online subscriptions. For instance:

> A journalist could probably deduct course fees for a photography class taken during the year if it is likely that the photography skills gained will improve income-earning potential.

> A filmmaker could probably deduct the cost of a subscription to *Qui fait Quoi* magazine as well as the cost of purchasing *Filmmaking for Dummies*.

On the other hand, it is unlikely that:

> A fashion designer could deduct the cost of a creative writing course.

> A photographer could deduct the cost of a subscription to *New Yorker* magazine.

> A graphic designer could deduct the cost of joining the Quebec Theatre Federation.

OTHER DEDUCTIONS

There may be additional deductions that are applicable to your particular line of work. Consult with a professional association, the tax office, or an accountant familiar with the needs of self-employed artists or small business owners.

Also, keep in mind that various publications are available from Canada Revenue Agency for artists in different lines of work.

> Performing arts: 525-R

> Visual artists and writers: 504-R2

> Dispositions of Cultural Property to Designated Canadian Institutions: 407-R4.

Check with Canada Revenue Agency and Revenu Quebec for guidelines and publications specific to your line of work.

FAQs FOR THE SELF-EMPLOYED ARTIST

Below are several frequently asked questions related to the financial needs and obligations of the self-employed artist. Note that the information below in no way replaces the professional advice of an accountant, bookkeeper, or business consultant. In fact, we recommend that you speak to an accounting professional who is familiar with the needs of self-employed artists.

I only use top-of-the-line materials for my work. Can I deduct the full cost of my materials or only the cost of average-priced materials?

The taxman expects your expenses to be reasonable and relevant. For example, you'll have a very tough time convincing the taxman that you need to drive a Ferrari. When it comes to the specific tools and materials of your trade, the situation is a little less clear but you'd better be able to justify your expenses.

I've received a grant to complete a project. Is this considered income? Do I have to pay taxes on it?

Yes and yes. Grant money is considered taxable, and the taxes are not withheld by the granting agency. Therefore, make sure to set aside a portion of the grant money for tax time, keeping in mind you will also be deducting some expenses related to production/project costs.

It's been two years since I've filed taxes. What do I do? Am I in trouble with the law?

There is no penalty for filing a tax return after the deadline if you don't owe anything. On the other hand, if you do owe back taxes you'll be charged interest for every day you're late and a late filing penalty on top of that. Don't let your taxes get away from you! If the process is overwhelming, get help from an accounting or tax-preparation professional. Even if it costs money, it'll end up costing far less than the penalties.

I've been in business for five years and I've had five straight years of loss. I'll probably have losses again this year. What will happen? Will I be audited?

Nine out of 10 small businesses lose money within the first years of operation. However, if you keep losing money over longer periods, you'll probably be asked to prove you're running a business, not just a hobby.

In order to claim business expenses, there needs to be a reasonable expectation of profit. No one goes into business to perpetually lose money. After six or seven years of ongoing losses, the government may want to meet with you in person to assess your tax situation.

If you can't prove that you have a reasonable expectation of earning an income from your work, then it will be considered a hobby, and the expenses will no longer be deductible from your other income. In fact, it's even possible that the government will force you to pay back taxes.

Do I need to hire an accountant? How much will this cost me?

Accountants charge by the hour, so a more complicated tax return will take more time to complete and will cost more. Depending on the accountant and the complexity of your business, it could cost anywhere from $50 to several hundred dollars. The more organized you are, the less it will cost in accounting fees. Larger businesses can expect to pay much more. Although an accountant isn't strictly necessary in many cases, they are experts at doing taxes. If funds are tight, consider bartering some of your art for accounting services. Several of the artists we interviewed have done that.

Doing your own tax returns by hand is time consuming, especially if you're self-employed. But it's certainly possible. There are several easy-to-use software applications for both Mac and PC that walk you through every line of the tax return. You can get many of these applications free or inexpensively online.

While you don't need to be a tax expert to complete a tax return by yourself, the chances of making mistakes is much greater. This might delay your tax refund or even negatively affect the amount you're entitled to.

It's a good idea to get the tax forms and tax guides from the post office during tax time, February to April. You can also download them directly from the Canada Revenue Agency (www.cra-arc.gc.ca) and Revenu Quebec (www.revenuquebec.ca/en).

OTHER ACCOUNTING CONSIDERATIONS

If any of the following apply to you, then you must register for federal and/or provincial registration numbers (which can be done at each government's tax office):

> You have sales above $30,000 a year (GST/QST/HST numbers).

> You are incorporated (Business Number and Quebec Registration Number).

> You do import/export (Import/Export Numbers).

> You employ others and pay them wages—not applicable to contracted labour (Payroll Number).

For useful information on starting a business or any required registration, see the following web pages:

Canada Revenue Agency: www.cra-arc.gc.ca/tx/bsnss/sm/menu-eng.html

Revenu Quebec: www.revenuquebec.ca/en/entreprise/demarrage

FASHION DESIGNERS

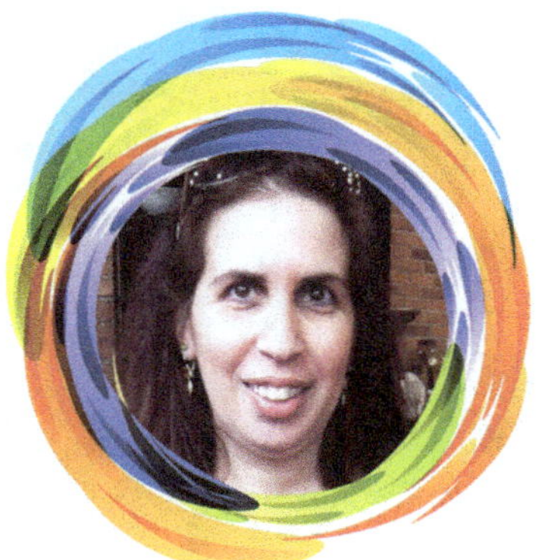

Ev Arad

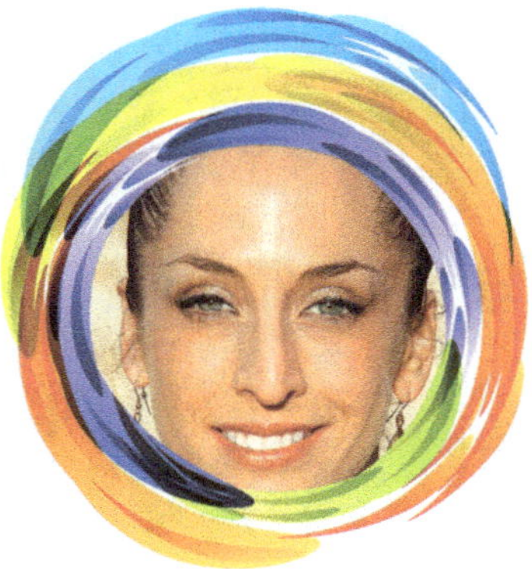

Manika Gaudet

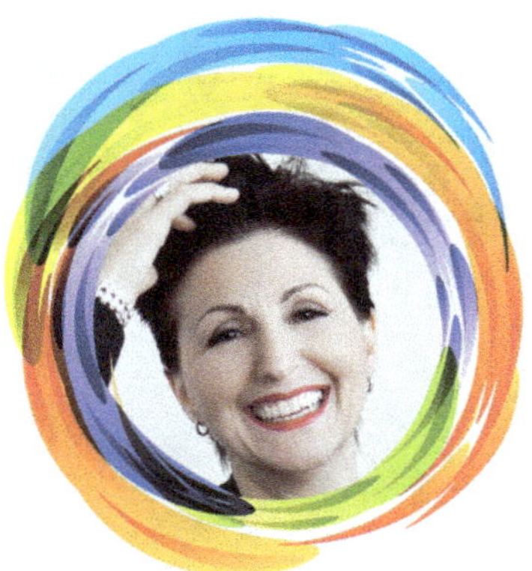

Marisa Minicucci

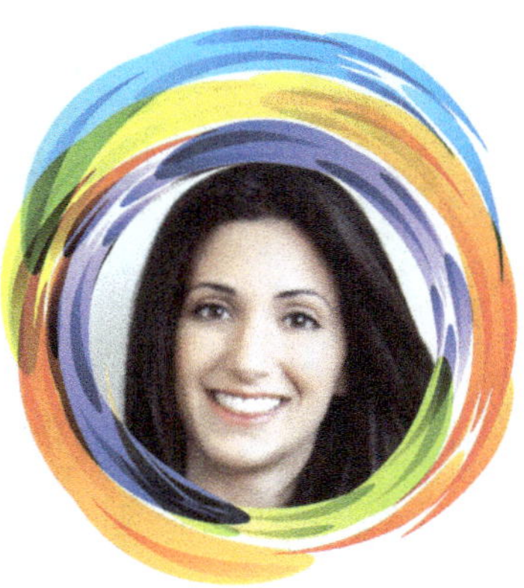

Anissa Marcanio

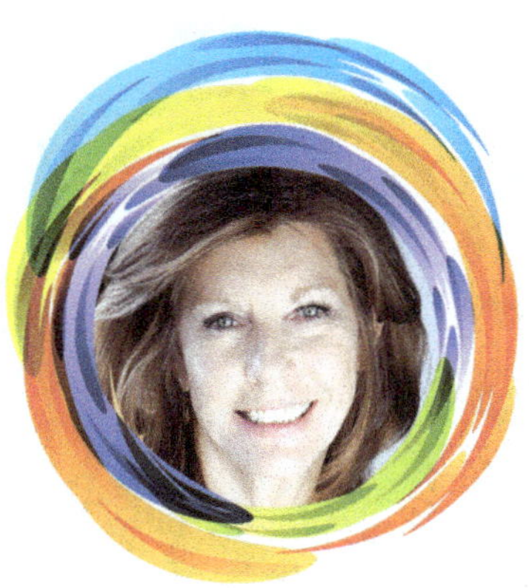

Hilary Radley

FASHION DESIGNERS

Don't buy into the feeling that the financing people are more important than the designer. Without the designer there would be nothing for them to finance.

- Marisa Minicucci, MINICUCCI x MARCANIO

SO YOU WANNA BE A FASHION DESIGNER?

When most people think of fashion design, the fashion world's most stylish names are conjured up: Calvin Klein, Donna Karan, Vera Wang, all waltzing down an Italian catwalk in front of an audience filled with the world's most beautiful people.

But, let's face it, creative design isn't the exclusive domain of New York, Paris, and Milan. Walk into many chic Montreal boutiques and you'll find the racks are filled with gorgeous creations from home-grown designers. Of course, if you're reading this because you have a passion for fashion, you're already well acquainted with Montreal's fashion scene. In fact, you could probably name ten hot, local designers before you even make it to the checkout counter.

Graduates of design programs engage in a wide variety of creative occupations. If our expert advice piques your interest in design, you may want to further investigate the following related fields listed in the National Occupation Classification (NOC), published by Employment and Social Development Canada:

> Clothing designer

> Costume designer

> Couturier

> Fabric designer

> Fashion designer

> Fur designer

> Jewellery designer

> Patternmaker

> Shoe designer

> Window display designer

THE EXPERTS

We spoke with the following accomplished designers to get a view behind the catwalk curtain:

Ev Arad is a fashion and jewellery designer, and author of several best-selling interior design books. She is also the owner of Impact Galerie in Old Montreal, where she sells her own creations and the work of artists from all over the world, particularly Israel. Graduating from a three-year fashion design program in Milan, Italy, Ev rounded out her fashion education with courses in interior and industrial design. Her work is inspired by nature, ancient cultures, and even fairy tales. "Creating new collections is always such an exciting process; I am always surprised that, after so many years, I can still develop a new idea into a full line." Have a look at what Ev is creating at www.impactgalerie.com.

Manika Gaudet graduated from Campus Notre-Dame-de-Foy in 1999 with a dream to create fashions that make women of every shape and size feel beautiful, comfortable, and confidently feminine. Upon joining BGN&CO, a Quebec-based fashion house renowned for creating stylish and original clothing, Manika quickly rose to the position of head designer. After over a decade at the helm there, Manika undertook her greatest aspiration: starting her brand Manik Fashion. Clientele gravitate to Manik for its novelty, distinctive hand-painted designs, and uncompromising cut and comfort. See more of her work at www.manikfashion.com.

Marisa Minicucci and her daughter **Anissa Marcanio** are the mother-daughter collaborative, MINICUCCI x MARCANIO (MM). Marisa is an accomplished designer and businesswoman in the Canadian fashion industry. Her thirty plus years of experience play an integral role in the venture, backing the budding brand with knowledge and expertise in design, entrepreneurship, and product confection. Her reputation for quality garments and detail refinement is detectable in all MM products. Anissa participates in the development of the brand's profile, bringing to the table a curiosity for technology and a passion for visual imagery. She is responsible for keeping the product and image progressive and dynamic. See their creations at www.wearmm.com.

Hilary Radley worked in TV costume design and as a college lecturer before beginning her fashion design career. As an astute businesswoman and artist who always pushed the boundaries of fashion design with revolutionary uses of textiles, Hilary quickly made a name for herself as North America's "queen of outerwear." Hilary's eponymous company is a leading internationally recognized fashion label. Designed and developed in the Montreal-based Hilary Radley Design Studio, the women's outerwear collections have expanded into a distinctive lifestyle brand. The Hilary Radley and Hilary Radley New York labels are sold in major department and specialty stores across Canada and the United States. See www.HilaryRadley.com for more.

Here's what they had to say, designer to designer:

WHO NEEDS FASHION DESIGN SCHOOL?

According to the National Occupational Classification (NOC), an aspiring designer usually needs a university degree or college diploma in design to land their first internship or job in the industry. Most of our panel of experts concur, though jewellery designer, Ev Arad, says that it's not quite as essential in her field. "It depends what kind of jewellery you want to make. If you need to do soldering or work with heavy metals, then you'll need at least one course in that." But no matter what segment of the fashion design field you're looking to enter, all our experts tell us you'll pick up necessary technical skills in school that you'd be hard-pressed to learn on your own.

"Many young fashion designers think they can just flip through magazines all day and be a designer," says Hilary Radley. But to be a great clothing designer, she says, it takes an intimate knowledge of textiles, including familiarity with fabric, colour, texture, and draping, best gained through an appropriate course of study. Radley also stresses the importance of drawing well, another skill that should be honed in design school. "For me, drawing is fundamental. I sketch all the time. Drawing is how you get your ideas down on paper."

Marisa Minicucci agrees that a degree in fashion is expected nowadays. "University is something they look for," she says. And while you're in school she suggests you broaden your knowledge beyond just design. "Learn a little bit about everything. Fashion is so broad. You could end up as the patternmaker and be in the pattern world or you could be a design editor. If you want to be the designer, you need to know a little bit about everything."

And one final thought came from Manika Gaudet for those of you still wondering if you need to bother with an education. "If you know how to build a garment and you're naturally creative, then maybe you don't absolutely need school. But school will prepare you for the other parts of the business, and they're just as important."

For jewellery design, even if you don't create a whole website, put together an album on Facebook or Flikr. And make sure you have excellent-quality pictures.

- Ev Arad, Impact Gallery

HOW DO YOU SHOW WHAT YOU'VE GOT?

To land a job in the industry, a portfolio of your work is essential. This is not only the results of NOC research, but what our Montreal fashion experts tell us as well. We'll let them tell you in their own words:

THEY WANT TO SEE THE WORK

Hilary Radley: "You need a portfolio with examples of what you do. When someone comes wanting to work for me, I want to see the work. For me, it's better if it's physical and I can see it. Don't just bring a CV."

SHOW YOUR TECHNICAL SKILLS ALONG WITH THE WORK YOU'VE DONE

Manika Gaudet: "Most companies use computers from A to Z, so it's good to show that you can use those tools. Of course they'll want to see what you've done, too. You can show your online portfolio or, depending on the company, they might want a physical binder showing your work."

HOW INVOLVED ARE YOU IN FASHION?

Marisa Minicucci: "Besides your portfolio, you need to show what activities you've been part of. How involved are you in fashion? What have you done? Are you part of the fashion world, volunteering, organizing shows? Let me see how involved you've already been."

GET PROFESSIONAL PHOTOS DONE

Ev Arad: "When a new jeweller wants to work with me here in the gallery, they send me pictures. I can just look at the pictures and know if I want to see the collection. If I love it, I'll ask them to come in so I can check the quality, and then it's just about the price."

You cannot give up. You can never give up. The people who made it are the ones who didn't give up. There are a lot of talented people out there who just couldn't hack it.
- Hilary Radley, Hilary Radley Design Studio

GETTING STARTED

You may think that you've read enough Vogue and Glamour magazines to know what the fashionistas of rue Saint-Denis and Madison Avenue want to wear. You may feel divinely driven to dress the masses in your glam-inspired collection of couture-Creations-with-a-capital-C. Our experts, however, think otherwise.

Successful Montreal-based designers are unanimous: an internship or an entry-level position are the standard means of getting started in the industry and a sure-fire way to meet the people and make the connections you'll need to get ahead.

And you'll have to jump in with passion to spare. This industry can take a lot out of an artistic soul. So you'd better be certain there's no other place you'd rather be.

Here is what our experts told us about getting started and making it work:

YOU NEED A PASSION FOR FASHION

Hilary Radley: "You have to have a passion for it. If you have no passion for fashion, you won't ever make it. What does that passion mean? You're totally immersed and obsessed with clothes. You go out and watch women on the streets just to see what they're wearing."

YOU'VE GOT TO LOVE THE INDUSTRY

Marisa Minicucci: "You have to really love the industry, not just because it's fashion and you really like to dress yourself. There's a lot more to the industry than loving to wear clothes."

KEEP YOUR EYE ON THE PRIZE

Hilary Radley: "A true designer is as close as you can get to being a real artist in fashion. Creating something from nothing. Following your instincts and your gut is number one. There will be a lot of people who won't want you to do that. It's a very tough and competitive business. Most people think that being at the bottom is the toughest, but being at the top is even harder."

MASTER YOUR CRAFT

Manika Gaudet: "You have to know how to build a garment from A to Z. A lot of people think that a fashion designer is someone who's good at drawing and has good ideas. But you need to know a lot. I started by being a patternmaker and an assistant. That gave me a great base to work from."

GET AN INTERNSHIP

Manika Gaudet: "Do an internship in the industry, even if it's for free, even if it's just for a few weeks. Get to know the industry and see if it really is for you. School and work are two completely different things. Some people have trouble jumping from one to the other. The companies who hire you will want you to work the way they do. It's a lot of adapting, and it's not for everyone."

TUCK SOME EXPERIENCE UNDER YOUR DESIGNER BELT

Marisa Minicucci: "Get experience elsewhere first. Go work for a bigger company to start off. You don't have to stay there forever if you want to start your own thing, but get that experience."

Manika Gaudet: "It's good to know what's going on in the industry before you go out on your own. School is one thing, but you should try to get hands-on experience. Some designers start on their own as soon as they finish school, but I think you need to be prepared first."

LOOK FOR A GOOD FIT

Hilary Radley: "Wanting to learn and being willing to work isn't enough to get a job with a designer. When I'm hiring I have to know your tastes are similar to mine. Ideally, if we look at designs or flip through magazines together, we should like the same things."

FIND A COMPANY THAT SHARES YOUR VALUES

Anissa Marcanio: "Find a company that you respect for their morals and ethics. You might go with a company because you like their style and then realize you don't share their values. What they have you doing as an entry-level position won't sit well with you."

BE PERSISTANT

Hilary Radley: "Landing an internship is really a matter of getting your portfolio to the companies where you want to work and then hammering away on the door until you get an answer. I get a lot of resumes and I don't even know where half of them end up. I know that sounds terrible, but the point is that it's really about being pushy."

DISCOVER YOUR PLACE IN THE INDUSTRY

Manika Gaudet: "Only a quarter of the people who did fashion school with me actually became designers, most did other things in the industry. There's so much surrounding design to get into. You can become a patternmaker, a buyer, a manufacturer, or you can work in production. There's a lot to do, especially in Montreal."

DON'T BE AFRAID TO TAKE THE LEAP

Manika Gaudet: "Ultimately, if you want to go out on your own, be prepared but don't wait forever. You can become too comfortable working for someone else and not move forward. You'll never know for sure if you're really ready, but take your own aspirations seriously. There will be a couple of hard years. It's always seven days a week, but if you're prepared for that amount of work, it's very gratifying."

It's good to have pictures of normal people wearing your clothes, not just models. People need to see themselves in your clothes too.

- Manika Gaudet, Manik Fashion

TAKING IT TO THE NEXT LEVEL

So, you landed that all-important first job in the fashion industry. You probably learned more about the business in your three to five years on the inside than you could have in a lifetime of design school. You saw a side of the industry your teachers never told you about, and you've lived to tell the tale.

But now your head is crammed with a myriad of ideas on how to dress the world; creative juices are throbbing through every vein in your body. You eat, drink, and dream design. It's time to put your creativity to work for someone else: you.

Relax. You knew this day would come. Now is the time to concentrate on business financing, accounting, and marketing, which, you'll soon learn, are every bit as important to your success as the cut and colours of your spring collection.

We've also asked our fashion experts for some advice on getting your creations from the cutting floor to the catwalk and beyond.

I. THE FASHION BUSINESS

You may have aced all your patternmaking classes and gotten glowing recommendations from your internship supervisors, but what do you really know about the business of fashion? Of all the artistic disciplines in this book, a career in fashion may require the most business savvy. All the experts we spoke to are as much businesswomen as they are designers. Read on for their advice on making it as a designer/entrepreneur.

START SLOWLY

Ev Arad: "Start from home; don't open your own place right away. If you have your own place, you'll be worrying about overhead expenses and concentrating on what will sell well rather than on what you love to do. And if you lose your passion, you'll be finished."

TAKE A BUSINESS COURSE

Hilary Radley: "As a fashion designer, one of the main things I've observed is that people with some business background tend to do better. In design school, they didn't teach any business basics, which is a mistake. I learned the hard way. You should definitely get some business education if you can."

HONE YOUR LEADERSHIP SKILLS

Marisa Minicucci: "I've met some really great young designers who work perfectly on a team, but wouldn't be able to lead a team of cutters and sample-makers. It depends on what level of designer you want to be. If you want to run your own fashion business, leadership skills are incredibly important."

WATCH YOUR DEADLINES

Marisa Minicucci: "When I worked with a partner, I could take more time with the creative side. But even then I had the production to worry about, I had deadlines, I had decisions to make. You have to be organized and quick on your feet.

Anissa Marcanio adds: "In fashion, if you don't meet your deadlines, that's it. You're done for that season. You're done."

SET REGULAR GOALS

Manika Gaudet: "Organization is really important. I don't mean having a clean desk, but organizing your day and setting goals for yourself. At night I write down what I think I'll do tomorrow and during the week. I usually put down too much, and I'm never able to get half of it done. But at least I have concrete goals and I'm always moving ahead."

KNOW YOUR NICHE

Marisa Minicucci: "Know who your target market is, and be very specific. Your product needs to be niche, not broad. You can't just say, "I love fashion and I'll do all kinds of things." Know your niche and know exactly how your product will fit in it. Will it be a full collection or will it just be shoes?"

START CLOSE TO HOME

Ev Arad: "Start by marketing yourself to friends. Do home shows. Before Christmas, make presents for family and friends and their friends. Slowly you'll spread the word."

BE OPEN TO NEW MARKETS

Manika Gaudet: "I've found that young designers want to design things for themselves. It's easier to design things that you like and that look good on you, but don't be afraid to venture out into different markets. It can be very worthwhile to design for a clientele that isn't exactly like you. Fashion goes a lot further than personal aesthetic. For instance, we need more designers creating for [plus size] markets."

YOU DON'T HAVE TO DO EVERYTHING YOURSELF

Hilary Radley: "One of the strengths I've had is the ability to know I can't do everything well. Manufacturing was not one of my fortés and administrative work isn't high on my list either. So I concentrated on what I was good at: designing, conceptualizing, starting with a fabric, and getting to the final product. I hired others to take care of the parts that, for me, were weaknesses."

Manika Gaudet: "I try to deal with as much as possible myself, but I have an accountant because I want that to be in good hands. I have assistants and I hire people to help out with technical stuff and marketing. Sometimes I barter or engage in cross-promotional exchanges with people to limit my costs and maximize efficiency."

Marisa Minicucci: "When I first started my own business that's when I got my own lawyer. You have to have that. They'll know how to set up your business, register your trademark, and make sure it's protected. They're key to starting a business."

Ev Arad: "Most of the good artists I know aren't good sellers. If you're an artist, you're probably a very sensitive person. If people don't buy your work or you get criticized, you likely take it to heart too much. If you're the sort of person who can't sell their own work, find somebody who can do it and give them a commission."

SURROUND YOURSELF WITH THE RIGHT PEOPLE

Hilary Radley: "Thinking you can do it all is not the smart way to go. Financing, for instance, is a big burden, especially for an artistic person. Finding a partner is extremely important. It's a huge step. If you look at the big fashion designers today, they've all got great business partners. So you've got to surround yourself with the right people."

Marisa Minicucci: If you just want to do custom-made stuff, then maybe you can work on your own. But if you want to sell your product at large, you'll need to associate with other people. Have a clear picture of what you want to do and where you want to go and then find the right people to work with. When I started out, I found a partner who had a master's in finance. I was very close to the product and he was close to the administration. Although we each had influence on both sides of the business, we would defer to each others' judgement for certain decisions."

YOU NEED TO BE A TEAM PLAYER

Hilary Radley: "You have to be able to work in a team; if you can't do that then you won't make it in this business. It's hard when it's your own thing and you have to let other people in, especially when your name's on the label. But you have to be able to trust other people."

II. FINANCING AND MAKING MONEY

You've heard our experts talk about the need to involve other people in your business, and financing is among the top things you'll need help with. It's especially tough nowadays to secure grants and loans for fashion, so you'll likely be looking for creative ways to fund your venture. Well, no problem; you're a creative-type, right? There's everything from slow-as-you-go self-financing to partnering with a major manufacturer to consider. Take a look and see what our experts advise.

BANK FINACING IS HARD TO COME BY

Marisa Minicucci: "Banks don't finance the fashion business anymore. They don't believe in the industry. You used to be able to go to the bank and show them your written orders and they would give you the loan. Now they don't believe in those receivables. Now you're putting up your house as collateral."

GRANTS ARE FEW AND FAR BETWEEN

Manika Gaudet: "For fashion and design it's harder to get grants, and it's a lot of work to apply. Fashion design isn't included in most of the regular government and arts council funding systems. You need to be a well-established designer to be eligible."

Marisa Minicucci: "There is some government funding, but they want a lot of things in advance of the financing, and by the time you've given them all they require, you've missed a season."

CHECK OUT FASHION CONTESTS

Manika Gaudet: "I see a lot of fashion contests on different levels. Shopping centres will hold competitions for emerging designers. TV shows will hold them as well. They're not for everyone, but winning could give your career a big boost."

WATCH YOUR DEBT LOAD

Ev Arad: "My advice to jewellers is don't start taking loans from the bank right away. You don't need all that stress while creating your business. Start small. Make five rings and sell those five rings. Then take that money and make ten rings. The more you earn the more you make, the more you sell. That way, if you make a small mistake at the beginning it's just a small mistake. If you start big, then any mistake is a big mistake."

YOU CAN WORK ON A ROYALTY BASIS

Hilary Radley: "When I started designing coats as a freelancer for a manufacturer, I always worked on a royalty basis, and my name was always on the label. But I didn't handle any of the financing. I owned my own studio and my own name. I worked for a year for nothing, because royalties don't come in right away. That year was tough, but I did it. Then the ball was rolling and I never looked back."

CASH FLOW CAN MAKE OR BREAK YOU

Marisa Minicucci: "When you're starting out it can cost you $5,000 or $10,000 to go to a trade show. When you're building a line, you need to pay for the show, you need to pay for the material to produce your orders, you need to ship them. It might be six months before you collect anything, and meanwhile you need to support yourself. And while you're shipping your first collection, you're producing your next one and paying for your next show! Make sure you have the cash flow to keep you afloat."

WATCH THOSE PENNIES

Ev Arad: "Always put money aside. If you're selling a lot, you never know what will happen in six months. You'll need time to make your collections and time to sell them. And when you're designing and making, you won't be making any money."

FIND THE RIGHT MANUFACTURING PARTNERS

Hilary Radley: "I was always self-financed. It's not right for everyone, but I never wanted to be the manufacturer, and I never wanted to finance. I knew my strengths and all I wanted to do was design. My strength is in creating. I didn't want to have to worry about the manufacturing. Some people can spend twelve to fourteen hours a day in the business. I'm not like that, so I contracted with a manufacturer right from the beginning."

LICENSING IS ONE OPTION BUT YOU LOSE SOME CONTROL

Hilary Radley: "Licensing is tricky. It's a nice way to ease yourself out of the manufacturing business and it's great to get royalty cheques, but you stand a chance of losing the integrity of your product. I trust my licensers and I've been with them for a long time. But you have to insist on certain things in the contracts."

III. GETTING VISIBILITY

It's no surprise that our fashion mavens all stressed the importance of developing a strong name brand. It's the most basic step in gaining any kind of visibility in the market. And in this business, your name can mean everything to your customer. So think long and hard about what your brand will represent. After that, our experts have a host of suggestions on how to get your collection seen and talked about, from fashion shows to Facebook ads. They've done it all.

DEVELOP AN IDENTIFIABLE BRAND

Ev Arad: "Focus on one collection and create a strong brand. Don't keep switching to something new. People will start to recognize you and your collections. If you're doing silver jewellery, do only silver. If you're doing modern, do only modern. If you mix them up too much no one will recognize your style."

Manika Gaudet: "It's very important to have a cohesive brand. Before I launched my line, I wanted to make sure I had something that reflected my style but that I could also apply to a diverse market. So it has to be consistent, unique, and adaptable at the same time."

PUT QUALITY FIRST

Marisa Minicucci: "It used to be that you designed a certain type of product and that's what you were known for. But now that our brand is well established, we're starting to branch out into other types of products like housewares. Your brand has to represent what you believe in and what your values are. But mostly you want people to recognize the excellence of your products, no matter what they are."

THE POSSIBILITIES FOR VISIBILITY ARE ENDLESS
Hilary Radley: "If you're just starting off, you can call a fashion reporter to come photograph your collection. That's the most straightforward way to get visibility. Once you're big enough, in-store presentations are good; you can meet your customers directly. You can also go to shows for buyers in the local market or in New York where it's bigger. And there's even fashion TV today. There are a million different things you can do."

GIVE OUT THOSE BUSINESS CARDS
Ev Arad: "I make sure everyone who comes into the store leaves with a business card. I get so many customers through word of mouth. I tell all my customers that they have to tell their friends about us. If someone is enthusiastic I say, 'Take five cards!' That's important, especially since I'm selling online as well. They could be sitting at home and buying from me."

FASHION SHOWS BUILD YOUR IMAGE
Manika Gaudet: "Fashion shows are something you should definitely consider. They don't make money directly, but they create visibility for your line. But remember: you're not just creating a shopping experience, you're creating a magical world for your audience. They have to "experience" your vision. For me, it was a great way to build my image."

TRY A POP-UP BOUTIQUE
Manika Gaudet: "Since it's hard to get known and picked up by retailers in the early stages of your career, I started organizing cinq-à-sept pop-up shows in boutiques to showcase my line. The boutiques get to see how people react to your line and it's good for them too as it attracts new people to their store."

OPEN AN ONLINE SHOP
Ev Arad: "Open a shop on eBay or Etsy. Start selling online. At least people will get to know your work—if they like it they'll tell their friends and you'll start growing an audience."

GOT ANY CELEBRITY CONNECTIONS?
Marisa Minicucci: "I did a dress for the Oscars, for Annie Proulx, the writer of Brokeback Mountain. She found us and liked our whole philosophy. That was great publicity. Another couple of Montreal designers put a suit on Kate Middleton, which she wore during her Canadian tour and that took off like crazy. Those are the things that get you real visibility."
Manika Gaudet: "I was a personal shopper for celebrities, and because they always wanted to have something different to define themselves, I offered some of my pieces to them. That way I had Quebec actors and singers publically wearing my line. It worked for everybody and brought me great publicity."

PR FIRMS CAN GIVE YOUR IMAGE A BOOST—FOR A WHILE

Ev Arad: "I used to use a PR agency, and I would pay them a monthly fee. They would advertise our new collections and send out press releases. Sometimes it worked and sometimes it didn't. For the first six months they got us covered everywhere, in lots of magazines and in the Gazette. The second six months, not anything. Zero."

LISTEN TO YOUR MARKETING TEAM

Hilary Radley: "You need to be able to listen to your marketing and advertising team and let those departments do what they know how to do. Some designers are great self-promoters, but if you don't have that, then you need to trust other people."

CHOOSE THE RIGHT SOCIAL MEDIA

Manika Gaudet: "I have Facebook, Twitter, Pinterest, and an Etsy store, but I have a hard time being active on everything. My Facebook page is the most important because I can update it easily. It's visual, it's accessible, and I can pay to have it reach more of my market. If you put a lot of effort into one social network, especially a visual one, it will help you a lot."

SHARE YOUR PROCESS WITH YOUR CLIENTELE

Marisa Minicucci: "People get interested in a product by knowing more about it. You want to reach people who aren't in the fashion world as well, so you need to be talking about things other than your product. We talk about our process and about the workers behind the scenes. We get people interested in who we are rather than just the end product."

GET HELP WITH YOUR ONLINE ACCOUNTS

Manika Gaudet: "A lot of people jump right into social media without any real understanding. It's important to get advice from people who know what they're doing. For instance, Facebook changed its algorithm to make it less effective for people who don't pay to boost their business posts. You need to know those kinds of things. If you don't, get help."

CONNECT WITH BLOGGERS AND STYLISTS

Manika Gaudet: "To publicize your line, you have to work with bloggers and stylists. Invite them to your events; try to make connections and network with them. If they can't attend, send them amazing photographs they can use. That's very important."

Marisa Minicucci: "I get the media's attention by sending products to stylists, bloggers, artists, anyone with influence. If they like your product, you might be featured in an editorial. That's great, especially in the United States media. Magazine coverage online or offline is good too; it helps to get you noticed by people who have influence in the fashion world."

INDUSTRY NETWORKING IS KEY

Manika Gaudet: "I know networking isn't for everyone, but it can really make a difference. So, how do you network? Check out what's happening in the market. Pop-up boutiques are for designers to get together and they're good places to make contacts. You can usually find them on Facebook and through other online fashion groups."

Hilary Radley: "Networking can start when you're in school and continue from there. Where you network depends on what kind of help you're looking for. There are all sorts of places you can connect, for example through organizations for designers and at conferences, etc. There's even a specific artist conference held by YES each year. I've spoken there myself. And if you approach me after a conference, I'll be happy to talk with you."

DON'T GET CAUGHT UP IN YOUR OWN HYPE

Hilary Radley: "One problem with getting lots of media attention is that you can get caught up in all the hype. Don't believe your own BS. I see so many young people who get in the papers a few times and start believing their own PR. Press helps but it's not the end of it. You can't take a bit of success for granted. If you don't have product out on the street and people wearing your clothes, you have no credibility."

At a certain point you can't be calling people at midnight about something for the next day. You need to be able to stop and prioritize other things in your life.
- Marisa Minicucci, MINICUCCI x MARCANIO

LIVING AS A FASHION DESIGNER

The world of good-looking people and gorgeous things can be hyper-competitive and, frankly, pretty dirty down under. That's what we're hearing from our experts, who've been knee deep in it for ages. So what's an open-hearted designer to do? Don't despair; it's still possible to live the dream, but do it with your eyes wide open, that's all we ask. If the designing life is what you've chosen, heed our experts' advice. It's worth more than its weight in gold brocade.

STICK WITH YOUR PRIORITIES

Manika Gaudet: "You'll have to deal with unexpected situations all the time, so know your priorities. Sometimes you'll be offered opportunities that seem very attractive, but you have to evaluate them versus your goals. You have to learn how to say no to things sometimes."

BE PREPARED TO TAKE CRITICISM

Marisa Minicucci: "For me, accepting critique is second nature, because I've been in this business for thirty years. But you have to understand that you'll be constantly criticized. You critique everything and you're constantly being critiqued. But not necessarily in a negative way. You'll bring your stuff to fifty different stores and get fifty different opinions on the buttons, on the shoulder, on the leg…"

YOU CAN'T TAKE THINGS PERSONALLY

Anissa Marcanio: "If you're a sensitive person by nature then I don't recommend the garment business. It's an incredibly competitive industry these days. You have to be hardened to the fact that people are always out for themselves. The only thing they want to know is how you can make them money or what skills you have that can benefit them. If you take that personally, you're not going to get anywhere in this industry."

YOU MIGHT BE WORKING ON BEIJING TIME

Marisa Minicucci: "You've got to be an early bird in this industry because of all the time zones you'll be dealing with. If you work with China, you have to be ready to deal with their issues at 7:00 a.m. If you're working with Europe, our 9:00 a.m. is their 3:00 p.m. If you're not up early enough, their day is done before you can get to them."

FIND YOUR WORK-LIFE BALANCE

Hilary Radley: "Balance is a terribly important thing. I've never been a workaholic, but I love what I do. You need to know what your priorities are. Having children makes it more difficult to run your own business, but it's possible. We travelled a lot together, and I had a house in

Vermont where we could go to decompress. You need your downtime; it will make you more productive in the long run."

FAMILY SUPPORT IS A BIG ASSET

Ev Arad: "I'm really lucky that my husband supports me. Five days after my son was born I went back to work, and my husband stayed home with our son for the first year. He did it with love, because for me it was just normal to go right back to work. I'd suggest finding [a life partner] who isn't an artist. You need to be with someone different if you're an artist. They will balance you and support you."

KNOW WHEN TO CALL IT A DAY

Marisa Minicucci: "The days are not 9:00 a.m. to 5:00 p.m., they're often 24/7. But if nothing is working and you're really stressed out and you have deadlines to meet, you have to be able to say, 'no, I'm done for the day' and go home."

SOME FINAL THOUGHTS

Our designers have some final thoughts they'd like to share. They were like you, once upon a time, and remember what it was like to make the leap into that brave new world of fashion. Yes, they made some mistakes, and so will you. But we're sure that having their words to mull over before you jump will give you a softer landing. For the record, here's their parting advice:

KNOW WHEN TO GO OUT ON YOUR OWN

Manika Gaudet: "After graduating, I worked for twelve years for other people. I think I could have worked for myself and started my line sooner, but I worried that as a small designer I'd end up doing everything myself—even the stuff I didn't like. So maybe I waited too long for that reason. Now I do a lot of things myself, but because I have so many contacts in the industry, I can contract out a lot of stuff. So don't be afraid to take that leap. You won't have to do it alone."

TRUST AND VALUE YOURSELF

Marisa Minicucci: "Sometimes I didn't trust my instincts. When you're looked at as the 'artist,' people don't always take you seriously, and they're not comfortable with you making certain decisions. But don't underestimate your instincts. Make sure you understand the business part of it and learn as much as you can. But if you don't understand part of it, it's okay to ask someone to explain it to you four times. You need to understand instead of just trusting someone else completely. Even though you're the artist, you're as important as the business people."

FASHION IS A BUSINESS FIRST, ART SECOND

Anissa Marcanio: "If you're sensitive about your creations, this won't be an easy industry for you. The fashion showroom isn't like an art gallery where the price is what the artist expects to get for the work. In a showroom, the buyer will immediately ask for a discount, no matter how long or hard you worked on something. In this business, it's all about money. Know that going in."

YOU'LL HAVE TO MAKE HARD CHOICES ALONG THE WAY

Hilary Radley: "At a certain time in my life I made many of my choices for love and lifestyle more than for my career. I found I wasn't able to maintain both as well as I would have liked. Those life choices weren't massive, but they tipped the scales a little bit and changed the trajectory of my career. There comes a time in the life of any artist where you'll have to make tough priority choices. Think about that in advance, what you want and where you want to go."

FOLLOW YOUR HEART

Ev Arad: "I remember my father telling me, 'What will you do with fashion design? Go and do something else; be a doctor or a lawyer.' So I always hesitate to say things like that to my own daughter, who wants to study music. You should go with your passion. Even if you don't eventually become a musician or a jeweller, you should follow your passions in life. If you do, no matter what, I believe the right things will happen."

FILMMAKERS

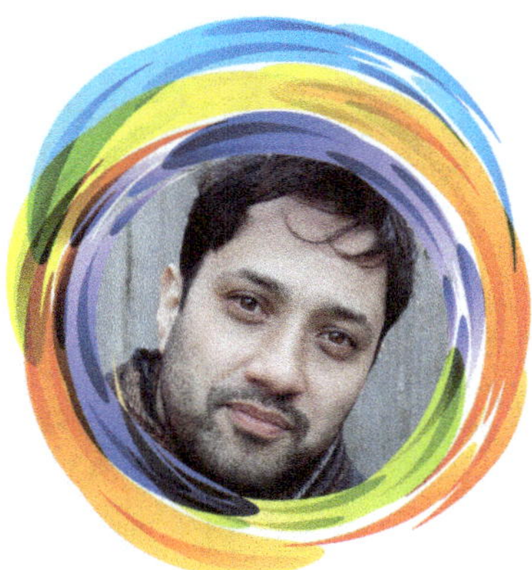

Mila Aung-Thwin

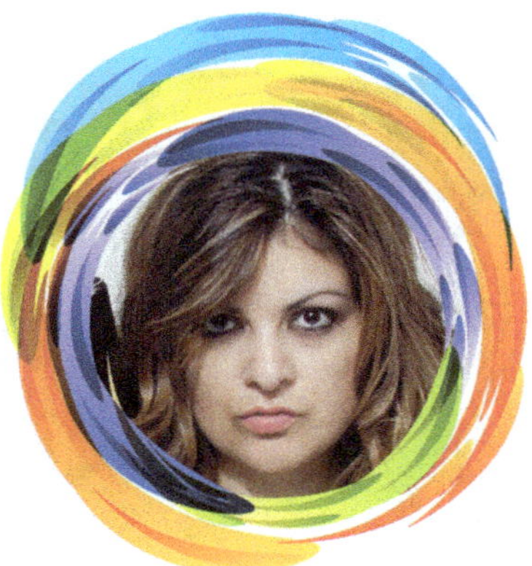

Patricia Chica

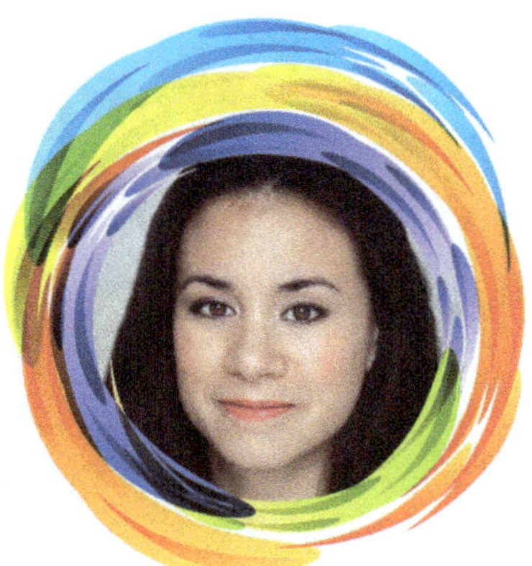

Karen Cho

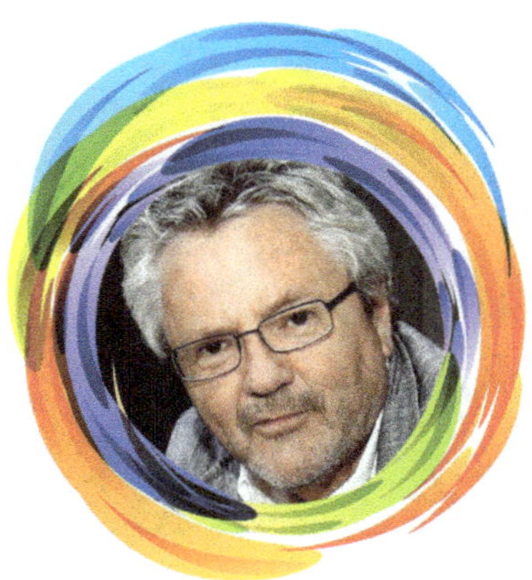

Kevin Tierney

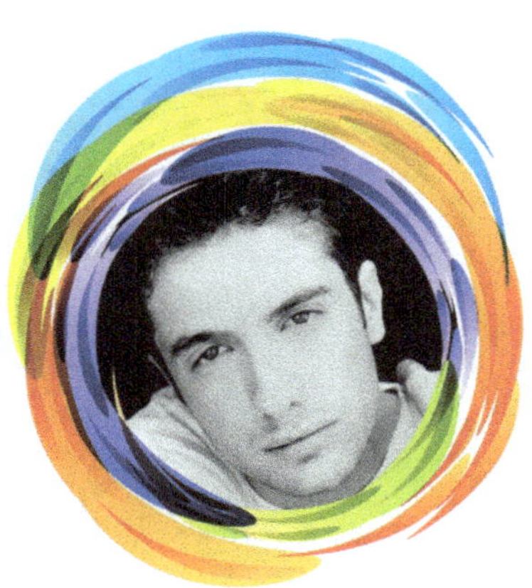

Jacob Tierney

Don't be afraid to take risks, especially at the beginning when you have nothing to lose.
- Karen Cho, multi-award-winning filmmaker

SO YOU WANNA BE A FILMMAKER?

The first time you got behind a camera and held it in your hands, you knew there was no place you'd rather be. Your mission is to show your stories. You are a filmmaker.

Whether it's another buddy movie you plan to shoot (this one is different, we know), a 400-minute avant-garde art flick, or a take-no-prisoners guerrilla documentary in artsy Montreal, there will surely be people who will connect with your film.

In this section, we feature the advice of five successful Quebec-based filmmakers. And while we focus on directors and producers, there are a variety of occupations in the industry that you may want to investigate further if filmmaking is your passion. Here are some possibilities included in the National Occupation Classification, published by Employment and Social Development Canada:

> Audio and video recording technician

> Broadcast journalist

> Broadcast technician

> Director of photography

> Camera operator

> Film director

> Film editor

> Film producer

> Gamer

> Screenwriter

> Videographer

For professions related to acting and other performing arts, please refer to the Performers section of this book.

THE EXPERTS

We spoke with the following accomplished filmmakers to get their take on "take one":

Mila Aung-Thwin is a co-founder of the Montreal production company EyeSteelFilm, which produces and distributes documentaries from around the world. He has produced more than twenty feature documentaries over the past decade including *Up the Yangtze* (2007, Golden Horse winner), *Last Train Home* (2009, winner of two Emmy Awards), *Rip: A Remix Manifesto* (2009, IDFA Audience Choice Prize winner), and *Forest of the Dancing Spirits* (2013, IDFA First Appearance Prize). In addition to producing, Mila is also a director, editor, and writer. He currently serves as president of RIDM, Montreal's international documentary festival. For more on Mila check out www.eyesteelfilm.com.

Patricia Chica is a thirty-five-time award-winning genre director specializing in psychological dramas, thrillers and edgy documentaries. She is fluent in English, French and Spanish and has built an international cult following. Patricia's acclaimed films have been presented at over 200 film festivals, in theatres, art centers, universities and on television around the world: *The Promise* (2000), *Rockabilly 514* (2008), *Day Before Yesterday* (2010), *Ceramic Tango* (2013), and *Serpent's Lullaby* (2014) just to name a few. Her latest film *Serpent's Lullaby* was part of the Coup de Cœur selection at the Short Film Corner of the 67th Festival de Cannes. Patricia is presently attached to direct a few feature films with producers from Canada and the US. Check out her work at: www.PatriciaChica.com

Karen Cho is a Chinese-Canadian filmmaker known for her socially-engaged documentaries. Her films explore themes of identity, immigration, and social justice. Karen directed the award-winning *In the Shadow of Gold Mountain* (2004), a documentary about the Chinese Head Tax and Exclusion Act, and the Gemini-nominated *Seeking Refuge* (*Terre d'asile*) (2009), a film following asylum seekers in Canada. Karen's film *Status Quo? The Unfinished Business of Feminism in Canada* (2012) won Best Documentary at the Whistler Film Festival and had over sixty-seven community screenings across Canada. Karen is currently working on an experimental docu-fiction and cooking up her next batch of cultural subversion. Get a better look at www.storyboothmedia.com.

Kevin Tierney is the producer and co-writer of *Bon Cop, Bad Cop* (2006), the first-ever bilingual film made in Canada, and the highest grossing movie in the history of Canadian cinema. His most recent production, *French Immersion* (2011), was his directorial debut. Other films include *Good Neighbours* (2010) and *The Trotsky* (2009), both written and directed by his son, Jacob (see below), *Love & Savagery* (2009), directed by John N. Smith, and *Serveuses demandées* (2008), written and directed by Guylaine Dionne. Over the past fifteen years, Kevin Tierney's television productions have been nominated for a total of eleven Emmys and twelve Geminis, including two Outstanding Mini-Series, Best Series, and most recently, Best TV Movie for *One Dead Indian* (2006). For more on Kevin's projects click www.parkexpictures.ca.

Jacob Tierney's feature directorial debut, *Twist* (2003), received Genie nominations for Jacob's screenplay, as well as for Best Actor and Supporting Actor. His second feature, *The Trotsky* (2009), won the 2011 Genie Award for Best Original Screenplay, Best Original Song, and the User's Choice Award for its star, Jay Baruchel. Jacob also won both the writing and directing awards for the film at the 2010 Canadian Comedy Awards. Jacob also directs frequently in the television world. To see more about what Jacob is up to check out www.garygoddardagency.com/clients/jacob-tierney.

Here's what they had to say, filmmaker to filmmaker:

WHO NEEDS FILM SCHOOL?

There are differences in opinion over whether an aspiring filmmaker needs a university education to make movies. The short answer is "probably not." But, making great flicks requires extensive technical knowledge that goes beyond what you may have picked up shooting YouTube shorts. If you expect to be taken seriously by your peers, you'd better know how to talk the talk.

A film or communication studies degree introduces you to the technical side of filmmaking. It also allows you to study film history, film styles, and the works of the most influential, controversial, and important names in film. Film school is also a great opportunity to play with high-tech equipment and work at a slower pace than frenzied movie sets shooting to deadline.

So a university degree can't hurt, and, if you take a proactive approach and follow your teachers' recommendations and advice, it can actually prove to be quite helpful. If you decide to enrol in film school, make the most of your experience: network, get involved with as many projects as you can, volunteer, and seek out the films and festivals your professors recommend.

Although film school will arm you with an array of skills, don't forget that when you're looking to make it, no degree beats the experience gained by jumping into the industry wherever you can. And, if at all possible, start making films with whatever technology is at your disposal!

Director Patricia Chica puts it this way, "Get an education, but a quick one. A PhD in film won't necessarily make you a better filmmaker or earn you more money. If you want to make films, start making films now. I've noticed that there are two different kinds of film production graduates: the ones who take it for granted that because they have a diploma, they'll get a job and get paid, and the ones who know that they have to prove themselves."

I remember telling myself in my early 20s that if I start at the bottom, I can only go up. If I start at the top I can only go down.

- Patricia Chica, multi-award-winning director

HOW DO YOU SHOW WHAT YOU'VE GOT?

Let's be blunt here: you need a portfolio of your work if you're ever going to be more than the bringer-of-lunches or the giver-of-coffee on set. A quality portfolio will help you make a lasting impression and might even contribute to your next big break. Here is our experts' specific advice:

HAVE A DEMO REEL

Mila Aung-Thwin: "I won't even look at the CV if someone has a good demo reel. Everyone sends me their Vimeo links, and it's very easy to see if they have any skills. It cuts through a lot of unnecessary talk. You need to have already taken some steps towards your artistic direction. If I look at CVs, I scan through for experience in the field or if you have specific skills with editing software, for instance."

PUT YOUR PORTFOLIO ONLINE

Karen Cho: "A demo is important, but even more so is a website. You'll need a bit about yourself, your vision as a filmmaker, your up-to-date CV, clips from a film or whole short films, and any press. When I'm researching a film I often have to cold-call people and their first question is, "Who's Karen Cho?" and then I can direct them to my website. You should also exist on IMDB if you can, but you can't just have student films. You have to have a film that's played at festivals or been broadcast."

REFLECT YOUR DRIVE AND PASSION

Kevin Tierney: "The CV should reflect where your drive has taken you. This is a self-promoting, self-generating industry. Produce a short film, produce an animation, anything! Write a piece. Not just, 'I went to school.' Everyone went to school."

"BUT I'VE NEVER MADE A MOVIE BEFORE; WHAT CAN I DO?"

We assume that if you've read this far into the filmmaking section, you have some sort of creative bent. We trust that you're accomplished in whatever medium you've chosen to express yourself in.

Don't feel constrained if you've never made a film. But as Kevin Tierney advises, you should have produced something tangible. So whether you write, take photos, paint, or design clothes, make it clear that you have vision, talent, and boundless creativity by sending a portfolio of the very best of what you have accomplished to date.

You've got to have the skills of a businessman and the soul of an artiste.
- Kevin Tierney, Producer Bon Cop, Bad Cop

GETTING STARTED

You've sat through Andy Warhol's controversial film Empire, an eight-hour shot of the Empire State Building, and thought, "I could do better than that!"

Or perhaps your favourite fruit and vegetable store is closing after servicing the neighbourhood for seventy years and you've thought to immortalize this historic spot, the quirky grocers who ran it, and their loyal customers on film.

Or maybe you want to tell a good old-fashioned love story that unfolds on a winding staircase on St-Urbain Street, plays out on Montreal's most romantic boulevards, and ends in tragedy on the banks of the Lachine Canal.

What now? Although you might have all the talent in the world, if you want to pursue a successful career in film, you still need to pay your dues. Our panel of award-winning filmmakers agree that the best place to start is at the bottom, and to move up from there.

Here is what our experts told us about breaking into the film industry and making it work for you:

FIRST AND FOREMOST MAKE SURE YOU HAVE THE PASSION AND DESIRE
Mila Aung-Thwin: "You have to really want it more than anything else, because it's not a logical business choice. If you look at filmmaking, the competition is so fierce and the remuneration is just not there. You need to have a desire that's stronger than anything else."

And once you've checked that off…

CONSIDER INTERNING OR VOLUNTEERING ON A FILM SET
Patricia Chica: "Get an internship, especially when you're attached to a school. You'll immediately appeal to an employer. They'll take a chance on you, and you'll be allowed to make mistakes and improve yourself. Not only that, but you can get noticed. You might get the job next time. I'm very loyal to all of my interns, that's how I find the right talent that suits my personality. The ones who are good, I want to keep them."

BUT DON'T VOLUNTEER INDEFINITELY
Mila Aung Thwin: "A lot of the industry is built on people who are coming out of school and are willing to work for nothing just for experience. The music video industry is a big example. If you work as an intern on a huge set, you might not learn or make anything. Be careful not to be taken advantage of. It's one thing to spend a couple of years working under one of the best

cinematographers—you couldn't pay to learn those sorts of skills. But if your job is fetching coffee, don't do that for a couple of years. Do it for a couple weeks then move on."

CONSIDER WORK IN RELATED FIELDS
Jacob Tierney: "Acting was my Starbucks job. I would take jobs that I didn't necessarily want just for the money, and everything is a learning opportunity. I'm super lucky that I got to work in the same field I'm in now."

GRAB YOUR OPPORTUNITIES WHEN THEY COME ALONG
Karen Cho: "I was working on this independent 'B' movie as a production coordinator, and they totally took advantage of me. I was making maybe $60 a day. A bigger production company called me and asked if I wanted to be an assistant editor on The Heist. And I said no—out of loyalty to this 'B' movie. I probably should have said yes, because then I could have made contacts and been on the editing room floor. I guess the wisdom there is know when to jump ship."

BE A JACK OF ALL TRADES
Karen Cho: "On your way up, learn all you can about the different roles. As an independent filmmaker, if you're low budget, you might have to do all those jobs."

FIND A MENTOR
Kevin Tierney: "Look for people who can mentor and help you. This is totally plausible. If somebody came to me and actually knew what I've done and was genuinely interested, I wouldn't mind letting them hang out for a while. I'd read their project, it's not that big of a deal."

START BUILDING YOUR NETWORK
Jacob Tierney: "You need to find a community. Go to local screenings and events and meet people in the same field as you. Find your peers and get to know them. You'll find people to work with and compare your work to and, eventually, who knows, they might end up being your best supporters."

JOIN PROFESSIONAL ASSOCIATIONS
Karen Cho: "For networking, there's the English-Language Arts Network, www.quebec-elan.org, there's the Montreal Film Group, www.montrealfilmgroup.com. There's Women in Film and Television and New Media, www.fctnm.org. Recently, I've joined a lot of unions and guilds, but I don't know if I would do that as an emerging filmmaker. It's a lot of money out of pocket at the beginning."

MAKE A SHORT FILM
Jacob Tierney: "A short film is a calling card. You can't expect to make publicity off it, unless it's really controversial or something. What you can hope for is the chance to make another movie. Hopefully a feature. Take that opportunity when it comes."

It's the hardest job, but the most beautiful job in the world.

- Patricia Chica, muliti-award-winning director

TAKING IT TO THE NEXT LEVEL

Congratulations. Scorsese came to town and you landed a production assistant job on the set. You befriended an important figure in the Montreal film scene and from then on the jobs have been coming in steadily.

You've seen the way things work on a set. You've made some key contacts and maybe a few shorts of your own along the way, and now you're confident that you have the skills to make and sell really good movies.

But do you really have what it takes to get your film shot and onto the big screen? You may have a movie concept to end all movie concepts, but unless you have some basic knowledge of the film business, it's more likely to sit on your hard drive than to play in the local multiplex.

We've asked our film experts for some advice on how to get your film made and from the editing suite to a theatre near you. Here's what they had to say:

I. THE BUSINESS OF MOVIE MAKING

CHOOSE PROJECTS YOU REALLY BELIEVE IN

Mila Aung-Thwin: "[Because of the tremendous commitment required] a project has to feel fun, even if there's no value attached to it. It has to be innovative. If we believe in our work and want to brag about it—that's the rule of thumb. Otherwise it's not worth it."

FIND THE RIGHT PARTNERS

Mila Aung-Thwin: "You'll have to ally yourself with people who have complementary skills. I started my company with someone who was more of an established filmmaker. You need to find people who are compatible with you and who are right for the specific tasks that you require. And they should share your values."

NURTURE YOUR FILM COMMUNITY CONTACTS

Jacob Tierney: "One thing I can't stress enough is the community. You have to meet people, deal with other people, expose your work to other people. If you can develop certain skills—writing, editing, VFX—you can use them to help [colleagues] with their projects. That's a great way to get to know people and work with them. Everyone needs people to participate in their projects."

DON'T BE AFRAID TO ASK FOR HELP

Karen Cho: "Don't be afraid to ask for advice from people you've worked with in the past. I'm pretty shy myself, but you just have to force yourself."

BE PREPARED TO PLAY MANY ROLES

Kevin Tierney: "When I was working with people in LA, I would get a phone call with someone saying, 'Can I speak to business affairs?' So I would put them on hold for a few minutes and come back and say, 'Hi, this is business affairs.'"

BE READY TO DEAL WITH AMBIGUITY

Mila Aung-Thwin: "Being able to juggle the unknowns is crucial. Will it rain tomorrow? Will my camera show up? You have to make the best of what you have, and you have to be able to improvise. That's a big part of being a documentary filmmaker."

YOU'LL NEED YOUR BEST COMMUNICATION SKILLS

Mila Aung-Twin: "You have to have really good people skills. In film, you have to be able to communicate well and work with others. Communicating what's in your head and getting it on screen is key."

MAINTAIN A TEAM ATMOSPHERE

Karen Cho: "The people you meet on the way up are also the people you meet on the way down. You can be nasty to people on set, but two years can go by and that production assistant you yelled at might be the producer on a big show and you have to beg them for money. When you're on a film crew, it's really important to maintain that team atmosphere."

DON'T LET OPPORTUNITY PASS YOU BY!

Patricia Chica: "After my first short got noticed at the Sarasota International Film Festival, Jim Carrey's agent called me up from Los Angeles to request a screener, which I never sent. He was looking for an up-and-coming foreign director for Jim's next film. A year or two later, a movie comes out [that he was connected to] with Jim Carrey: *Eternal Sunshine of the Spotless Mind* directed by French filmmaker Michel Gondry. I said, 'Oh my god, where would I be if I'd sent in my demo and screener to that guy?' I'll never find out!"

II. FINANCING AND MAKING MONEY

Making films is an expensive business, and our filmmakers had a lot to say about financing. Expect to put in eighteen-hour days and maybe your RRSP too! Happily, Canada has a granting system you can access, but be warned of the bureaucratic quagmire you'll encounter if you're looking for the big bucks. Our filmmakers also advise that you hedge your bets by keeping a few projects in the pipeline at all times. Financing can always fall through at the last minute, so be ready to sail another ship. Here are the specifics:

BE PREPARED TO INVEST YOUR OWN MONEY

Patricia Chica: "I've been financing my own independent work since the beginning. I've sold my condo, used my retirement fund, my credit cards, my savings. After getting noticed for my independent film work, I am now getting private investors financing my films.

TAP INTO THE GRANTING SYSTEM

Mila Aung-Thwin: "We're very lucky in Canada for the number of foundations and organizations that will help. We have the National Film Board and the Arts Council. Both the Arts Council and the Société de Développement des Entreprises Culturelles [SODEC] have a first tier financing for young filmmakers up to age thirty-five. And you can make a ton of films with the money they give you."

START SMALL: GRANTS WITH NO STRINGS ATTACHED

Mila Aung-Thwin: "The bigger sums of money you get, the more strings will be attached. Try to find grants that are just that. They give you the money and they want to know how you'll spend it, but that's it. Further along you'll get investors and tax rebates. Either they're trying to make money, which is a hard thing to promise in film, or they're government investors who are trying to build the industry. You need to understand the staggering amount of bureaucracy that goes with higher amounts of financing."

LEARN THE ART OF THE PITCH

Karen Cho: "To apply for grants, learning how to write well is really important. You've got to be able to pitch really well."

DON'T BE SLOPPY

Kevin Tierney: "There's a lot of competition for every cent. Filmmakers need to be serious and professional about financing. You have to be credible and do your reports and your homework. You can't be sloppy."

TRY ALTERNATIVE FINANCING

Patricia Chica: "I used Indiegogo a little bit, but not as much as I wanted. And I also create events within the filmmaking world where people pay for tickets to get into the Wrap Party. My last two had a burlesque show performed by the film's actors where guests got to interact with me and the team, and therefore discover the world of the movie, before it even got released.

ALWAYS HAVE A FEW PROJECTS IN THE PIPELINE

Kevin Tierney: "You need to nurture the pipeline. You need to invest your time properly. It's cyclical: you get busy and then you won't be busy at all. Don't put all your eggs in one basket."

KEEP ON TOP OF THE BUREAUCRACY

Mila Aung-Thwin: "One of our most successful films lost a lot of money because of a technicality that was totally avoidable. We gave in our tax evaluation after the deadline, and it was costly. We're perfectionists in the artwork, but not the bureaucracy. We didn't need to have that happen to learn from it. It was right there in the rules. Just read the rules!"

GET A GOOD ACCOUNTANT TO MAXIMIZE TAX BREAKS

Karen Cho: "I have an accountant. I think the money is well spent, just for tax reasons. You should get an accountant who knows and understands the ups and downs of the entertainment industry. They can get you a lot of tax breaks."

FRANKLY, YOU SHOULDN'T GET INTO FILM FOR THE MONEY

Jacob Tierney: "In my experience, the people who are successful are the people who just do it. This is not an industry to get into if you want to make money. You won't be making money for years and years. You've just gotta love it."

III. GETTING VISIBILITY

It's not surprising that filmmakers know all about exposure. Most of their advice about visibility is simple: get yourself and your films out there, at film fests, online—any way you can. Meeting the right people in this industry will most likely happen when you're out there making films, showing films, and watching other people's films. The festival circuit is a natural venue for rubbing shoulders with industry types and your devoted fans. And once you've got a bit of a fan base, nurture it like it's your own family. Our experts had these tips to offer:

ESTABLISH AN IDENTIFIABLE BRAND

Patricia Chica: "My style and my signature are in all of my films. I have a very strong personal brand that I have been polishing over the last ten years. I don't take every project. If it's not to my taste or if it's not in alignment with my creative purpose, then I won't work on it. Now people know that about me, and they'll pitch me the right projects."

GET OUT THERE TO GET NOTICED

Patricia Chica: "When I go to FanExpo or ComicCon, I go in full costume: latex, feathers, big hair, makeup, everything. I show up and people get excited, curious and intrigued. They line up to get my autograph and take pictures with me. I upload it all on my phone right away. And those people will add me to their networks. Even if they forget about me after the Expo, I'll always be appearing on their feed. And it works!"

SUBMIT YOUR WORK TO FESTIVALS

Mila Aung-Thwin: "Film festivals are huge, and they're great for filmmakers because once you've had a film at a festival, you've arrived. Even at a little festival, you're important."

Jacob Tierney adds: "It's even easier now. A lot of festivals are online, you don't even have to attend."

SCREEN YOUR FILMS ANYWHERE YOU CAN

Patricia Chica: "Don't miss an opportunity to put your film on a screen in front of an audience, even if it's not the best venue. Even if it's in a garage projected on a sheet. Get out there and let people discover your work!

DON'T LET THE FEAR OF PIRATING HOLD YOU BACK

Mila Aung-Thwin: "The biggest mistake people make is getting scared about pirating. If your film gets pirated it's because people really want to watch it. That can be a calling card and you can turn that into a proposal for funding for your next film. So don't sit on your work."

PERSONAL NETWORKING IS KEY

Patricia Chica: "Do the leg work. Network in person. Go to film markets and film festivals, and show up to your screenings. You are your own business card."

VOLUNTEER FOR JURY DUTY

Karen Cho: "You can volunteer to be on a jury. You watch maybe sixty hours of programming, and you're on a jury of peers. It's a great way to network!"

NURTURE YOUR FAN BASE

Karen Cho: "Because my films are socio-political, I get really involved in whatever community the film is discussing. I will do screenings, talk with audiences, and maintain networks within the causes that my films talk about. There are a lot of newspapers and journals within these groups. Through them you'll get great coverage."

MAXIMIZE THE POTENTIAL OF SOCIAL MEDIA

Patricia Chica: "It's important for every artist these days to generate a cult following by building and engaging with their own audience. My main sources of social media are Facebook, Twitter, YouTube, and Vimeo. [Managing them all] takes a lot of hours and now I've hired someone else to help do it. On a slow day it's two hours minimum. It's not just about posting stuff, it's about interacting with fans; having a conversation and telling a story. They're the ones who pay for your art, so you have to pay them some respect. Last year I stopped posting for five days because I was so busy; a half hour after interrupting my account, I started getting messages saying, 'Oh my god, what happened to your Facebook?' That's when you know you have an audience."

GET HELP WITH SOCIAL MEDIA IF IT'S NOT YOUR THING

Jacob Tierney: "You should get to know people who are great at [social media], and get them to help you. You need so many people to get involved in your projects. You don't have to have every skill set."

DON'T FORGET ABOUT TRADITIONAL MEDIA

Mila Aung-Thwin: "Having an article written up about your work, and having it uploaded and shared around, is the best. We try to build up relations with journalists. Keep in mind that they're desperate for stories. They need new content every day. Whenever the company does anything legitimately interesting, there will always be at least five to ten journalists who will want to talk about it."

You have to be able to turn off the computer, turn off the cell phones. Declare that at seven o'clock you're not going to answer any more emails.

- Jacob Tierney, multi-award-winning filmmaker

LIVING AS A FILMMAKER

So, what life skills do you need to make it in this fast-paced industry? Our experts stressed the cooperative nature of their field, which requires excellent people skills, composure, and confidence. It also won't hurt to be uber detail oriented, since you'll likely have lots of expensive balls in the air all the time.

One big challenge is money management, both personal and professional. When you're in a business that can run scorching hot one minute and icy cold the next, keeping your own budget balanced takes incredible discipline. You'll need to save, save, save when the bucks are rolling in, because they won't roll in forever. Finally, our filmmakers admit that managing relationships when the work often requires a 24/7 focus can be difficult. Each of them has made different choices about how to fit family and friends into their hectic schedules. Consider their words of wisdom:

KEEP A WORK-LIFE BALANCE: EASIER SAID THAN DONE

Mila Aung-Thwin: "You're going to have an initial honeymoon phase, where the people around you will give you leeway. With my wife and my family, it was always, 'Boy, he's really living the dream! He won't be around, but we're proud!' That only lasts a certain time. After a while they're not excited for you anymore and you have to learn pacing. You need to be able to rebalance after that initial thrust. Separating work and taking time off is important."

FIND A NICHE THAT SUITS YOUR LIFESTYLE

Karen Cho: "Now that I'm [starting a family] I'm trying to move more into post-production; it's more stable work. I'm trying to move into writer and story editor jobs. The hours are long but they're flexible. It's more stable work with higher pay."

MAKE SURE YOUR FAMILY UNDERSTAND THE DEMANDS

Patricia Chica: "All of my boyfriends have been artists, because they need to understand [my] lifestyle. I don't have kids, and that was a conscious decision I made. My movies are my children, my contribution to society."

DON'T FORGET YOUR REST AND RELAXATION

Jacob Tierney: "You have to remember to sleep. People who haven't slept are the most useless people. Their brains don't work, they have no energy. Go to bed! Don't think that you can show up to work after three hours of sleep. You can't, you're incompetent. And on a movie set you're going to get hurt and you're going to hurt other people. If you're not taking care of yourself, you're not helping anyone."

NOURISH YOUR PEER COMMUNITY

Mila Aung-Thwin: "In some industries, your peers are competing with you. In our field, your competition is your best audience and your best allies. I've worked with producers who were my best assets, even though technically we were competing for the same money. Surround yourself with generous people. Your peers will become your friends, either in productions or festivals or applying for grants. If you make enemies, they will take the opportunity to take you down. I've seen that happen before."

CONSIDER SEPARATING YOUR PROFESSIONAL AND PERSONAL ONLINE ID

Karen Cho: "On Facebook, you should probably keep both a professional account and a personal one. And I try not to tweet about how 'my cat barfed on the floor.' I would keep a separate account for that sort of stuff."

WATCH THOSE PENNIES

Karen Cho: "You have to be frugal with your money. It's feast or famine. I know from having worked in the industry that I'll network and take on a bunch of jobs at once, and I'll work six to seven days a week for a whole year. I know at any moment it could dry up. I don't change my living habits in a year where I make more money. You've got to bank that money to have it for a year when you have nothing."

FINAL THOUGHT

Director Jacob Tierney gets the last word here. It's something all of us can take to heart:

GET READY FOR LIFELONG LEARNING

Jacob Tierney: "You'll make tons of mistakes along the way, but your career will develop so slowly that it ends up making you smarter. I've definitely seen people torpedo their careers; it's the usual stuff: substance problems, attitude problems, egos running rampant. What's so wonderful about working in the arts is that you're always learning; there's no point when you're done. It's always changing. None of the successful people I know have the attitude that they're here to teach you what they know. They're here to learn and participate."

BECOME A BETTER FILM AND TV NETWORKER
By Ezra Soiferman, Director of Montreal Film Group

I love our city and I love making films here. I've always felt a big part of making films was meeting talented people to help create them with me. Over the past twenty years, I've sharpened my networking skills to a level that gives me confidence and reassurance each time I attend a business event, party, or festival.

Here are ten tips on how to step up your networking game:

10. BE (OR BECOME) CURIOUS
Let's face it, if you don't give a hoot about meeting new people, this whole networking thing's gonna be awfully hard. Train yourself to be curious. Open your eyes and ears. Cultivate an appetite for unexpected encounters, for the thrill of not knowing how the next conversation with a stranger might make your day or lead to the next big (or little) thing. The more you want to learn about people, their projects, and their personalities, the richer everything should be.

9. WALK UP TO PEOPLE AND SAY HELLO
As a kid and teenager I was shy. But I also liked fun. Eventually I discovered it was really just more fun to challenge myself to approach people and start up a conversation than to sit watching things happen from the sidelines. Often, I'll just walk over to a stranger at a networking event and throw down my tried-and-true "What's good?!" It's amazing the variety of responses I get to those two positivity-seeking, out-of-left-field ice-breaking words.

8. BE YOURSELF
This is pretty self-explanatory. Nobody wants to meet a carbon copy of the person they just met five minutes ago. Don't try to be someone else. Just as you should be developing your own artistic style and sensibility, you should also develop your own networking style and it should be firmly rooted in who you are deep down—your real self. Find this person and this voice and introduce them to the world, one new encounter at a time. I think you'll be impressed with whom it helps attract. Oh, and stick to the truth. Don't make stuff up. Keep to the facts and let your natural personality shine. Be real and watch what happens.

7. INTRODUCE PEOPLE
Nothing says classy more than helping good people out by putting them in touch with other good people. They appreciate it and it reflects well upon you. Plus, you'll feel good when you see they've gone on to create cool things together. Networking should be about helping the whole industry grow and not just trying to grow your own thing. It may sound trite, but I believe it to be true: we all grow when the industry grows. So, mention this person to that person when you see a good fit. Offer to put them together by email, or even better, bring the person

you're talking to over to that other person on the opposite side of the room if you think they really should meet. From my experience, chances are that if the match makes sense on a gut-feeling level, it'll also click in real life when you make it happen. Be a connector.

6. IT'S A SMALL TOWN

As big as our city is, and as much as it's true that there are always new people to meet in our town and our industry, you'll likely cross paths with many of the same people over and over throughout your career. So be nice and make a good first impression (and second impression and third, etc.)

5. LISTEN

Don't hog the conversation. Let the person you're talking to talk. Yes, make sure they learn who the heck you are, but don't leave them feeling like you sucked the air out of the room by not shutting up for a minute. This is a back and forth kind of thing.

4. KEEP THINGS MOVING

Don't take up anyone's time more than you should—two to five minutes is a good chat length at a busy networking event—unless you're both really clicking. Better to cut things a bit short (remember the old adage: 'leave them wanting more'), thank the person for the nice chat, and offer them a card, than to have them feel that you're being a tad (or way) too clingy. When you're ready to end the encounter, politely excuse yourself by saying something to the effect of, "It's been a pleasure meeting you, but we should both have time to meet other great people like ourselves. Let's talk again for sure. May I offer you my card so we can stay in touch?" Oh, and if they wrap things up before you, don't be put off. Networking events are meant to give people the chance to meet a lot of other people.

3. BRING CARDS

If you make a good impression, folks will probably want to know how to reach you. Have a small stack of business cards at the ready in your pocket or purse. And when you hand a card to someone, do so proudly and confidently—that's a bit of you you're passing along. The energy you present it with might just be that spark to help a person decide on the spot whether one day you'll merit a follow-up, or help them think positively about you when they consider contacting you in a month or a year from now. Also, when you offer your card, always ask for a card in return. And consider writing a short and sweet follow-up email in the subsequent day or two saying how much you enjoyed meeting them and expressing how you look forward to staying in contact in the future. Add a link to your website so they can become familiar with your work. Don't assume they'll look for that card you gave them in order to find the link themselves.

2. IF NOTHING ELSE, SMILE A LOT

Even if none of the above tips are useful, smile when you're at a networking event or walking the halls of a film festival. People take to that. Why, that smile of yours might even move someone to approach you to ask, "What's good?!" At the very least, you'll brighten up the room. We can always use a bit more sunshine in our industry and our world.

1. AND FINALLY... I ONCE HAD THE FOLLOWING EPIPHANY: NETWORKING ISN'T THE SAME THING AS NOTWORKING

Whether you're between jobs or swamped with several projects, you should always make time and space to meet someone new or to follow up with an old colleague. This is, I dare say, the stuff that makes the world go round. New ideas, new possibilities. Get out there and schmooze it up. The effort you put into meeting people will pay off with more than just dream gigs, boatloads of money, and an overflowing Rolodex... Meaningful networking will make a career in the arts feel less isolated, more enriching, and hopefully a whole lot more fulfilling.

0. (BONUS TIP) PUT YOUR BEST FOOT FORWARD AND GET OUT THERE.

I, for one, am looking forward to meeting you at an upcoming industry event.

Ezra Soiferman (www.EzSez.com) is a documentary filmmaker and street photographer based in NDG. His quirky, unexpected films (Man of Grease, Tree Weeks, Posthumous Pickle Party, etc.) have appeared on numerous TV networks and at a wide array of film festivals worldwide. Ezra is also the director of the Montreal Film Group, a film/TV industry networking group with over 2,500 members who gather for networking events at bars around town. Join them all as a proud fellow MFG member at www.montrealfilmgroup.com.

MUSICIANS

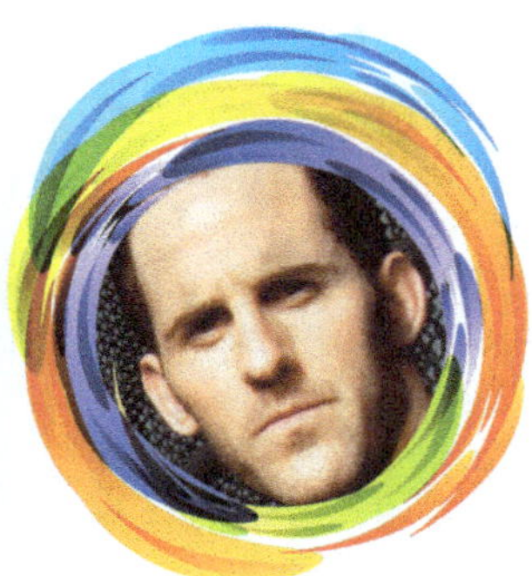

Charles "Chuck" Comeau

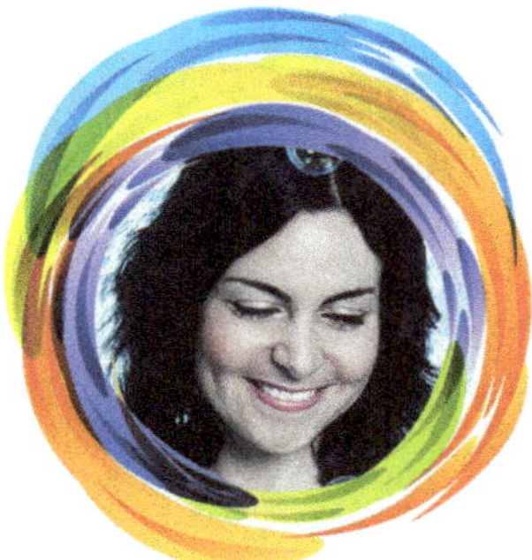

Jennifer Gasoi

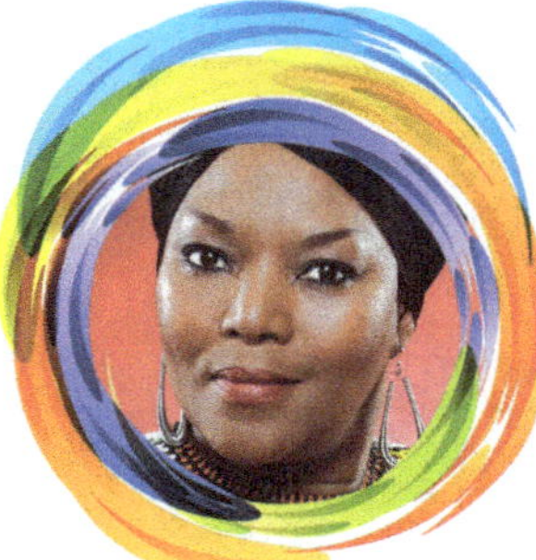

Lorraine Klaasen

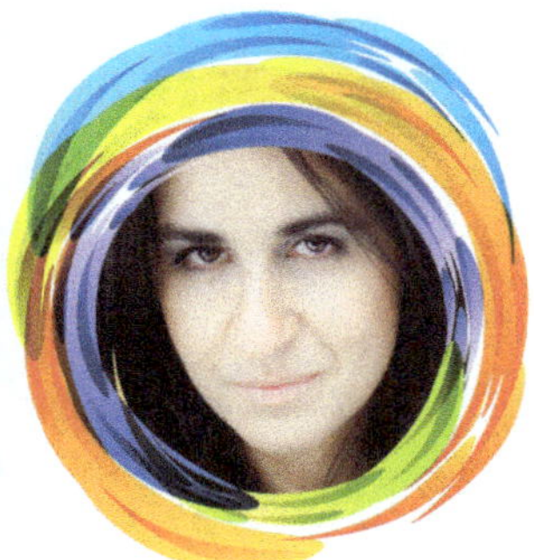

Misstress Barbara

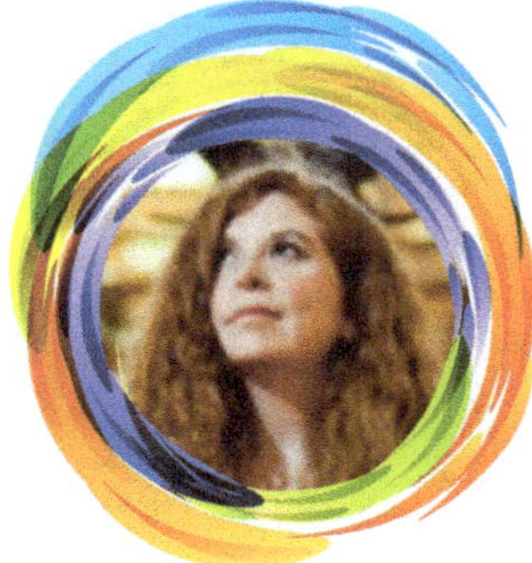

Katie Moore

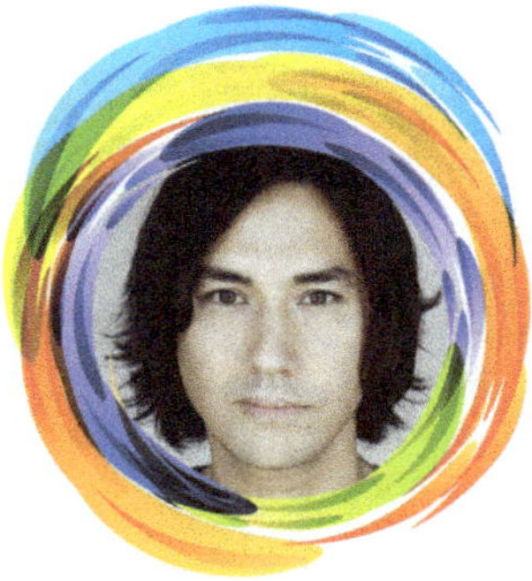

David Usher

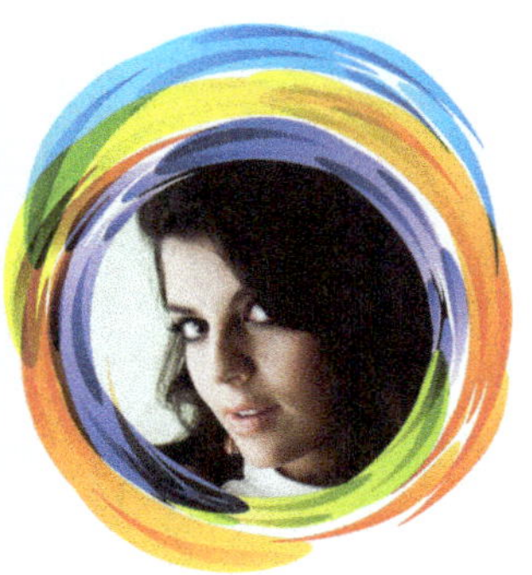

Nikki Yanofsky

I fell into music for fun. I wrote songs because it made me feel good, as therapy. I remember thinking I wanted to be a singer, but in the same way I wanted to be a fireman.

- Katie Moore, singer/songwriter

SO YOU WANNA BE A MUSICIAN?

The living legends who inhabit the world of music captivate fans and critics alike. But down here on Earth, far from the glamour of superstardom, the working musician's life is often fraught with toil and trouble.

We won't lie: making it in music takes more than great pitch and an ear for harmony. But, as you'll read in the pages that follow, if you map out your goals, stay focused, and treat music like the career it is, success is definitely within your grasp. In this section, a host of successful musicians share their tips on getting ahead in the industry.

Musicians work in a wide variety of creative occupations. If our expert advice piques your interest in the business, you may want to further investigate the following fields:

> Accompanist

> Arranger

> Artistic director

> Composer

> Concert singer

> Conductor

> Lyricist

> Music director

> Music teacher

> Musician

> Record producer

> Session musician

> Songwriter

> Sound engineer

> Stage musical director

> Vocalist (singer)

> Voice teacher

THE EXPERTS

We asked the following musicians to sing the praises and discuss the perils of their craft:

Charles "Chuck" Comeau is the drummer and one of the main songwriters for Simple Plan, which he helped found in 1999. The Montreal-based band has since gone on to sell nearly five million albums in Canada and the United States, and more than ten million albums worldwide. Through the Simple Plan Foundation, the JUNO-award-winning band has donated more than one million dollars to youth-focused charities since December 2005, helping both young people in need and children facing life-threatening illness in Canada and abroad. See more about Chuck at www.simpleplan.com.

Jennifer Gasoi is a Grammy-award winner and two-time Juno-nominated singer/songwriter/producer who has made a name for herself as one of Canada's hottest children's performers and recording artists. Jennifer has a unique gift for writing and performing upbeat, intelligent jazz and world-based children's songs that adults love too. Jennifer is passionate about living life to the fullest and creating music and live shows that reflect this passion. Through her music, she inspires kids and adults to live from the heart, stay true to themselves, and follow their dreams. Check out more about Jennifer at www.jennifergasoi.com or "Like" her at www.facebook.com/jennifergasoimusic.

Lorraine Klaasen, the daughter of legendary South African jazz singer Thandie Klaasen, is one of the few South African artists who have preserved the classic sound of 'township music.' Born and raised in Soweto, and long since based in Montreal, Lorraine has electrified audiences worldwide with her dynamic stage presence and showmanship. In February 2008, Lorraine released the highly charged album *Africa Calling* on the Justin Time label. Her latest CD, *A Tribute To Miriam Makeba*, won the 2013 Juno Award for World Music Album of the Year. And in 2014, Lorraine was honoured with SOCAN's Hagood Hardy prize for Singer-Songwriter of the Year in the World Music category. Find out more about what Lorraine is up to at www.lorraineklaasen.com.

Misstress Barbara is an internationally renowned electronic artist who has performed alongside music heavyweights such as Bjork, the Prodigy, Tiesto, Carl Cox, Richie Hawtin, and John Digweed. Her DJing and production have earned her several awards, including Best Breakthrough Underground DJ at the UK Underground Music Awards, a Best Dance Album of the Year nomination at the 2010 JUNO Awards, and Best Montreal DJ in 2014. Barbara has also released two of her own albums: Juno-nominated *I'm No Human* (2009) featuring collaborations from Brazilian Girls, Björn Yttling, and Sam Roberts, and *Many Shades of Grey* (2012). Check out all Barbara has to offer at www.misstressbarbara.com.

Katie Moore is an uncompromising songstress whose haunting music lies somewhere in the no-man's-land between country, folk, soul and Americana. She has performed at SXSW, Montreal International Jazz Festival, Calgary Folk Festival, Hillside Music Fest, Festival de musique émergente, Dawson City Music Fest, and Pop Montreal. Her effortless timbre has been sought out to accompany various musicians including Feist, Patrick Watson, Chilly Gonzales, Plants and Animals, and Socalled. Katie's own music has won the SOCAN ECHO Songwriting Prize, and Quebec's GAMIQ award for Folk/Country Album of the Year. See more about what Katie is up to at www.katiemoore.ca.

David Usher is a musician, entrepreneur, author and activist. With his band Moist and as a solo artist, he's sold over 1.4 million albums and toured worldwide. When he's not making music, David is passionate about using technology to build new businesses. His company, CloudID Creativity Labs, works on a range of innovative projects from building web platforms to consulting for clients like Cirque du Soleil and Deloitte. David sits on the board of McGill's Institute for the Public Life of Art and Ideas and is the founder of Amnesty International's Artists for Amnesty. Check out David and his new book, *Let the Elephants Run*, at www.lettheelephantsrun.com and www.davidusher.com.

Nikki Yanofsky has covered plenty of territory since her auspicious start as the youngest headliner in the history of the Montreal International Jazz Festival at age twelve. She's topped both jazz and pop charts, and sold out festivals and major theatres worldwide. In 2010, she sang to 3.2 billion people at the Vancouver Olympic and Paralympic Games. She's worked with luminaries such as Herbie Hancock, Phil Ramone, Wyclef Jean, and Stevie Wonder. In 2014, under the guidance of her mentor, Quincy Jones, Nikki had her highest album debut with her sophomore release, *Little Secret.* Find out more about Nikki at www.nikkiyanofsky.com.

Here's what they had to say, musician to musician:

WHO NEEDS MUSIC SCHOOL?

As with other performing arts, an educational background can open the doors towards a career in teaching or administration should you become unable to perform at some point in your life. But unless you're interested in working in a highly technical field, for instance as a sound engineer, hands-on learning in the industry and mentorship under a trusted professional beats any kind of formal educational program.

Chuck Comeau, the drummer for Simple Plan, would agree. He quit McGill Law School to pursue his incredibly successful music career. One of his top pieces of advice is to find a mentor in the field. "Try to find someone to coach you. Even if they haven't signed to a big label or sold a million records, they might have some really good advice and experience to pass onto you. Don't be afraid to ask. The worst thing they can say is no."

On the other hand, if you have an opportunity to get some quality music education, it can't hurt. Singer/songwriter Katie Moore says, "I don't have any formal music education myself, other than a few piano and guitar lessons, but if you're in Quebec and you're going to go to CEGEP, why not do the music program? It's not crucial for the music business, but every little bit helps."

Whichever route you take, there will be lots of lessons to learn along the way. And that's where our experts come in. They've been there and done that, and they're here to offer you the Coles Notes version of Making it in Music 101.

Everyone has a unique expression and gift to share; be true to yourself and have the courage to follow your heart.

- Jennifer Gasoi, children's singer/songwriter

HOW DO YOU SHOW WHAT YOU'VE GOT?

To land a job in the music industry, a demo of your work is an absolute requirement. The National Occupation Classification survey determined this; our panel of musicians confirms it. In their own words, this is what you need:

MUSICIAN "MUST HAVES"

Jennifer Gasoi: "You need a website. It can be simple, in fact the simpler the better—people have very limited attention spans these days. And you'll need a press kit, including a bio, a description of what you do, a list of where you're playing, contact info, a video, and pictures. A tagline is also helpful (i.e. what you do in a line or two), along with active social media sites and YouTube videos."

APPLYING FOR GIGS

Katie Moore: "In this business you don't really apply for jobs, you apply for gigs by shopping around your press kit to festivals and venues. If you're a singer/songwriter, you need to show a bunch of songs that you've written and recorded. I don't think it needs to be a CD anymore, everything is digital, but if you've played live, you should have a video of that to show you in a live setting."

LIKE THE PIED PIPER: IT'S ALL ABOUT THE MUSIC—AND THE FOLLOWING

David Usher: "The bottom line is that you're judged by the quality of your music and by your following. If you play live, it's all about the music you play and how well you engage a crowd."

I think in this industry there's a quiet respect for those who are not for sale but still have an open mind to work together.

- Nikki Yanofsky, singer/songwriter

GETTING STARTED

You may lead the choir every Sunday with the spirit of a rock star or perhaps you tore the coffeehouse down at a recent café gig, but don't be going diva on us yet. Without a bit more practice and some professional guidance, you risk pulling the plug on a potentially successful musical career.

The message from our musical mavens is clear: You alone are responsible for developing your image, your style, and your talent, and for selling that package to industry pros.

In their own words, here are some tips from our panel on moving your gig from metro corridors to the Metropolis:

BELIEVE IN YOURSELF

Chuck Comeau: "You're going to hear the word 'no' a lot, from a lot of people. And a lot of people will worry for you: your parents, your friends. They'll tell you to think about doing something else. Blocking that out is part of the process. Obviously, be aware of the comments and criticisms you get, they might not all be wrong. But keep your eye on the long-term game."

LOVE IT OR LUMP IT

David Usher: "You've got to do it because you love it. Music is a difficult business to make a living in; it's always been that way. When I was starting, there were a few record companies and they were the gatekeepers. Now you can play shows and make your own records, but you have to figure out a way to get an audience. That's the hard part."

Nikki Yanofsky: "Make sure you can't imagine yourself doing anything else. This job is not an easy one and there are a ton of people trying to 'make it.' If you can picture yourself being happy doing something else, then do it. Because those who really want it can't live without it; not because of the fame or fortune they may get, but because they love it."

Chuck Comeau: "If it's a hobby, that's not going to cut it. It has to be what you want most in the world. It has to be in your blood and in every fibre of you. If you don't have that fire, think about something else. There will be some days that are really terrible, and the only thing that will keep you going is knowing that there's nothing else you'd rather do. The people who have that will be miles ahead of everyone else."

MAKING MUSIC ISN'T THE SAME THING AS "MAKING IT" IN MUSIC
Katie Moore: "Playing music is so enjoyable and wonderful, but that doesn't mean you should try to make a living off it. It's a really hard career. Once you start making it your business, it becomes something totally different. I write the songs that I want to write and I'm not going to autotune my voice; I record my songs live. I do it for fun because I love it."

KNOW WHY YOU'RE MAKING MUSIC
Jennifer Gasoi: "Always tune into why you are doing what you do. This will help guide you when you have big decisions to make. I learned how to be business savvy and practical as I went along, but ultimately passion and a deep inner calling has driven my career."

STAY TRUE TO YOURSELF
Nikki Yanofsky: "Don't conform to what you think will work in 'the biz.' Make sure you stay true to yourself, especially if the type of music you do isn't considered mainstream or popular. People will reward originality and they will know if you're faking it."

KEEP ON KEEPING ON
David Usher: "We have a lot of rejection letters in our vaults that we [received] for the same music we eventually got signed for, the exact same recordings that were hits in the end."

NO DOESN'T MEAN NEVER
Katie Moore: "If someone is saying no to you, they might just be saying no now. You can ask them again in a month or in a year and maybe their circumstances will have changed."

DEDICATION IS MOST OF THE EQUATION
Chuck Comeau: "I made a choice to drop out of McGill Law School to pursue music full-time. I knew that if I got to twenty-five or thirty and looked back and wished I'd really gone for it, I would regret that for the rest of my life. The biggest risk I took was to take two to three years of my life to devote completely to the band. [Dropping out of school is] not the best advice to give everyone, I know, but it worked out for me."

IT'S NOT A MERITOCRACY
Katie Moore: "If someone wants to be a doctor and they work really hard at it, they're going to be a doctor, barring some weird thing. With music, there's no secure path, a lot of it is luck and timing—things you have no control over. It's not a meritocracy."

HONE YOUR CRAFT
Nikki Yanofsky: "One of my favourite quotes, by Will Rogers, is, 'Even if you're on the right track, you'll get run over if you just sit there.' Everything comes with hard work and practise. Work on your craft and your technique. Gig a ton, write a ton. Satisfaction is the death of ambition."

Chuck Comeau: "Don't think that every show you play or idea you come up with is amazing right away; it's probably not. Whatever song you think isn't amazing, go back and rework it a million times. Practise a lot and get tight as a band or solo act. You only get one shot at a first impression. Be ready."

Jennifer Gasoi: "Become excellent at what you do. If you are offering a quality product and experience, and you have confidence in what you do, your chances of success are much greater."

Lorraine Klaasen: "It is one thing to take lessons from a teacher and another to go on stage in public. Tape yourself, and hear your mistakes. With time, the stage is the best teacher."

KNOW HOW TO SHOWCASE WHAT YOU'VE GOT
Nikki Yanofsky: "You need to know your sweet spots when you perform live. If you can hit a high note well, then do it. But don't overdo it. Confidence is key, and having the power to hit highs or hit lows or do really fancy runs and stuff like that is great, but sometimes less is more."

IT'S ABOUT THE BEST TEAM, NOT THE BEST TALENT
Chuck Comeau: "A lot of people think they need the best singer and the best drummer and such for a great band. That's just not true. You need the best team, and people you can get along with."

IMMERSE YOURSELF IN THE FIELD
Jennifer Gasoi: "If you want to be a musician, go to live shows, watch YouTube videos of your favourite bands, take classes, practise, collaborate with other musicians, join music organizations and networking groups in your field of interest. Immerse yourself."

FIND THE STYLE AND RANGE THAT SUITS YOU
Lorraine Klaasen: "Young singers today sing too much like the singers they hear on the radio. They sing in a key that is not theirs. Work with a pianist; they're good at telling you your range."

REACH OUT TO OTHER MUSICIANS
Chuck Comeau: "Nowadays you have more access than ever to your favourite musicians through Facebook or Twitter. For instance, a guy tweeted me about his cover of one of our songs on YouTube. I checked it out and it was fantastic, so we met up and now I'm trying to help him out. We even wrote some songs together. And all he did was send me a tweet. The worst people can say is no."

IT'S LOTS OF HARD WORK AND LUCK

David Usher: "The harder you push the luckier you get. And if you write a great song and you put on enough pressure, you'll have a better chance of making it. But it's not guaranteed. There are a million great songs out there that, for whatever reason, haven't clicked. But you're much more likely to have something happen if you're doing all the rest of the work—not just the music. In our case, we played, we did independent tours, we borrowed money to buy a crappy old van and we went out on the road, back and forth across the country, we made the video and album ourselves. Nothing would've happened if we hadn't done all that stuff."

THE STRUGGLE FOR RECOGNITION IS ONGOING

Chuck Comeau: "After getting signed, that's when the real work starts and you have to distinguish yourself. You have to earn it every day. Every record is a make-it-or-break-it moment in your career. You've got to keep your fan base interested and the industry curious about what you'll do next."

LET YOUR AUDIENCE GUIDE YOU

Lorraine Klaasen: "My best teacher has always been the public. If they are enjoying the show, then I know I am doing something right. If not, I know I have something to work on. And you have to realize that fans are coming for you not just your music. You have to have a pleasing personality. My personality has played an important role in getting people to come see me. I make each person feel special for coming to see my show."

Creativity doesn't operate within a vacuum. Very few people are allowed to just be creative and think solely about their art. Most creative people have to run the business of creativity underneath that.

- David Usher, musician and author

TAKING IT TO THE NEXT LEVEL

You've done so many charity gigs for free, they should probably make you a saint. But, when you set out to make it in music, you don't remember taking a vow of poverty. And now you'd like to take it up a notch, you're looking to upgrade to better equipment and hire professional musicians to back you up. You need to start earning cash.

From the sublime pleasure you bring to your audiences to the artistic contributions you make to Quebec's cultural scene, we agree that it's about time you got paid for your services.

Now is the time to think like a professional and an entrepreneur. You can't do it all, so hire professionals to help you round out the administrative edges of your career. Get educated on things like contract negotiation, copyrights, royalties, marketing strategies, and financial tips for stretching your income to last through the slow times.

We've asked our music industry experts for some advice on making your talent work for you. Here's what they had to say:

I. THE MUSIC BUSINESS

EDUCATE YOURSELF ABOUT THE BUSINESS

Chuck Comeau: "Don't just think, 'I'm the artist, I'm not worrying about the business side.' If you don't care, people will notice and think they can get away with stuff. I recommend a book called All You Need to Know about the Music Business by Donald Passman. He manages to break down this very complicated business into a way people can get it."

Jennifer Gasoi: "Having a solid foundation and knowledge of the industry will go a long way. Educate yourself on the basics of the business. Get a good accountant, learn about the music industry, learn about key organizations such as SOCAN and SoundExchange. Create a foundation for financial success."

BEWARE OF BAD CONTRACTS

Chuck Comeau: "Don't just sign a contract because someone is giving you a little money. You have to be careful. You can make some short-term decisions for the money, but be careful not to lock yourself into something that you're going to regret down the road. Some things you think are super great at the time might not look so great when you're selling out shows."

FOLLOW THROUGH ON YOUR PROJECTS
Jennifer Gasoi: "Sometimes the last 10 percent of your project is the most challenging, but it makes all the difference. You may create a fabulous CD, but it's important to follow through with all steps involved, including marketing, distribution, and PR."

GET PROFESSIONAL HELP
Misstress Barbara: "I have a bookkeeper, an accountant, a few lawyers for different things (trademarks, contracts, etc.), and a booking agent. But I've been self-managed for most of my career after having bad experiences with managers in the past."

SURROUND YOURSELF WITH GOOD ADVISORS
Chuck Comeau: "We've had the same agent and manager since the day we started. It's important to have people who are loyal and who care for you. There's something to be said about keeping the same team together. Our advisors know we want to know everything, and that the final call is always made by the band."

Nikki Yanofsky: "You need honesty from your advisors. You need people who aren't afraid to tell you the truth."

PAY A PUBLICIST WHEN YOU TOUR
Katie Moore: "If you do a tour, you should have a publicist and pay for publicity. You might think it's too expensive, but in the end it's an investment. There's no point touring across the country if no one knows you're doing shows. And get a publicist for Quebec and another one for Canada. It's rare for someone to know both Quebec and the rest of Canada intimately."

BUT DON'T WASH YOUR HANDS OF THE BUSINESS SIDE
Chuck Comeau: "You've got to at least learn about the business side. You can't be thinking, 'It doesn't matter, someday I'll have people doing all that for me.' One day you might, but nobody will care about your business as much as you do. A manager might have five to seven different bands, and a label will have twenty-five bands, and a lawyer will have a bunch too. But you only have one."

Katie Moore: "When I started working with a manager, I thought I didn't have to worry about the whole business aspect of music. But that's not true; it's still your thing. When you get people to help you, they're only representing you in the world. They can act on your behalf, but they're not you. You need to stay on top of things and communicate what you want."

David Usher: "We have lawyers and managers and agents, but we're always very involved with our contracts and every aspect of our business from touring to merchandise to everything else. You need to be in control of your own destiny."

Katie Moore: "If someone's doing your accounting, you should still check it over, because ultimately it's your money, not theirs. When you're signing contracts with venues, you should keep track of the percentages. You might not get cheated on purpose, but people make mistakes."

II. FINANCING AND MAKING MONEY

The music industry business model has been turned upside down in the last decade. Making money by making music is a whole new game, and the big players are scrambling like everybody else to figure it out. For emerging musicians, lots of the traditional pools of capital are drying up, but there are new ways to raise money popping up all of the time. Crowdfunding is just the latest darling. Our experts have lots of opinions on how you might navigate these shifting tides. Hear them out:

BE PREPARED TO SELF-FINANCE
Misstress Barbara: "All through university, I had three jobs in order to buy my own records and studio equipment. All the money I earned went towards building my studio."

David Usher: "The bridge money that used to take an artist from small to big is disappearing fast. That's what record companies used to do. They used to discover artists and bridge that gap from small to big, and now that money only exists for a very few. So you have to bridge that gap yourself."

TECHNOLOGY CAN REDUCE YOUR PRODUCTION COSTS
Chuck Comeau: "We had to borrow money from our parents. But these days, you can do a lot of the work yourself to save money. It used to be that you had to go to a studio and pay for a studio hour. Now you can make all your demos on your computer. You can use software to make a good record for a dime. That makes a huge difference."

GRANTS ARE HARD TO GET, BUT KEEP TRYING
Katie Moore: "I've gotten grants for songwriting and to make an album. But they're hard to get and it depends on so much, like who's on the jury. Just keep applying again and again. I haven't yet gotten a Canada Council grant. There are so many great people applying; it's like a lottery."

Jennifer Gasoi: "Seek out organizations that may be able to fund some of your projects. I have been fortunate to have received financial support from a few organizations including FACTOR, Canada Council for the Arts, and YES Montreal."

HAVE A TOP-NOTCH GRANT APPLICATION AND DEMO

Katie Moore: "To get a grant it's really important to have a good quality demo. If you're just doing something on GarageBand, it's not going to go anywhere. The jury needs to listen to it and think, 'Oh this is awesome.' And you need to have a great marketing plan. It's worth hiring someone to do that for you because you're a musician, not a marketer. You can also hire a grant writer. Personally, I didn't write the grants I got. My manager did it. I have an English degree and I do proofreading for part of my living, but it's very different putting your own project into words."

TRY NEW FINANCING MODELS LIKE CROWDFUNDING

Katie Moore: "I self-released an album using Kickstarter, and it got great publicity because crowdfunding was new back then. There was a lot of buzz around it. Within ten days I'd raised $5,000. Recently, some guy in Cleveland put up thirty tracks of silence on Spotify, and he ended up getting a lot of money. He said if people listened to those silent tracks, he'd give a free tour. And everyone said he was a hero. Try something new if you can."

BUT BUDGET PLENTY OF TIME FOR YOUR CROWDFUNDING CAMPAIGN

David Usher: "Kickstarter and other crowdfunding campaigns are great ways to raise funds, but they're very, very time-consuming. All those promises you have to fulfil on the back-end are a lot of work. Especially for music, there are a lot of back-end gifts. Just be cognizant that you'll have to mail all that stuff out and do everything you promised."

GET OVER YOUR AVERSION TO MONEY MANAGEMENT

David Usher: "In my circle, there tends to be a disconnect between art and money. We don't really focus on money much and we don't tend to manage it very well. And that is the truth. But if you're like that, you have to get over your aversion to managing money and figure out how to deal with it. If you don't really focus on it, it's easy for it to get all confused."

KEEP A BUDGET

Katie Moore: "I realized a long time ago that I had to keep a monthly budget. Before that, I really had no idea how much my life cost. As a freelancer, you might get a large amount of money and then nothing for another month, and you have to stretch it out. The budget helped me realize where my money was going. When I first started a budget I'd say, 'Oh my god, I'm going for coffee every day and it's a fortune!' Stuff like that."

PAY YOURSELF FIRST

Lorraine Klaasen: "At the beginning, my whole idea was to pay everybody first, and I'd come home and have nothing. Pay yourself as you go along. There is also a lack of security that self-employed artists have, so put something aside for yourself for the future, as you begin to make money."

FIND OTHER SOURCES OF INCOME

Lorraine Klaasen: "In June and July, Montreal thrives. But what happens the rest of the year? That's where the business part comes in. You have to look for other opportunities to continue making money. In my case, I started networking with people, and now I am able to perform in the Caribbean during slower months."

Katie Moore: "I have my own projects but I'll tour with other people too. I like being busy, so I do proofreading and editing work that I can bring with me on tour."

WHEN THE MONEY'S FLOWING, SAVE FOR RAINY DAYS

Misstress Barbara: "You never know when your best years will end. So it's important to be smart with your money while you're making some. It's funny because when you make the most money, you have no time to spend it, and when you work less and make less, you have more time to spend it. But that's when you should really be careful."

III. GETTING VISIBILITY

You've got the songs, the CDs, even a few faithful groupies. Now what? How do you reach that larger audience? The one that will help you turn those weekend gigs into a global tour? Our panel wasn't shy with their advice:

PUT YOURSELF OUT THERE

David Usher: "Now, more than ever, you need to put yourself out there. If you're an artist who plays live, then you have to play. You need to get out there in every way possible, and that includes social media, playing gigs, and everything else there is."

Jennifer Gasoi: "I've gotten almost all my gigs through word of mouth. The way I created visibility with fans was by getting out in the world and playing music. My career was built on grassroots gigs, connecting with musicians, kids, parents, daycare organizers, and schools.

Chuck Comeau: "Don't be too selective when you start. Don't wait for the perfect show. That doesn't mean saying yes to every contract you're offered without checking it out first. But if someone offers you a festival gig, even if it's unpaid, go for it. Do whatever you can to get exposure. You never know who's going to be there."

BUILD A FAN BASE

David Usher: "Record deals are few and far between, but if you're looking to go down that road, all they're looking at are the numbers. And even if you're not looking for a record deal, you still need to have a massive following, because if you're independent, it's all about your reach."

Chuck Comeau: "When we first started out, we opened for Sugar Ray in the United States. After our set, we'd jump into the crowd and talk to everybody and sign our CDs and T-shirts. Every night we were selling 100 to 150 CDs and our label couldn't believe it. And it was because we were right there with the fans. That's how we built our hard-core followers."

SUPPORT THE COMMUNITY AND THEY'LL SUPPORT YOU

Lorraine Klaasen: "I support in order to be supported. I pay to go to different community events and I appear at these events. People see you and then it is easier to invite them to your shows. I also volunteer in the community. I give singing lessons to youngsters and help out in other ways. That way, people see me and they know me. I develop my audience that way. Basically, I'm not just sitting by the phone, waiting for it to ring. I'm out there and I know what is happening in the community."

YOU ARE YOUR BRAND, SO BE AUTHENTIC

Nikki Yanofsky: "I've always just been myself and I'm surrounded by people who don't try to make me be anything I'm not. The common denominator with everything I've worked on has really been building a brand that is real. If you aren't faking something, it's very easy to stay true to it."

BUT THAT DOESN'T MEAN YOU CAN'T TRY NEW THINGS

Misstress Barbara: "I became a brand by being myself and doing what I felt was right at the moment. Although I've been a DJ and techno producer for many years, at one point I came out with two pop albums where I sing. My fans got all confused and thought I had dropped DJing for singing. I probably should have followed my brand of techno and never released those albums, but that's what I felt like doing and I am proud I did it."

BUILD AN ONLINE FOLLOWING WITH SOCIAL MEDIA

Chuck Comeau: "Labels don't want to build a band, that's expensive; they want to see that you can build your own buzz. Whether it's through your Facebook page or your Twitter, you need to build up your followers. If you have ten thousand followers on Twitter, a label will say, 'Wow, they have that many followers and they're unsigned? There must be something going on with them.' That's the new business card: how many views you have."

Nikki Yanofsky: "Social media is the most effective way of building a real relationship with my fans. It has been extremely rewarding and important. Without the support of my #niksters, none of my success would have been possible. Get on sites like SoundCloud and YouTube and show the world what you have to offer; make an Instagram and Twitter account and show your human side too."

Misstress Barbara: "Nothing beats social media nowadays. I post pictures once in a while because I know my fans love to see what I'm up to in my everyday life, and I also post news on my upcoming music releases and gigs."

SOCIAL MEDIA IS TIME CONSUMING BUT ESSENTIAL

David Usher: "Doing all that social media stuff is time consuming and draining. It definitely takes away from the artistic side. But without it, unless you've got some kind of patron, you've got to do it. A lot of people thought that social media would be the answer [to the lack of record label support] because it gives this equal voice to everyone. But at the same time, it made the pool enormous. To cut through the noise, you have to find your own ways to be remarkable."

NOTHING BEATS A PERSONAL TOUCH

Chuck Comeau: "People might forget the song you wrote but they'll never forget how you made them feel. You've got to connect with your fans in a real way. Sign autographs and take photos with them. Contact them over email if they send you messages. Cut out the middleman whenever you can."

DON'T FORGET ABOUT TRADITIONAL MEDIA

Misstress Barbara: "I have a lot of success with traditional media thanks to the music I've released. The press needs reasons to talk about you, and usually when you're a musician, you're the best one to talk about the music you make."

RESPECT THE JOURNALISTS COVERING YOU

Chuck Comeau: "A lot of bands arrive late to interviews, they blow them off. I was a journalist once and it would always give me a bad impression of the band when they did that. Try to treat these interviews as a real job, like a pro would. Don't think it's not important, that you're a rock star and you don't need to do it. You do."

TAKE INITIATIVE!

Lorraine Klaasen: "People won't come to see you if they don't know you. Call local radio stations, get interviews. Take initiative."

Katie Moore: "I was on [the CBC radio show] Q and met the producer, and had his email. A while later, when I was in the running for the GAMIQ Songwriter of the Year Award, I sent him an email and asked if he'd play my song on Q, and he did!"

CHUTZPAH DOESN'T HURT WHEN YOU WANT ATTENTION

Chuck Comeau: "When we were just starting, I called every record label and told them I was the manager of the band, which wasn't true, and told them, 'Hey they're fantastic, you've got to hear them.' Nine out of ten never called back, but one guy who did ended up signing us to Atlantic Records. My point is, you have to be a little ballsy if you want to get noticed."

If you want a really high-level career, then some things will have to take a back seat. You have to be ready to go to bed thinking about music and wake up thinking about music. That comes with the territory.

- Chuck Comeau, drummer, Simple Plan

LIVING AS A MUSICIAN

You've probably gathered by now that living the life of a working musician isn't all about cashing big cheques and trashing hotel rooms. The folks we interviewed chose this life because they couldn't see themselves doing anything else. And they've got some sage advice for those of you still reading who want to join them up on stage.

STAY FOCUSED

Jennifer Gasoi: "It's essential to have focus, especially when you have a specific project in mind, like creating an album or touring. I've been working with a business/life coach for fifteen years who's kept me on course, so that I can stay focused in my business as well as in my personal life."

Chuck Comeau: "If you want to make it in this industry, you really have to focus. You have to make your music a big priority. When we were first getting attention we were traveling eleven months of the year, doing three hundred shows. That's just what it took."

COMPARTMENTALIZE

David Usher: "I use the Bill Clinton form of management. He was known as a master compartmentalizer, where he could put things into different places in his head, and then be able to switch between them very quickly. I often visualize [things in] my mind like that. I've got fifteen slots in my head for songs, a certain number for business, a number for public speaking, and a number for all the other ridiculous projects I've got going. As long as I keep thinking of it that way, I'm able to flip between these areas in my brain."

BE REFLECTIVE

Jennifer Gasoi: "If one path isn't working, and you keep knocking on doors and they're constantly closing, perhaps you need to re-evaluate your course. It doesn't mean giving up the dream, but it's helpful to develop skills that allow you to take a step back, reflect, and change course if need be."

TAKE CARE OF YOURSELF

Jennifer Gasoi: "Take care of yourself physically, mentally, emotionally, and spiritually. Eat well, exercise, spend time in nature, meditate, and do whatever activities help centre you. Do what it takes to stay grounded."

HAVE FUN!

Nikki Yanofsky: "Don't take yourself too seriously all the time. As John Lennon said, 'Time you enjoyed wasting is not wasted time.' You need to live in order to breathe that life into your work."

YOU CAN'T DO IT ALONE

Chuck Comeau: "The number one killer of bands is when people are fighting, so you have to build a band that can withstand the ups and downs. It's not easy when you're going on tour and you're with the band more often than you're with your wife or your best friends. You have to learn how to compromise and live with people. Don't put your stuff everywhere! Don't wake people up! You have to understand that it's a democracy and make sure everyone's happy."

Nikki Yanofsky: "Surround yourself with people you actually like spending time with and who have your best interest at heart. People who make you think and help you find ways to grow. Your team needs to inspire you."

Jennifer Gasoi: "Create a community that will cheer you on and support you as you move forward. This may include friends, family, mentors, or fellow musicians. Create a network of people who inspire you, people whom you admire and trust. These people will often take you further than the ones who appear glitzy and glamorous."

BE HUMBLE AND POLITE

Chuck Comeau: "People won't want to help someone who's really cocky and disrespectful. If you step on people's heads on the way up, they'll remember on [your] way down. It's a business of people and you need to make contacts with people who will do favours for you. Wherever you go, make a good impression. That goes a long way."

TOURING CAN BE HARD ON RELATIONSHIPS

Misstress Barbara: "Relationships can be hard to coordinate if you're constantly on tour. When I was at the peak of my career I had none. It was just impossible. Then I decided to take fewer gigs in order to have a better quality of life, and I can't complain about this now."

Chuck Comeau: "You have to understand that you'll have to sacrifice some things to have a high-level music career. Some people will have more trouble with that. If you're seeing someone, they'll have to be super understanding. You're married to your music."

FINAL THOUGHTS

For our last track, we asked our experts to tell us what mistakes they often see made by emerging musicians—mistakes they may have made themselves back in the day. They had plenty to say and plenty of advice to give. Here are some of their parting words:

GET OUT THERE AND PLAY MUSIC!

David Usher: "People ask me how to get a record deal, and I ask them if they play live somewhere. Half the time they say, 'No, but I'm going to start soon.' I tell them they need to start playing right away, because record deals hardly exist anymore. Playing live is going to be the major source of income for musicians. That's where the money comes from in the business right now. I'm not talking about Coldplay—but for practically everyone else—the money is from playing live and selling merchandise. So play all the time!"

LISTEN MORE

Nikki Yanofsky: "I think the most common mistake made in this industry is that the artist thinks they know best. The truth is, it is very important to trust your gut, but it is just as important to hear everyone in your team out. When you are too close to something, it is virtually impossible to be unbiased."

BE CAREFUL WHAT YOU SIGN

Chuck Comeau: "A lot of terrible deals are signed in the industry. The reality is you don't have to sign with the biggest label or the biggest manager. Those people probably won't have time to talk to you. Ask yourself if you want someone who has the time to dedicate to you, or someone who might have twenty other artists who are bigger than you are. It's a trade-off. And no matter what you do, don't sign something without a lawyer or someone with experience there to help you."

19 WAYS TO MAKE MONEY WITH YOUR MUSIC
By Dave Cool, Director of Artist Relations for Bandzoogle

One of the biggest challenges musicians face is generating income. Gone are the days when a band could rely solely on music sales and touring to earn a living.

Part of the reality of being a working musician today is the need to diversify your revenue streams. Although sales of recorded music have gone down significantly in recent years, new sources of income have become available to musicians.

Here's a list of 19 ways to generate revenue through music:

1. CD SALES
If you're going to be playing live shows, having CDs on hand is still a good idea. They make great takeaway souvenirs that can easily be signed for your fans.

2. VINYL SALES
Vinyl sales have surged in recent years. Again, if you'll be playing live shows, printing a small batch to have at your merch table can help generate extra income.

3. DIGITAL SALES
You should be selling digital music through your own website to make the most money, but also through online retailers. Keep in mind that online retailers take a percentage of sales (i.e. iTunes takes 30 percent, Bandcamp takes 15 percent). Some digital distributors that place your music in stores like iTunes and Amazon will take a cut on top of that.

4. STREAMING
Although per-stream payouts from music streaming services tend to be small, they can add up over time. Also, these services help new fans discover your music and shouldn't be seen solely as an income generator.

5. LIVE SHOWS
Money made from live shows can vary greatly, but it's still a reliable way to earn income. Not only can you make money from selling tickets, but it's also one of the best ways to sell merch.

6. PHYSICAL MERCH
Income from physical merch can depend on the amount of live shows you play. If you go out on tour, be sure that you have some T-shirts as well as smaller items like buttons and stickers that you can sell to fans after the show.

7. DIGITAL MERCH

You can also sell digital merch items like PDFs, videos, and images to your fans. Things like lyric books, live concerts, sheet music, exclusive photos, artwork, and more.

8. CROWDFUNDING

Crowdfunding can be a great way to generate income for your music career. A well-executed crowdfunding campaign can help you raise enough money to offset the cost of producing and marketing your album.

9. GRANTS

Organizations like FACTOR and Canada Council offer various grants for music projects. CIRAA offers monthly micro-grants to Canadian musicians for live performances. There are also some provincial arts organizations and music industry associations that have grant programs for musicians.

10. SPONSORSHIPS

If you've built up a fan base, some companies are willing to sponsor musicians to reach those fans. Sponsorships can range from cash to free products, services, and equipment.

11. PUBLISHING ROYALTIES

You should be signed up to a performing rights organization so you can collect royalties on your music. This includes public performance royalties (radio, TV), mechanical royalties (sales through retailers, streaming, etc.), and sync royalties (commercials, film, TV).

12. DIGITAL ROYALTIES

Whenever your music is played on services like SiriusXM radio, Pandora, and webcasters, they must pay royalties. Sign up for a free SoundExchange account to make sure you're collecting those royalties at www.soundexchange.com.

13. LIVE PERFORMANCE ROYALTIES

When performing original material in a bar, restaurant, club, or other music venue, you can earn royalties from those performances. Visit www.socan.ca to find out how to collect those royalties.

14. LICENSING

If you get your song placed in a film, commercial, or TV show, chances are they're going to pay you a licensing fee. These fees vary greatly, depending on the budget for the project, and how much they want to use your particular song.

15. YOUTUBE

On YouTube, whenever your music is used in videos that are running ads, YouTube pays a portion of that advertising money to the rights holders of the song. Digital distributors like TuneCore and CD Baby can help you collect that money, as can Audiam.

16. SESSION WORK

Another way to make some extra money is to put yourself out there as a session musician. As a singer or instrumentalist, you can do session work for other musical projects, or even for music used in advertising.

17. SONGWRITING/COMPOSING

If you're a songwriter, you can write songs for other musicians or compose music specifically for film and television.

18. COVER GIGS

Playing cover gigs at bars, restaurants, weddings, and other private events is sometimes frowned upon by musicians. The reality is that those shows can pay really well and allow you to get paid to play your instrument.

19. MUSIC LESSONS

Many musicians teach their instrument to others to help generate revenue towards their own career. This can be a nice way to supplement your income and allows you to hone your craft at the same time.

Dave Cool is the Director of Artist Relations for musician website and marketing platform Bandzoogle. Find more of his writing at www.bandzoogle.com/blog.

NEW MEDIA ARTISTS

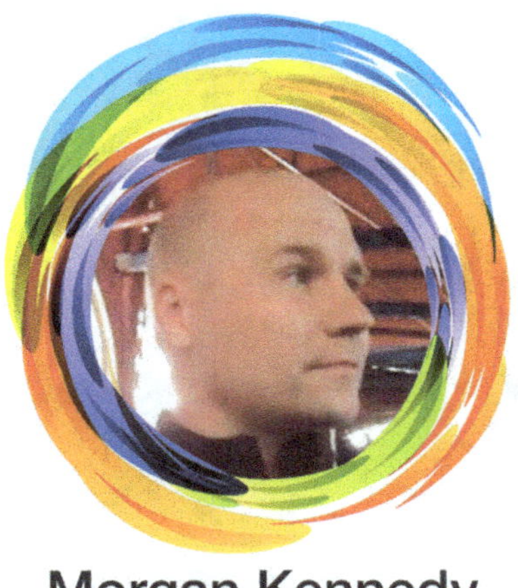

Morgan Kennedy

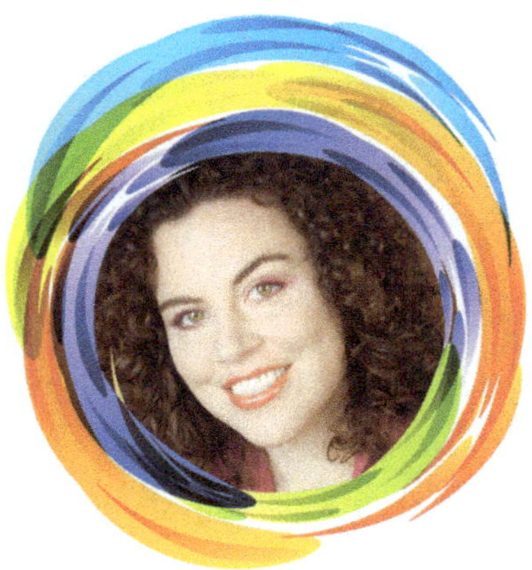

Jill Murray

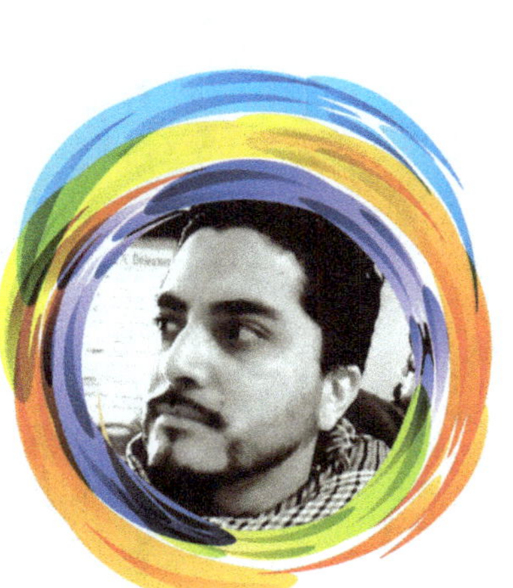

Rommel Romero

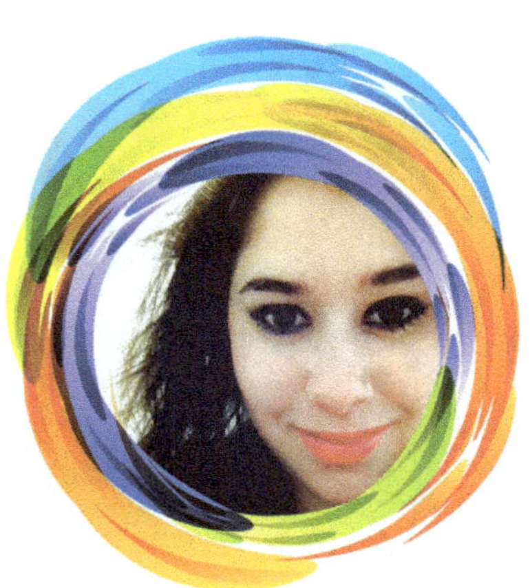

Tali Goldstein

Pay attention to those things in your life outside of work. Because no one in this industry is going to tell you, 'Don't stay too late at the office.'

- Morgan Kennedy, game user researcher, Ubisoft

SO YOU WANNA BE A NEW MEDIA ARTIST?

You've spent more hours than you care to count hunched over your keyboard, fingers flying, point count rising, villains vanquished. You're a gamer; the virtual world is your home away from home. But not everyone understands.

Each night someone bangs on your bedroom door, "Dinner!" It's someone from that other world, where people eat and sleep and go to the office. Stuff too mind-numbingly boring to even contemplate.

Then one day you hear of a place where people actually spend their time, undisturbed, in that virtual realm. Five days a week, and sometimes weekends! And they don't just inhabit the world, they *create* the world.

Too mind-numbingly awesome to even contemplate?

Well it's real; it's a place called New Media.

Sound like someplace you'd like to visit? Here are just a few of the portals included in the National Occupation Classification, published by Employment and Social Development Canada:

> 3D modeler

> Animation programmer

> Computer programmer

> E-commerce (electronic commerce) software developer

> Effects (vfx) aftist

> Graphical user interface (GUI) designer

> Interactive media developer

> Java programmer

> Level designer

> Multimedia developer

> Software developer

> Special effects programmer

> Texture artist

> Video game developer

> Video game writer

> Web programmer

And there are new portals opening up all the time, including several of those used by the experts we interviewed for this chapter. The folks we interviewed are all in the gaming sector, but as you can see above, New Media is a much wider field and getting wider all the time.

THE EXPERTS

Tali Goldstein is Minority Media Inc.'s line producer/publishing. With an extensive background in film, Tali has won numerous awards from prestigious film festivals worldwide, including the Berlin International Film Festival, the Licorne d'or at Amiens International Film Festival, and the Golden Plaque at Chicago International Film Festival. As line producer for Minority Media, she successfully shipped three games: the critically acclaimed *Papo & Yo* (Windows, Linux and OS X ports), the App Store chart-topping *Loco Motors*, and *Spirits of Spring*. Her creative leadership has helped Minority establish strong relationships with major game publishers like Sony, Steam, Apple, and Amazon. Check out Tali's latest projects at www.weareminority.com.

Morgan Kennedy was the first hire at Concordia's Centre for Technoculture, Art and Games, and joined Ubisoft Montreal in 2010 as playtest coordinator for the studio's Kinect projects. Currently conducting user research on an unannounced title, he is passionate about improving usability and user experience for games, websites, and apps. With wide and deep experience ranging from running focus groups, interviews, and rapid prototyping sessions on smaller projects, his current focus is on long-term iterative tests with hundreds of players focusing on a single brand: Assassin's Creed. For more information about participating in user research at Ubisoft Montreal see playtest.ubisoft.com.

Jill Murray is a freelance game writer, narrative designer, and novelist. She wrote for games such as *Assassin's Creed: Freedom Cry* and *Assassin's Creed IV: Black Flag*, and won a 2013 Writer's Guild of America award for her work on *Assassin's Creed: Liberation*. She is the author of two young adult novels, *Break on Through* and *Rhythm and Blues*, published by Doubleday Canada. Her talks on writing and games have been featured at the Game Developer's Conference, GDC Next, and Gamercamp Toronto. In past lives she worked as a web designer and graduated from Ryerson Theatre School's Technical Production program. Learn more about Jill's work at www.jillmurray.com.

Rommel Romero is media relations and social media manager and writer at Minority Media Inc. Rommel's comprehensive knowledge of online media and public relations first landed him the job as Minority's community manager, where he was responsible for actively engaging with the company's growing fan base across social media. After helping triple the size of Minority's online community within a year, his role expanded to include public relations and marketing strategy coordination, media relations, market research, promotional coordination with publishers, and business partnership development. As Minority's writer, he also plays an active role in conceiving and producing the company's outward-facing written material, including website content, pitches for private investors, and grant writing. See more about what Rommel is up to at www.weareminority.com.

Here's what our experts had to say, artist to artist:

WHO NEEDS A DEGREE?

All the experts we spoke to had some sort of higher education—though not always in the field they're working in today. New media, after all, is new. And much of the technology that drives this booming industry didn't even exist five years ago. And five years from now, it will all have changed again! So what's an aspiring new media artist to do?

"Stay in school," says Morgan Kennedy, game user researcher for Ubisoft. "It's rare for someone to make it in this industry without a degree. Certainly if you're a programmer you have to show that your work is of the standard they're looking for. Study math. Study more math than you think you should because, no matter what, you'll always end up needing it for this business."

Study math?! Well, yes, if you want in on the programming side, which is a large part of the industry. And maybe that's bad news for some of you. But the good news is that you can find your way into new media in a number of other ways. The industry isn't *just* about programmers and techie-types. New media needs creative types too, like you! Writers and filmmakers, visual artists and performers. In fact, this business loves nothing better than a basket of creative skills in the people they hire. Take game writer Jill Murray: "During theatre school, I taught myself HTML, CSS, and JavaScript, and using these tools worked in web development for a decade after graduation. Then I began writing novels about a third of the way into my web career, and I kept up my freelance development contracts until I realized I wanted to write for games and found a game writing job."

Supporting Jill's experience, Morgan stresses the need to develop a variety of abilities, and points out that a formal education can help with that. "It's especially important that students get a broad range of skills [math, research, writing, creative thinking] so they can take advantage of the different opportunities that come up." And he mentions one other fact that's worth considering, especially for work in the new media field: "It's normal to have seven careers throughout your lifetime, so skills that are transferable are especially important."

When they're looking for a job, most people submit CVs and conventional things like that. But the best way to find work is to get to know people.

- Rommel Romero, manager and writer, Minority Media

HOW DO YOU SHOW WHAT YOU'VE GOT?

HAVE CONCRETE EXAMPLES OF YOUR WORK

Jill Murray: "The best thing I can advise for working in games is a portfolio of completed work. This can include some student work. But between the time when you decide to enter the industry and the time you find your first paying gig or full-time job, it's important to make your own games. Find others who need help on their games, form teams to make games, participate in game jams… You see where I'm going with this. Make games!"

Morgan Kennedy: "The most important thing is to have examples of your work. Either games you've developed or, if you're a researcher, research you've done in relation to games. You need evidence that you can do the job. It's such a competitive and demanding industry, they need people who are already up to speed on the work, which is why there's such an emphasis on people with experience."

Jill Murray: "For game writing, you have to demonstrate top-notch writing skills. When hiring, I like to see a portfolio with at least three short, vivid samples that demonstrate an ability to write dramatic scenes that advance story and character. They don't all have to be from games, and sometimes it's better if they're not. As a writer, you can't always control what you get to work on, and not all games include good dramatic writing. Secondly, I like to see a few samples of technical or lore writing."

DEVELOP PERSONAL PROJECTS TO SHOW

Tali Goldstein: "If you're an awesome graphic designer and you have really good 2D skills, but not much experience, make a beautiful CV. The other way is to have a portfolio. It's very important in this industry that you have personal projects. If you don't have any experience in the field, make your own piece of work that you're proud of. If it's 2D art or film, it doesn't matter, as long as it shows your skills."

BRING YOUR PORTFOLIO TO THE INTERVIEW

Tali Goldstein: "Always bring your personal projects to an interview, even if they don't ask you to. Always. Sometimes someone will see something and it'll catch their eye. I've seen that happen."

CREATE A WEBSITE

Tali Goldstein: "Display your work in a way that you can be proud of. If you can make your own website, do it. That way you can present your portfolio online and in person. And don't be shy to show people!"

PROBLEM SOLVERS GET NOTICED

Rommel Romero: "If you're interacting with a [gaming] company on Facebook or Twitter, people will often post questions to the company pages like, 'I have this problem….' If you present a solution, you get noticed by the company right away. And you look bold. From then on, if you've made a good impression, the moment they have a job opening they'll think about you. That can help you cut a lot of the red tape getting into the gaming industry."

DEMONSTRATE HOW RELEVANT YOU ARE

Tali Goldstein: "When I'm looking to hire someone, I don't want them to just talk about themselves. That's boring, it won't keep people engaged. I want to see how relevant their discussions are to the industry. If they share things that are relevant like new articles or their opinion on important subjects, that's impressive."

If you want to work in games, you should, naturally, be the kind of person who's going to lots of game industry events—just out of sheer passion for the medium. So when you apply for that job, you'll be a part of the community already.

- Morgan Kennedy, game user researcher, Ubisoft

GETTING STARTED

It's no wonder you've got your eye on a career in gaming or new media. They've got some super-hot, well-paid, creatively satisfying jobs. And it doesn't hurt that several of the industry's big guys have massage tables and fridges full of goodies on the premises. So much for the starving artist!

But that sought-after status comes with a downside: it means that you, your brother, and your neighbour's three sisters are all applying for the same lone position. So what can you do to set yourself apart? Our experts have some tips on how to prepare yourself for that big break.

FIGURE OUT WHY YOU WANT TO WORK IN NEW MEDIA

Morgan Kennedy: "Be extremely sure that it's what you want to do because the process of getting a job in this industry doesn't stop once you have a job. It's just as dynamic and competitive and challenging after you have the job. There's such fierce competition to get into gaming, and that continues once you're in it. You should expect to work harder in the industry than you did trying to get into it. So figure out why you want to do the job; you'll have that to remind yourself when things get challenging later."

BUILD UP YOUR SKILL SET FIRST

Morgan Kennedy: "I wouldn't recommend trying to get a job in the gaming industry before you have experience in some related area. I'd suggest going for a job in your particular field first, [or] in an adjacent industry like film or TV. So that when you do apply for the games job you've already got experience. It looks much better on your resume."

HONE YOUR CRAFT

Jill Murray: "Whatever your field is, seek out constructive advice and feedback on your work from peer groups, and develop your craft before submitting your work to recruiters."

FIND THE SYNERGY BETWEEN YOUR TECH AND CREATIVE ABILITIES

Tali Goldstein: "Try to learn as many software applications as possible, and get comfortable with as many new platforms and engines as you can. Being polyvalent is very important in this industry. The technical side is not always easy for artists, but discover how different software and engines can facilitate your creative side."

RESEARCH, RESEARCH, RESEARCH

Jill Murray: "Never wait to be told what you need to learn, or which skills you need to have to succeed. The information is out there and the future belongs to those who love research."

INTERNING CAN GET YOUR FOOT IN THE DOOR

Tali Goldstein: "I started interning at a film company in Brazil when I was sixteen. There was no game development at that time. To enable my career, I decided it didn't matter that all I was doing was serving coffee, I just needed to be breathing that creative air. And I made an impression, so when they had a job opening they gave it to me. That internship was so important for my career."

DON'T LIMIT YOUR OWN POSSIBILITIES

Morgan Kennedy: "A couple of years after trying to get into the industry, I was ready to give up. Then about two months later I was offered a job at Ubisoft. So don't be limited by your own sense of what is possible. Decide what you want to do, but don't rely too much on your own plan of how you'll get there; it can blind you to opportunities. All you need to do is stay conscious of opportunities and be ready to take them."

CONNECT WITH MENTORS AND EMPLOYERS AT GAME JAMS

Tali Goldstein: "Many game jams have mentors available to give you advice over the course of the event. This is invaluable. And it can even get you noticed by potential employers. I met one of the people I hired for my team at a game jam."

STAY INFORMED AND INVOLVED

Tali Goldstein: "Find out what other people are doing and how they're seeing the changes in the industry. Go to events where people are interested in your art. Communicate and ask for advice. You've got to educate yourself constantly in this business."

Be a kind and generous member of your creative community. Volunteer for the organizations that support your craft; get to know the people who will surround you for the duration of your career.
- Jill Murray, freelance game writer

TAKING IT TO THE NEXT LEVEL

The new media field is a business as much as it's an art. In fact, most of the experts we interviewed are working at medium- to large-sized companies. In this way, a career in new media won't look like the career of the typical filmmaker or visual artist. But make no mistake, most people who land jobs or contracts in new media will have spent many years honing their craft in related artistic endeavours, usually as freelancers. And most will go back to being freelancers at some point in their careers. New media is the most dynamic of industries, and life in that fast lane can take many twists and turns.

Here's what our gaming gurus have to say about incorporating new media into your long-term creative work life:

I. THE NEW MEDIA BUSINESS

ONCE YOU'RE IN, HAVE A GOOD EXIT STRATEGY

Morgan Kennedy: "Statistically, the average person will only stay in this industry for five years. That's the average developer lifespan because it's such an intensely dynamic field. Your career will look very different over the course of five years; the whole industry may look very different in five years. The amount of time you spend in the industry relative to your life is quite small, and because of that it's important to have a good exit strategy. For instance, you may do 3D modelling for your whole life, but you'll be doing it for movies and other industries, not just gaming. No one else will tell you that. It's certainly not something told to students."

LEARN THE BUSINESS SIDE OF YOUR ART

Tali Goldstein: "No matter what part of this industry you're in, try to understand the business side of your field. It's very important because if you don't educate yourself you might not have a very long career. I'm a games producer now, but I started as a filmmaker. I had to learn every aspect of that business because I had no resources to pay other people. It wasn't easy to let go of the artistic side sometimes, but by learning the business side, I was less dependent on others. Having that package of skills [artistic and business] got me my producer position. There are so many free classes and resources for educating yourself on the business of different art forms. You need to take advantage of them. YES has a lot of those available!"

IF YOU FREELANCE, GET PROFESSIONAL HELP

Jill Murray: "As a freelancer, my weak point used to be taking care of the business side of things. Luckily, game development can also be a full-time job. Working independently again, I hire professionals to help with key points of enterprise management: a lawyer to set up the initial incorporation, a great accountant for taxes—year round, a therapist for practically everything else. FreshBooks.com is a lifesaver on the bookkeeping front.

SETTING AND STICKING TO GOALS IS KEY

Tali Goldstein: "Time management can be really tough in this business. You have to establish lots of goals to know when you want to have things done. One thing that's extremely important is setting aside time to work on the bureaucratic stuff. It helps to compartmentalize that part of the job."

II. FINANCING AND MAKING MONEY

Whether you're in this business as a freelance game developer looking to finance your own venture or as an employee in a major new media company, our experts had some words of advice on money matters.

BE PREPARED TO SELF-FINANCE YOUR OWN GAMES

Jill Murray: "The best way to finance your own games is to take any job that can contribute to your work, and then use that money to save for your venture and invest in your education. Those savings will also sustain you in creative periods where a full-time job is not manageable. You need to have a goal and a system for managing your money—it might not come naturally."

GRANTS MAY BE AVAILABLE

Tali Goldstein: "You shouldn't rely on grants and government funding for the rest of your life, but it's a great way to start your career. One thing we used to use a lot was the Canada Media Fund (CMF), which has an experimental games stream. You pitch your project to them and you can get a lot of federal money for it. It's worth checking out! You need to show that you're serious with a business plan and a marketing strategy. You also need to show that you can get money from other sources."

LEARN TO MANAGE YOUR MONEY

Jill Murray: "All creative careers can benefit from a healthy relationship with money: how to save it, knowing when and when not to invest it in your work or education. An essential companion skill to this is learning how not to feel left out when all your friends go out to dinner while you stay home, writing."

SAVE WHILE THE MONEY IS GOOD

Morgan Kennedy: "With few exceptions, any job in the gaming industry will pay reasonably well. Max out your RRSP contributions so that your employer matches it. They all offer it. It might not be on your mind when you're in your twenties, but definitely do it."

III. GETTING VISIBILITY

Once again, whether you're just getting started as a freelancer or are employed by a large new media company, you need to be concerned with your own reputation and visibility as an artist. As we've heard, the average person may only stay in the industry for five years, but you're an artist for life! Your gig at the major gaming firm may well result in an offer to produce a web series, or design a phone app, or storyboard a feature film. Who knows? You and your creative skills may be in high demand, but it's a competitive world out there. Staying visible, in person and online, is key to a sustainable and satisfying career.

SEE AND BE SEEN IN THE LARGER INDUSTRY

Morgan Kennedy: "I try to speak at at least one regional or international conference per year just to stay visible within the larger industry. It's a small industry and it's international so that's important."

GO TO GAME JAMS

Tali Goldstein: "Game jams are great. They're little festivals that universities and organizations will put together. You can find them everywhere, especially in Montreal! The jams bring in people from all areas of development: artists, game designers, producers, and programmers. They're given an idea and then have to design a game in a day or over a weekend. There are game jams specifically for women as well. There's even a Mother's Day game jam! They're very casual events and let you develop your skills in a non-judgmental environment. Some amazing projects can come out of them too, and sometimes people continue to work together afterwards. It's a great way to meet your peers and make contacts. You get a lot more out of that than just sitting alone with your laptop."

GAME JAMS BUILD YOUR CONFIDENCE

Rommel Romero: "Build up your confidence by going to game jams. You'll meet your peers and other artists who are entering the field at the same time. It's a good first step for meeting people and seeing what they're working on. You'll see those people again along the way, and you'll already have that casual acquaintance. They'll know you and your work already."

JOIN THE INTERNATIONAL GAME DEVELOPERS ASSOCIATION (IGDA)

Morgan Kennedy: "It's important to think of yourself as someone who makes games and is part of that world. For young people especially, joining the IGDA is a good idea. It has its largest chapter here in Montreal and puts you in the right environment."

ATTEND INDUSTRY EVENTS

Tali Goldstein: "IGDA has chapters all over the place, and they put on conferences. There are meetings every month and plenty of opportunities to meet people in the industry. You need to apply to get in, but if you prepare yourself, you can do it. It's a great networking place and it's very casual. Many important people in the industry are invited to come and talk about what they're doing. A lot of artists are introverted, but you need to force yourself to interact. If you're shy, bring a friend. You can walk around and meet people, and when you're feeling tired, you can go back to your friend and recharge. And it's easier to get into conversations when you're two sometimes."

SHARPEN YOUR NETWORKING SKILLS

Tali Goldstein: "If networking makes you uncomfortable, practise with a friend first. It looks so easy, but it's not. It's very hard to introduce yourself in such a way that makes you feel proud and conveys what you do. It's very important to be prepared. Even if you just Google 'How to introduce myself,' there's information out there. Go to a friend who you think expresses themselves well and ask for help. And practise your handshake. Whatever you do, don't have a weak handshake."

We also asked our experts about networking via social media. As you might imagine, lots of people will only know you through your online presence, so keeping it polished is essential.

TAP INTO LINKEDIN GROUPS

Tali Goldstein: "Start on LinkedIn with the giant groups that are about things you're interested in. There are always people saying 'We're going to have this meet-up' and 'We're going to this event.' Then prepare yourself and go to those events, and go!"

DON'T FORGET, YOU'RE BEING WATCHED

Tali Goldstein: "On social media show yourself in a way that you can be proud of. Don't forget that people are always looking. You want to be professional."

IT'S ALL ABOUT CREDIBILITY

Rommel Romero: "Social media is at the core of how you present yourself as a professional. It's important to present yourself in a way that is consistent with your personality, but still projects what your talents and goals are. Stay on top of what the industry is doing on a business level so that you can contribute to the online conversation. You want to understand the industry and you want to build up credibility. Social media is key for doing that."

DON'T FOCUS ON YOUR PERSONAL BRAND MANAGEMENT

Jill Murray: "Use social media constructively to find like-minds and interesting projects. Converse with and support your fellow artists. But don't get too distracted by self-promotion or spin. It's easy to fall into a trap where your personal brand management becomes a pursuit of its own, and your casual celebrity exceeds the quality and energy of your creative output. It can sustain you for a time, but it's not the best way to build career longevity because it doesn't grow your expertise, or interests, and the media machine needs constant feeding and attention that would be better invested in your work."

And if you have a personal project that needs visibility, our experts have some advice for that too:

SEND OUT A PRESS RELEASE
Tali Goldstein: "If you want some publicity for a personal project, send out a press release. You don't need to hire someone to do it. There are tutorials online. Just Google it. Get a template or ask for help. People will help you. Don't get intimidated by things you don't know how to do. Most of us are here because we learned by doing."

CONTACT THE BLOGGING COMMUNITY
Rommel Romero: "Get to know the bloggers and journalists who cover the types of games you make. If you have something to show, a game that you're working on and a tentative release date, go to the blogs. There are different tiers of blogs. There are amateur blogs made by people who are passionate but casual. Then the next level of people who are professional, making money independently. Then the top tier of career journalists who are connected to larger organizations. You might not necessarily have a pitch for the bigger blogs, but if you show up in the smaller blogs, it gets picked up by the bigger ones and moves up the chain."

Sometimes we spend a lot of time on things that we think are important, which don't actually matter very much to us in the end. Know what matters to you.

- Tali Goldstein, line producer, Minority Media

LIVING AS A NEW MEDIA ARTIST

So you've finally made it; you're living the life you've dreamed of since powering up your first Game Boy all those years ago. But this action-packed industry can have its trap doors and trip-ups, just like any good game. Sure, there's a massage table in the back room but who has time for a rub-down? And that condo you bought with your fiancé, will it still make sense if you end up living there alone?

The intensity and dynamism of the new media world is part of its appeal, but the artistic souls who inhabit it must take care not to get swallowed up. Our experts have some guidance to that effect. They've all survived, and so can you.

KNOW WHAT YOU WANT IN LIFE

Tali Goldstein: "Ask yourself what makes you, you. Make a list of your top five goals in life. And then calculate how long you spend on the different things you do in a week and see if they match your goals. If family is on the list, make sure you're devoting time to your family. If travelling is on that list, make sure you're saving money and making plans for travelling. How do you spend your day? If you have a job that's purely commercial and it's eating into your other goals, it might not be worth it. You've got to find the right balance."

TAKE TIME TO REFLECT

Morgan Kennedy: "When it was only a dream, what did you want to get out of your experience in the gaming business in the first place? Try to remember that. It'll keep you grounded. For me, I remember playing Prince of Persia while I was living in Vermont and realizing it was made in Montreal, and that it was only three hours away. At that point it seemed really unlikely that I would end up working here. It never really occurred to me that there would be an industry so close, and once I realized that, I decided that that's what I wanted to do. Now I'm here doing something that seemed impossible only a few years ago. It's important to remember that."

CHECK YOUR EGO AT THE DOOR

Tali Goldstein: "Try to leave your ego out of your projects. That can get in the way, especially in this industry. It's beautiful to be an artist, but you can't let your ego cost you opportunities. You're always part of a larger team."

FIND A WAY TO GET PHYSICAL EXERCISE

Morgan Kennedy: "You should think about developing an interest in a leisure sport or physical activity because you're not going to get a lot of physical exercise in front of a computer.

Especially since in your free time you'll probably be playing games. When the weather is nice I try to run outside of the studio three times a week during my lunch break."

DON'T OVEREXTEND YOURSELF

Jill Murray: "I stretch myself pretty thin on occasion, between project deadlines, talks, interviews, and travel. You have to be careful because, while it often pays off, there can come a point where the quality of your output can be strained, or you just start to react badly to stress, which is not only uncomfortable and bad for your health, but can negatively impact your relationships with people."

SEPARATE YOUR LIFE AND WORK

Tali Goldstein: "Establish some boundaries between your work and your relationships. Artists tend to work a lot. It never stops. I still struggle with separating my work and personal life even after fifteen years in the industry. There are periods of my life when I'm so involved in a project that I don't see anything else. There's no end. Sometimes you just need to stop and say, 'it's done.' Make sure you take breaks, even small ones during the day. For me, I make a point to leave the office at five or six o'clock to go swimming. It's hard. But you need to make a commitment to those small things."

FINAL THOUGHTS

In closing, a couple of our professionals had some final thoughts they wanted to leave you with, based on their own journeys into the new media world.

BE AMBITIOUS BUT WORK WITHIN YOUR LIMITS

Tali Goldstein: "A long time ago, I was working on a movie and it was way too ambitious. We were never able to sit down and finish it. It's very hard to let go as an artist, because everything seems essential. We had very little money and we spent it all on this unfinished work. We weren't able to make choices and cut the film enough to have a final product. It's the same with creating new media projects. Try to work with the financing and resources you have. Surround yourself with professionals who are realistic and serious about the project. Don't be overly ambitious with your art or you might end up with nothing."

FOLLOW YOUR OWN PATH

Morgan Kennedy: "It's really important to create meaning out of the events that happen in your life, especially in such a dynamic work environment. Make goals and achieve them, and then make new goals and achieve them—every step of the way. To know what those goals should be you need to develop your intuition to the point where you can rely on it. In fact, if anything I've said in this chapter goes against your own intuition, ignore me and listen to that instead.

PERFORMERS

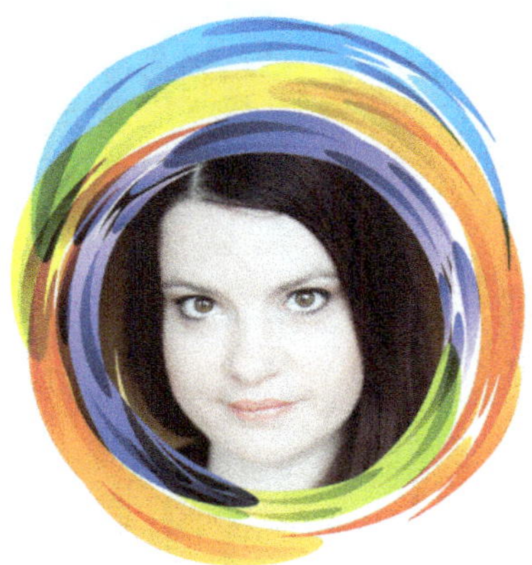

Amy Blackmore

Joey Elias

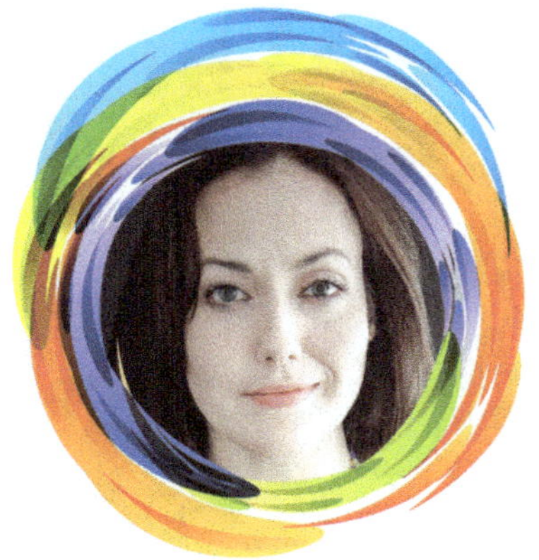

Holly Gauthier-Frankel

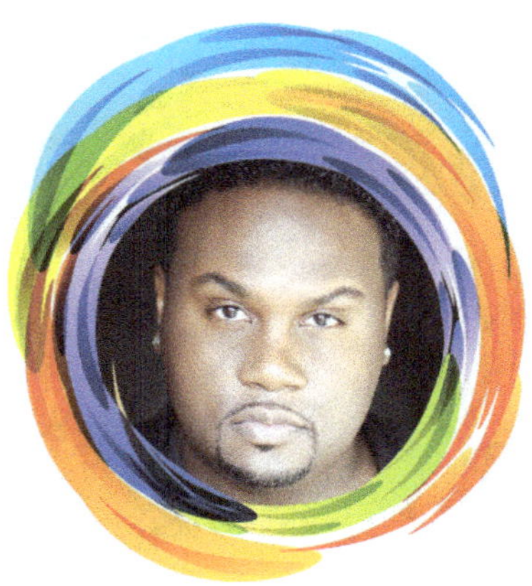

Tristan D. Lalla

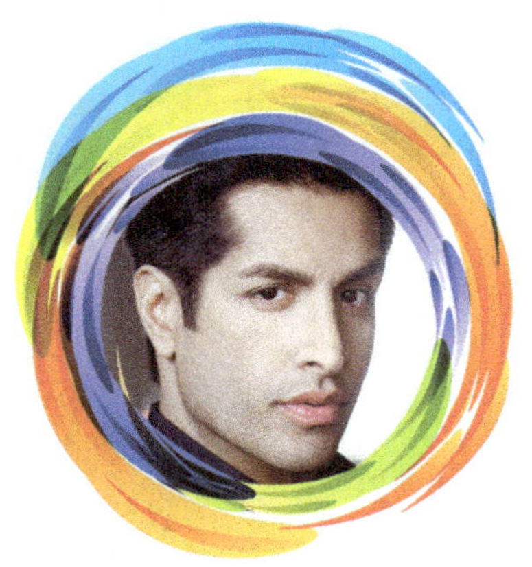

Sugar Sammy

As a performer, it's easy to conform to someone else's vision of what you should be. But true success is when you wake up in the morning and you're happy in your own skin.
- Amy Blackmore, Executive and Artistic Director, MainLine Theatre

SO YOU WANNA BE A PERFORMER?

Montreal has been called the "cultural capital" of North America, known worldwide for its world-class talent. Home of the Cirque du Soleil, the Montreal Jazz Festival, and the International Just For Laughs Festival, it's no surprise that the performing arts are big business in this city. In addition to the local scene, Hollywood films set up shop here year-round, taking advantage of the (relatively) low-cost talent, top notch studios, and stunning scenery. Performers with talent, drive, and a strong business sense can go on to make a solid living. And certainly not just on the silver screen or stage. Quebec's booming gaming industry is snapping up local actors to populate their virtual worlds.

A plethora of performing art icons call Montreal home. If, after reading through this section, you're interested in broadening your horizons in the performing arts, consider the occupations listed in the National Occupation Classification, published by Employment and Social Development Canada:

> Actor

> Artistic director

> Broadcaster

> Choreographer

> Circus performer

> Comedian

> Dancer

> Dramatic reader

> Extra, performing arts

> Narrator

> Performance artist

> Radio/TV announcer

> Voice actor

THE EXPERTS

We spoke with the following accomplished performers to get a peek behind the curtain:

Amy Blackmore is the executive and artistic director of MainLine Theatre, the Montreal Fringe Festival, and the Bouge d'ici Dance Festival. Amy is an award-winning theatre practitioner having worked with many companies including the Montreal Fringe Festival, the Montreal Highlights Festival, Crystal Pite's Kidd Pivot, POP Montreal, OFF-TA, and RUBBERBANDance Group. Recently, her work has been seen in MainLine Theatre's *The Mid-Life Crisis of Dionysus*, the Montreal Shakespeare Theatre Company's *Macbeth*, *The Rocky Horror Picture Show* by Shayne Gryn Productions, and Infinitheatre's *Unseamly*. A board member of the Quebec Drama Federation and the English-Language Arts Network, Amy believes in the power of community, openness, and opportunity. See more of Amy's work at www.facebook.com/AmyBlackmoreChoreography or @_amyblackmore.

Joey Elias has appeared in no fewer than fifteen Just for Laughs Festivals. He travels worldwide headlining and performing at festivals, top-notch comedy venues, and private corporate functions, twice venturing to Afghanistan to entertain Canadian troops. Joey has appeared in several films including *On The Road* starring Kirsten Dunst, *The Wool Cap* with William H. Macy, and *The Day After Tomorrow* with Dennis Quaid. Currently, Joey hosts the CJAD Comedy Show with Joey Elias and is touring his one-man show *In My Head and Out of My Mind*, which premiered at Just for Laughs in 2013. Joey also hosts the annual Joey Elias Charity Golf Classic to raise funds for diabetes. You can visit his charity website www.joeyeliasgolf.com for more information.

Holly Gauthier-Frankel is a multidisciplinary artist with over twenty-five years of experience in studio and stage performance as a singer and dancer, and she is also a writer and teacher. As a voice actor, Holly has lent her talents to hundreds of children's cartoons, foreign and local films, video games and albums, and has worked frequently for CBC, the National Film Board, and on many specialty channels. A skilled theatrical and cabaret actor, Holly has performed in plays and musicals in Montreal and Ottawa, and has performed in clubs in Tokyo, Toronto, New York, and Chicago. She works and lives in Montreal, Quebec. See more of what Holly is up to at lamandorla.ca.

Sugar Sammy is one of the hottest comedians on the international circuit, enjoying great success both at home and around the world. He has performed over 1,200 shows in thirty countries. His shows in Canada and India have sold 300,000 tickets since February 2012. His tour dates have won him the ranking among the highest-grossing tours in North America according to *Pollstar* magazine, and *Billboard* named him the top-selling Canadian tour for the twelve months ending April 2014. Sugar Sammy won the Comedian of the Year award at Quebec's Gala les Oliviers in both 2013 and 2014. So, where can you check him out? www.sugarsammy.com.

Tristan D. Lalla is an award-winning actor, poet, and honours graduate of the Dawson College Professional Theatre program. Selected credits include: for theatre, *A Raisin In The Sun, Othello, The Tempest, The Mahalia Jackson Musical, Man of La Mancha*, the Canadian Premiere of David Mamet's *Race, Glengarry Glen Ross, A Midsummer Night's Dream, Much Ado About Nothing, The Fairy Queen*; for film/TV, *How She Move, RED 2, Brick Mansions, White House Down, Betty & Coretta, Funkytown*, the cartoon *Bounty Hunters, The Bitter End, Misogyny Misandry*; for video games, *Assassin's Creed IV: Black Flag, Freedom Cry, Assassin's Creed Liberation HD, WatchDogs, Far Cry 2, From Dust*, and *Deux Ex Human Revolution*. Check him out online at Twitter/Instagram @tdlalla and at www.tristandlalla.com.

Here's what they had to say performer to performer:

WHO NEEDS A PERFORMING ARTS DEGREE?

There were mixed views on whether a formal education in the performing arts is an absolute necessity. Becoming a stand-up comedian, for instance, will have very different requirements than working as a voice actor. For the most part, the discipline that you choose to work in will determine the educational requirements. Many of our experts touted the training you can get outside a university or college setting. So even if you land a formal degree, don't think the learning will stop there. Not only will you continue to hone your craft, but there's a lot they don't teach you in school.

Tristan D. Lalla says, "In theatre school they teach you how to sing and dance and use your voice, but not how to take care of your finances and keep your affairs in order. Later, when that catches up to you, those lessons are learned the hard way." We'll talk more about that in this chapter, but suffice it to say, you won't necessarily learn everything you need in the classroom to make it as a professional performer.

There are some other things you should be aware of before committing to a formal education. For instance, some theatre schools don't permit their students to take on professional acting jobs during their studies. The ones that don't will often provide other forms of assistance to their students, but some young actors think this is unfair. On the upside, though, this policy allows you to focus full-time on your own artistic development. And that can be invaluable in the long-run.

If you don't have a proper headshot and a well-structured resume, you're not taken seriously. It's like having a soft handshake or a bad business card, or walking into a job interview with dirty socks and shoes.

- Tristan D. Lalla, actor

HOW DO YOU SHOW WHAT YOU'VE GOT?

Our panel of performing artists was loud and clear: You need a headshot in your portfolio and you need it done right! The headshot, usually an 8" x 10" size, will be sent along with the rest of your background material to casting directors.

A professional headshot can be expensive, but it's an essential investment early in your career that will pay off later. Not all professional photographers can produce a decent headshot, so ask peers or your local performing artists' union to recommend someone who can do a great job. You can also visit with several photographers until you find one with whom you feel comfortable. So, should you run off to the salon for a drastic haircut and have the seasonal colour palette painted on your face before your photo session? Or is au naturel the way to go? Well, put it this way, it should look like you—but better.

What else needs to go into your portfolio? You need a proper resume. List all the work you've done broken down into media (theatre performances, television appearances, film roles, etc). For an emerging performer, the information listed on your resume also goes beyond school and past experience to include eye and hair colour, special skills (like tightrope walking), languages spoken, and accents that you're capable of performing.

You should also include a demo reel if possible. Having this produced professionally in a studio is another worthwhile investment. If you already have numerous clips from TV and film work, hire a video editor to produce a montage of your clippings.

And if you have an interest in performing voice work (for commercials, cartoons or voice-overs), have a voice demo produced. Or you can record this yourself by reading out various ads in different tones and accents to show your range.

If you're looking to be a dancer, circus performer, or other physical performer, put together a video of performance clips along with your resume. If you don't have any professional performances to show, have someone film you at work in a gym or studio.

Here's the specific advice our performers had on showing what you've got:

MAKE A GREAT FIRST IMPRESSION
Tristan D. Lalla: "As an actor, your calling card is your headshot and your resume. Before you even show your talent to the casting director, you walk in and you hand them that. It's the physical manifestation of your talent. In thirty seconds they can say, 'I can see him as so-and-so.'"

DON'T SKIMP ON YOUR HEADSHOT
Amy Blackmore: "My personal cap is $150 on a headshot. It's worth having it in proper makeup and getting your hair right. My first headshot was a disaster. I'd gone out the night before and my hair was greasy and the photos were terrible! It's definitely worth investing a little money."

KNOW WHAT THEY'RE LOOKING FOR
Joey Elias: "For any comic starting out, have a demo tape, six to seven minutes, that you can show club owners where you want to perform. It's always good to keep a list of all the things you've done. If you've done a fundraising event, put it on your resume. That's what people will eventually hire you for. Charity events and stuff like that."

HAVE A SPECIALIZED PERFORMER CV
Holly Gauthier-Frankel: "On an acting CV you'll need your age, weight, what you look like, your training, the film, television, and theatre stuff that you've done, whether or not you're affiliated with any unions, and any special talents you have. You don't normally put in the commercials you've done unless you don't really have a lot of work yet. To do voice work you'll need to put together a demo and, if you can, get an agent to represent you."

TAILOR YOUR CV FOR EACH AUDITION
Amy Blackmore: "I think that casting directors are interested in range, in any special skill sets you have. I change my CV for every single audition, because I have a very diverse background. If you're auditioning for a drama, don't just have comedy on your CV. Have a little bit in there, but tailor it to the job."

THINK ABOUT CREATING A WEBSITE
Holly Gauthier-Frankel: "I have a new website and it's just an amalgamation of all the things I've been doing with some demos. I have everything on there along with my agent's details and contact information. I'd like it to be a tool that could help me get work in the future."

Whether you're going to do performing arts or become a baker, you've got to wake up every day loving what you do or there's no point.

- Joey Elias, comedian

GETTING STARTED

You were the sweetheart of your high school production of Swan Lake or your passion for performance led you to a myriad of long line-ups where you and scores of wannabe stars waited for hours until a casting assistant answered your prayers and made you an extra on the latest big production to hit the town.

But now you're ready to make the move forward with your career. You've got the talent; you just need a little push. Read on for our expert directions on getting started on the road to success:

RESPECT YOUR ART AS A CAREER, NOT A HOBBY

Tristan D. Lalla: "It's important to know that artistic careers are just that: careers, not hobbies. A lot of family pressure might tell you, 'Be a lawyer,' or 'Be a doctor.' But you can make a living doing what you love artistically without being apologetic and compromising other parts of your life."

THERE'S NO FORMULA FOR SUCCESS

Tristan D. Lalla: "Formulas for success don't really work. What works for me won't work for someone else. Find what works for you; take little bits and pieces from other peoples' experience and form your own method. Never rely on what someone else did to work for you in the same way."

BE DISCIPLINED WITHOUT PUNISHING YOURSELF

Holly Gauthier-Frankel: "Use gentle discipline on yourself; it's a harsh business. You have to be on top of your game, but you can't control any of it. Do all the work you can do to make yourself the best candidate for jobs you want, but don't try to fit yourself into rigid categories."

USE ALL YOUR LIFE EXPERIENCE IN YOUR ART

Tristan D. Lalla: "Whenever I'm working on something as an actor, I bring every other part of my life into it. It's important to be open to everything in your life that may feed into your playing a particular role. You never know, you might play a mathematician some day, so that level four math might help you out."

HONE YOUR CRAFT WHEREVER YOU ARE

Sugar Sammy: "To polish your stand-up, do open mics for a few months until you get better and better. Sign up for workshops offered at comedy clubs. Also, watch a lot of stand-up. The more you are exposed to it, the more you absorb it."

Joey Elias: "Before I got my radio gig, I delivered pizza. I taught swimming. I sold watches. I sold phones. As time went on, I thought, 'Let's try to sneak a joke in,' to whatever I was doing. If they laughed, then maybe I'd put it into my routine."

Amy Blackmore: "What you're doing is a craft. There are artists who succeed on a fluke, but they're rare. The artists who really do go far are the people who nourish and study their craft all the time, and then take it the whole way."

KNOW YOUR STRENGTHS AND WEAKNESSES
Holly Gauthier-Frankel: "Know yourself and your strengths and weaknesses because there's so much lack of control and fear in this industry, you can drive yourself crazy. If I'm not getting work, I explore why and what I can do about it. Can I go to a workshop? Should I host a workshop with friends? How can I take control of the problem?"

IMMERSE YOURSELF IN THE FIELD
Holly Gauthier-Frankel: "If you're interested in theatre, go join the theatre and see all the plays. Ask when the auditions are and who you should talk to to get involved. Ask where to bring your CV. A lot of people get jobs at casting agencies or as ushers in the theatre, and then they stay involved naturally."

DEVELOP YOUR PERSONAL NETWORK
Joey Elias: "It's important to have your own personal network. If you're a performer starting off, you're in this together with everyone starting around the same time. I love the fact that comics go out for drinks or coffee after a show. You become your own little network."

LOOK FOR GUIDANCE FROM SENIOR PERFORMERS
Tristan D. Lalla: "Networking with well-known performers is tricky because you don't want to come across as a sycophant. But if you're working with someone you admire, have the courage to ask their advice, and have the humility to take whatever they give you. Sometimes older actors will tell you things you don't want to hear. They'll say, 'I saw you in such and such and you were shit.' I got told that once! But they'll also tell you things like how to comport yourself on set and other things about the business. When those people give you advice, you listen. Be malleable, take it in, and like everything else, pick and choose what works for you."

Sugar Sammy: "Often, established comics in the audience will come up to you after your performance and comment on your work. Learn to take advantage of them and their expertise."

THERE ARE ALL KINDS OF MENTORS
Amy Blackmore: "Mentors can also be people who don't work in the artistic community. Maybe you're from a large family and your uncle is someone you look up to. Or you admire your boss at work. There are a lot of life lessons you can learn that are outside your craft."

DON'T BE AFRAID OF REJECTION OR CRITICISM

Amy Blackmore: "You'll get rejected a lot, especially when you're auditioning; it's just part of the process. You should learn from those rejections instead of being afraid of them. Take those into your tool belt for the next one. You might get rejected fifty times in a row before getting a role."

Tristan D. Lalla: "Be open to failure and getting knocked down. Those times build you up until that failure becomes something that you can anticipate and almost invite. It's fun to fail when you know how to succeed afterwards."

Joey Elias: "If you're going to go into the performing arts, you need to be ready to take criticism, whether it's valid or not. There's always going to be people who really enjoy your stuff and people who really don't."

BE FLEXIBLE

Holly Gauthier-Frankel: "Be as well rounded as you can be in your field. The performing arts have changed so drastically, it's becoming more important to be knowledgeable of all aspects of it. I anticipated doing more film and television, but then I wasn't really getting those parts. So to stop worrying about it, I focused on different things like my burlesque persona."

POLISH YOUR PEOPLE SKILLS

Amy Blackmore: "The performing arts is a collaborative form. You might be working for a director, but you're really working with the director. You need to know how to collaborate with other people and have very strong interpersonal skills."

REMEMBER YOUR PLEASE AND THANK YOUS

Amy Blackmore: "Simple stuff like please and thank you will go a really long way! In an audition, if you're on par with someone else but the other guy was a jerk, your politeness can make all the difference."

It's important to meet lawyers and doctors and people who aren't in the arts, because these are the people who will fund your work. Don't just stay in your little bubble with other artists.
- Amy Blackmore, executive and artistic director, MainLine Theatre

TAKING IT TO THE NEXT LEVEL

You've landed a gig with the performing arts troupe of your dreams. In your dreams, mind you, it was you placing the dressing room orders for sparkling water and sweet-smelling roses, not filling those orders.

Still, you did manage to get in front of the casting director on a few occasions and you impressed him with your classical interpretations or wild impersonations. You've been a character in search of an author for years and finally you've found someone willing to write you into a starring role.

We've heard from our experts that it's not all glitz and glam at the top, though it is a lot of fun once you get there. Professional performing artists have to work hard at promoting both themselves and their artistry. Believing in your power and purpose as an artist will sometimes take the poise and pluck of a Grecian hero.

Read on for what our panel of experts had to say about making it as a performing artist:

I. THE PERFORMING ARTS BUSINESS

TAKE TIME TO MANAGE YOUR CAREER
Amy Blackmore: "As an artist you tend to get overwhelmed and caught up in a million things. But you need to spend 10 percent of your time just managing your time and your career."

KNOW WHEN IT'S TIME TO GET AN AGENT
Sugar Sammy: "Don't get an agent until you feel like you can't handle your career yourself. When I look for an agent, I'm looking for someone who can open doors that I can't. I'm not interested in people whose contacts are the same as mine."

GET HELP WITH THE OFF-STAGE STUFF
Joey Elias: "When you get to a certain level, you realize there are little tax breaks you can get for being self-employed. There are so many loopholes that, back in the day, I didn't know about. You don't need to be spending $900 an hour on an accountant, but just have someone who knows that you can write off the clothes you wear on stage."

YOUR CAREER IS YOUR BUSINESS

Sugar Sammy: "Treat your career like a business. Get out there and market yourself. You have to be a good self-promoter."

SEPARATE YOUR ADMIN TIME FROM YOUR CREATIVE TIME

Amy Blackmore: "[As the director of Mainline Theatre], I've adopted a new practice of leaving my computer at the office. Otherwise my work life and my 'life' life both suffer."

II. FINANCING AND MAKING MONEY

Making money as a professional performer can be a bit of a rollercoaster ride. While some of our experts have been able to live off their artistic income for their entire careers, others have had to take the proverbial waitress job to keep afloat when times were tough.

Either way, they all advise to watch your wallet—even when the good times are rolling. Because, like all roller coasters, you can count on them plummeting down eventually.

In terms of financing, unlike filmmakers and fashion designers, it's relatively easy to make it as a performer with limited resources. There are a few grants available for certain categories of performance art but most of our experts simply self-financed their careers, and that's what they suggest you be prepared to do too. Here's their specific advice:

INVEST IN YOURSELF

Amy Blackmore: "I started off by financing my own work. It's risky to do that, and that's probably why I lost electricity back in the day. It takes money to make money, and you will end up spending your own money to make stuff happen. I think it's important to invest in your own stuff; it shows that you believe in it."

DON'T QUIT YOUR DAY JOB, AT LEAST NOT RIGHT AWAY

Joey Elias: "When you're first starting out, just don't quit your day job right away. You can't. It's a wonderful thing to be living the dream, but you've got to have that extra income. Doing stand-up, the first couple times you go on the road, you don't make a lot of money. You're probably going to lose money. I remember flying to Calgary on a $300 flight and the show only paid $250. But now I go back twice a year, and they pay my flight and all my expenses. I had to lose money at the beginning, knowing that if I last X amount of time, I'll make that money back. It's a lot like being a gambler."

YOUR ARTS COMMUNITY WILL SUPPORT YOU

Amy Blackmore: "It's important to engage in your arts community. Your kind actions will come back around if you ever try something like a Kickstarter campaign, which I recommend."

GRANT WRITING IS A LEARNING EXPERIENCE

Holly Gauthier-Frankel: "I applied for a grant last year and learned a lot from that experience. I didn't get the grant but they were very helpful and impressed. It was certainly worth a try."

DON'T STICK YOUR HEAD IN THE SAND

Holly Gauthier-Frankel: "I'm definitely a flaky actress type when it comes to finances. For a long time I was an ostrich with my head in the sand, ignoring all the letters and bills. Thankfully, I learned my lesson and started to look at myself as a business. I even incorporated in 2001. At first I didn't know what the hell I was doing, but now I have a wonderful accountant and agent who help me. Now that all that's in place, I can really start to build my business, as opposed to just living paycheque to paycheque and crossing my fingers."

EXPECT MONEY TO BE TIGHT

Amy Blackmore: "You have to be realistic and know that artists usually live in poverty at first. You have to save your pennies—which I didn't do. When I finally quit my waitressing job and decided to pursue acting full-time, that was difficult. I came home one day and didn't have any electricity. It took a couple days to find that money. I was begging for any work I could get at the theatre: mopping the floors, cleaning the toilets. But through all the auditions and rehearsals, I was still around the people I admired, and that was important."

BE PREPARED FOR FEAST OR FAMINE

Tristan D. Lalla: "I've never really had to deliver pizza or wait tables. Ever since theatre school, everything I've done has been in acting. When I finished school in 2004, I had three amazing gigs lined up, all lead roles. And then nothing for months. I would be sitting at home, just waiting; I thought it was supposed to be one thing and then it wasn't. It took a long time to adapt to that."

INVEST IN PROFESSIONAL SERVICES

Amy Blackmore: "Some people insist on learning how to do their own taxes but I think that's a waste. I don't need to know how to do my taxes if someone else can help me get them done properly. Spend 10 percent of your income on making sure your income is coming in right. I have an amazing accountant who does my finances. He has an artist rate and a corporate rate. I don't think people realize that those special rates exist. Ask other artists!"

Tristan D. Lalla: "I hire someone to do my finances properly. I've gone to school for theatre; my accountant's gone to school for accounting. It's important that the financial stuff is handled properly because, death and taxes, you can't escape them."

III. GETTING VISIBILITY

When asked about how to get visibility as a performer, our experts stressed the importance of maintaining a strong network. Who you know in this business can have a lot to do with how often you're invited to audition or work on collaborative projects. And networking helps keep you in the loop on what projects are in town and looking to hire.

They also stressed the importance of a having a "name brand." A performer's career can live or die on the strength of their name recognition. These days, cultivating media contacts and having an online relationship with fans can be what it takes to put you in the star suite. Here's their specific advice:

BROADEN YOUR NETWORKING HORIZONS

Amy Blackmore: "I think that the best [networking] organization is the English-Language Arts Network (ELAN). I work primarily in dance, and we can get stuck in our particular discipline and art form. But if you're working collaboratively, you're going to have to work with people in other forms."

UNIONS CAN HELP YOU PLUG IN

Holly Gauthier-Frankel: "Unions aren't casting agencies and they're not employers, but they're big networks with lists of casting agencies and workshops."

CHECK OUT THE QUEBEC DRAMA FEDERATION

Tristan D. Lalla: "The Quebec Drama Federation always makes sure that emerging artists have information about auditions and different theatre companies and films. I've been on a few committees with them over the years and they've been really supportive."

ACTING SCHOOLS ARE A GREAT PLACE TO NETWORK

Holly Gauthier-Frankel: "Join an acting school or acting gym (which is just a place where a bunch of actors will get together and read scenes). And improv groups are really great for networking too."

NEED AN "IN"? VOLUNTEER YOUR TIME

Amy Blackmore: "It's so easy to get in on what an organization is doing when you say, 'Hey I have some free time; do you need help with anything?' I had a friend do that at the Centaur Theatre and he had an incredible experience working with them."

A PERFORMER IS A "NAME BRAND"

Amy Blackmore: "I'm lucky because despite doing a lot of different things, my brand is my name. It's a unique name and it's easy to say. So I named my choreography company after myself and pretended to be big right away. You have to own it. If you want to be something, own it."

Tristan D. Lalla: "My real name is hyphenated, but when it came time to choose a stage name, we settled on Tristan D. Lalla because it rolls off the tongue. When people hear my name, they know I'll deliver."

Joey Elias: "You can brand yourself a certain way by marketing the character you become on stage. For instance, nobody is actually coming to see me, they're coming to see this wonderful character. But, then again, the cranky guy [that I normally play] doesn't show up to charity events. When I'm emceeing a Children's Hospital event, I'm more of a cheerleader."

BRANDING IS JUST RECOGNIZABILITY

Holly Gauthier-Frankel: "At one point I decided I wanted to be the Oprah of burlesque and feminist culture, but there's something about making yourself a brand that feels cold and impersonal. More than becoming a brand, I just think about how to become recognizable; how to get visibility."

HAVE A CLEAR AND CONSISTENT MESSAGE

Amy Blackmore: "The important thing in marketing is that your message is clear and that your visuals really match the words. At the Fringe Festival we did a campaign with a poster of a bee with #Fringebuzz on it. Even though we were planning on using other hashtags during the festival, we quickly realized that #Fringebuzz was the one everyone knew and recognized, so we stayed with that one."

INVEST IN YOUR ONLINE PRESENCE

Holly Gauthier-Frankel: "You've got to make sure the online tool you choose works for you and you're not working for it. I paid someone to design my website and make it swanky, but if I don't update my weekly blog or put content up, or keep telling people to go check it out, it won't work for me."

BE SELECTIVE WITH YOUR SOCIAL MEDIA

Amy Blackmore: "The key to social media is not attempting to do everything. Pick two or three formats—max—especially if you're working on your own. There are great resources to help you with this, like Hootsuite. It lets me do Facebook and Twitter and others all at once. You can schedule when things go out, and it lets you understand your whole picture. I put in the first fifteen minutes of my day and the last fifteen minutes of my day on social media and check it throughout the day—but not obsessively."

SOCIAL MEDIA IS PART OF YOUR JOB

Joey Elias: "Now networking is all about getting onto Facebook and LinkedIn and whatever. It's about how many followers and likes you have. Social media, in terms of networking, as much as I despise it, is part of your job."

FACEBOOK CAN BE CRUCIAL TO WORD OF MOUTH

Holly Gauthier-Frankel: "Facebook has been very helpful for me because a lot of what I did [as a burlesque performer] took off through word of mouth. Now I post pictures on Facebook every once in a while because they say that's what works; a post with a picture gets way more clicks."

SOCIAL MEDIA IS KEY TO VIDEO GAME PERFORMERS

Tristan D. Lalla: "I do voice work and full motion performance capture for computer games like Assassin's Creed. The fan base for that game lives online. They're waiting for any nugget of information, any leak. Once they found out I was in the game, they showed all kinds of love for me as an actor. My website almost crashed and my Twitter account gained two thousand followers, just from announcing the game."

CHOOSE THE RIGHT FACEBOOK PAGE NAME

Holly Gauthier-Frankel: "My Facebook is under my name, Holly, and I also have a Miss Sugarpuss [burlesque] page. My Holly page has far more friends and likes and connections, so I realized that I had far more power as Holly than as Sugarpuss. I also noticed a lot of performers being booted off Facebook and forced to use their real names, so my Holly page is better all around."

ENGAGE WITH YOUR FANS

Tristan D. Lalla: "If anyone reaches out to me, especially on Twitter, I'll write back right away. Because then they'll want to share it and hear about what else I have going on. It's important to give and take; without the support, you won't make it. Your career can't just be for you, your mom, and your grandma. It's important to acknowledge those who acknowledge you. When you don't, you ignore the momentum that you're trying to create."

PUT YOURSELF OUT THERE

Holly Gauthier-Frankel: "My burlesque persona really helped in getting me known. I was constantly dressing up and putting myself out there. At the time burlesque wasn't so big yet, so I was a little ahead of the curve, but I stayed true to my weirdo self and it worked!"

BE CONSCIOUS OF HOW YOU'RE PERCEIVED ON SOCIAL MEDIA

Amy Blackmore: "It's important to understand how you come across on your social media. Do you use slang, abbreviations, swear words? For me, it's something I don't do on my social media. Unless it's your brand, I'd say stay away from it. French and English are also very important here in Quebec. I'll tweet in both, sometimes in the same tweet."

POLITICAL POSTS MAY GET PUSH BACK

Joey Elias: "I got in trouble for posting political stuff a few years ago. I wouldn't recommend that when you're starting out. Use social media to build up your fan base before you get into the political stuff; you'll avoid the pettiness of the Internet. If you've got a funny one-liner, put it out there on Twitter, then people might come see you on stage. Just know that there are always people who want to cause crap for you. You've got to just push through that and promote yourself as much as you can."

TRADITIONAL MEDIA IS ALIVE AND WELL
Amy Blackmore: "There's a rumour out there that traditional media is dead or dying. I don't think that's true. I think it's worth trying to get in on it. Right now a lot of freelancers work for different places. People who work in print will also work online. They're paid to do ten tweets a day or something, in addition to their print articles."

FOSTER GOOD RELATIONSHIPS WITH JOURNALISTS
Amy Blackmore: "If you send out a press release a month in advance and don't hear back, just send another press release. Journalists appreciate the interaction. They need to cover stuff and you need the coverage. But don't harass them. Over the years you develop relationships with certain reporters and they'll start asking you what's going on."

Holly Gauthier-Frankel: "Having relationships with journalists has been helpful. I've been lucky to be friends with journalists and bloggers. I like to be friendly and nice to people and that usually helps get things out there."

Tristan D. Lalla: "I can call up any anchor at CTV or CBC or Global because I know them all through interviews and events. Those are important relationships and I don't exploit or abuse them. And it's mutual; if they call me up, I'm there for them. They know it's important to keep the relationship going too."

KNOW HOW TO WRITE A GOOD PRESS RELEASE
Amy Blackmore: "You want your press release to read like the article you'll read in the paper. Journalists work very hard, and they appreciate having a release that allows them to pull information directly and put it in an article. That's how it works. Have a well-written release that tells the story. You're not just putting on a show; you're putting on a show because you were in Africa for three years and got inspired."

DON'T OVER-DO THE PROMOTION
Joey Elias: "Working at a radio station helps me with promotion, of course. I have my own internal network, and also a very big external network. But I don't promote myself on my own show. You really want to make sure that you're not diluting your message and over-saturating the market with yourself."

CREATE YOUR OWN OPPORTUNITIES TO PERFORM
Sugar Sammy: "If the comedy clubs aren't helping you out, organize your own shows. When I was just getting started, I would do everything I was offered: bars, night clubs, charity events, and school events. And while you're there, invite other comics in to watch you perform."

Everyone bombs once or twice. The first time I bombed, I quit for two years. That was a bad decision. You have to keep going. Tape yourself at every show and see what worked and what didn't. Learn from your mistakes and just make sure you don't make them again.

- Sugar Sammy, comedian

LIVING AS A PERFORMER

The life of a performer is not for everyone, and maybe you're still wondering if it's for you. Can you handle financial roller coaster? The wild applause followed by stony-faced silence? The phone that rings one day with, "Congrats, you've landed the lead!" but then doesn't ring again for a month? Our experts have all said, "Yes, bring it on!" They know what that commitment means, and they've got some advice for you. Have a listen:

YOU'LL NEED OPTIMISM AND COURAGE

Holly Gauthier-Frankel: "You certainly need to have a sort of permanent optimism and be able to handle not knowing if you're going to make any money. And you have to have a lot of courage. People say confidence, but it's more about self-love. Actors can be really insecure. They want that applause and instant gratification. But you need to trust that what you have to offer is always going to be valid, just maybe not exactly where you thought it would be."

KEEP YOUR INTEGRITY INTACT

Holly Gauthier-Frankel: "When considering a project, always evaluate what you're feeling, and don't go against your integrity. I don't do a lot of television; when I was aggressively pursuing that, I was going in for roles that were uncomfortable. Every actor has done roles just for the money, and sometimes you have to balance that to pay your bills. But try not to dwell in that realm for too long."

BE OPEN TO CONSTRUCTIVE CRITICISM

Amy Blackmore: "You need a thick but open skin and to not get offended by feedback. Feedback can be really beneficial. Sometimes I work with young artists who get very defensive about their work, and it's a big turn off!"

TRY TO STAY ON AN EVEN KEEL

Joey Elias: "If you're having a bad day, you have to figure out a way to somehow channel that negative energy into positive energy on stage. I remember having to do a show the day my grandfather passed away. I took all that sadness and I had a really good show that night. Give yourself at least an hour a day just for yourself to decompress."

DON'T TAKE YOUR YOUTH FOR GRANTED

Tristan D. Lalla: "Take care of your body, because no one else is going to do it for you. And don't take your youth for granted, it's not here forever."

BEWARE OF THE DOUBLE STANDARD FOR WOMEN
Holly Gauthier-Frankel: "As a woman, you encounter a whole different set of rules, especially when it's an image-based project. For a long time, weight was a huge issue for the kinds of roles that I was being sent in for. Sometimes they would want me to be forty pounds lighter, and that just wasn't who I was. I made myself pretty sick for a while. Eventually, I chose my soul and my integrity as a human. When I placed more importance on that, other things started coming in."

DON'T FORGET TO SCHEDULE DOWN-TIME
Amy Blackmore: "Take time for recuperation after a project. We pour our heart and soul into a project, and as soon as one is done, we're tempted to jump into another one. The adrenaline won't carry you forever, so it's important to take some down-time. It's good to start working on the next thing to have something to look forward to, but you need a brain break."

Holly Gauthier-Frankel: "I make sure I go outside at least once a day and try to do at least one leisure thing just for me."

KNOW WHAT YOU WANT YOUR LIFE TO LOOK LIKE
Holly Gauthier-Frankel: "I have to evaluate what's important to me and what my life will look like. I don't think it'll look like other people's lives, but I really don't know what everyone's lives look like. I blame film and television for making other people's lives look so apparent. But that's just an illusion; everyone's lives are completely unique."

CREATIVE TIME AND FAMILY TIME ARE BOTH IMPORTANT
Tristan D. Lalla: "Make sure you have a solid foundation of either family or friend support. A lot of us get caught up in our work, but our work is not who we are, it's what we do. As actors it's our job to be a mirror for society and tell human stories, but if you haven't lived, you can't do that. So don't forget about your real life, because that's what your art should reflect."

Joey Elias: "Another comic recently told me, after coming out of a long relationship, "At first, everything is hunky-dory, but then they realize that they're going to be our second love, no matter what." And that's very true. I started when I was young and I didn't prioritize properly. I'm so passionate about what I do, trying to polish everything into this perfect little nugget of a joke. But now I would say give yourself enough time for creativity and enough time for family."

KEEP WORK AND LIFE IN PERSPECTIVE
Holly Gauthier-Frankel: "I try to balance it all out. When I'm on my deathbed, I don't want to be thinking about that toaster commercial I did. I want to be thinking about my friends and the things that matter."

DON'T TRY TO DO EVERYTHING

Amy Blackmore: "You think that being busy is a positive thing, which it is; it means you're doing well. But if you're too busy, you might be a jack-of-all-trades but master of none. It's taken me years to understand that."

MULTI-TASKING IS A MYTH

Amy Blackmore: "It's hard to know where your work starts and ends as an artist. Everything you do is your art form. Dance is movement. Everything is dance! I have a space in my house for choreography and another one for writing, so that I can really focus on each. Multi-tasking is a myth! The only people who do it are moms because they have no choice."

COMPARTMENTALIZE

Holly Gauthier-Frankel: "If I'm feeling really overwhelmed, I have my twenty minute rule, where I'll sit down and work on only one thing for twenty minutes, then take a twenty minute break. Then do another thing. It's a stress-managing technique."

LIVE ONE DAY AT A TIME

Tristan D. Lalla: "Right now I've got tons of work, meanwhile my mom wants to see me, my grandmother wants to see me; I was supposed to have a date. But next week I've got nothing! So I take every day one step at a time. It's like when you're driving at night, you know where you're going, but all you can see is the road in the headlights five feet ahead. That's how I have to live every day. Those five feet in front of me are what I have to accomplish and I just trust that the road will bring me where I need to go. There might be a detour, but I'll get there eventually."

DON'T BE AFRAID TO RE-EVALUATE

Holly Gauthier-Frankel: "Always re-evaluate and check in with yourself. Maybe you'll wake up one morning and realize, jeez, this isn't what I wanted. I sit on the fence a lot, especially when the work makes me tired. It's healthy to take a step back. A while ago, when I wasn't being offered roles, I created a burlesque persona. That got me in the papers and even got me some film roles, all because people recognized 'that burlesque performer.'"

FIND YOUR VOICE

Tristan D. Lalla: "As a kid, I couldn't speak until I was about eight years old. It was a thing that nobody understood. They tried to give me hearing aids and all types of weird stuff. They would put me in different art classes to get me to communicate and I'd make things and break things—I'm really good at destroying things—and really good at creating things. The point I'm trying to make is that acting is just another way for me to communicate. And I think all performers are somehow like that."

FINAL THOUGHTS

Our experts have learned a lot of lessons in their years on the stage and screen. Most things they wouldn't change, but some they might tweak a bit. Here's their advice taken from things they might just do differently if given a chance. Having a look might save you some grief, so read on for their final words:

DON'T GET COMPLACENT

Joey Elias: "About three or four years into my career I got a little too comfy. It's always nice to have a home club where you know everything's going to work out. But if you perform at one club all the time, and create a comfort level, you're going to suffer when you go on the road. You can make all kinds of local jokes in the area you're familiar with, but what about when you venture away? Those don't fly anymore. The advice I'd give to young performers is don't get too comfortable in one area."

LISTEN TO YOUR BODY

Amy Blackmore: "Before I understood about delegation, I was working with a group and doing everything myself. It was ridiculous. When you're in your early twenties, it doesn't seem to matter if you don't sleep. But that's not the case. I ignored a lot of the warning signs and ended up suffering from anxiety for a year and a half. As an artist, your body is your tool, and you have to really respect it. My biggest mistake was not listening to my body."

DON'T BE AFRAID TO FAIL

Holly Gauthier-Frankel: "My mistake has been that I really try to micro-manage things, maybe because I'm afraid of what might happen if I don't. I hold myself back a lot. I let my doubts get in the way and I get paralyzed. For instance, my website took a year and a half when it should have taken six months. I was terrified that I would be making the wrong choices. You've just got to do it! I wish I hadn't held myself back from doing certain things, even if some of them ended up being crappy."

TRUST THE ROAD YOU'RE ON

Tristan D. Lalla: "Everything I had to go through is why I am where I am. I've made tons of mistakes; hiccups and failures and stumbles along the road. But I wouldn't change anything. I genuinely believe that everything happens the way it's supposed to, in its own time. It may not happen the way you want it to, but it's always on time."

THE OTHER SIDE OF THE CASTING COUCH
An Interview with Andrea Kenyon, President of Andrea Kenyon & Associates

Casting director Andrea Kenyon has run her own casting agency in Montreal for over twenty-five years. In that time, thousands of performers have come through her doors, strutting their stuff to land roles in indie flicks and Hollywood blockbusters. And in those years, Andrea's seen everything! With all that experience under her belt, we asked her what advice she'd have for emerging performers, so when it's their turn to show their stuff they'd make the right impression. Here's what Andrea had to say:

Besides the headshot, what kind of experience do you want to see on a CV? Do roles in student films or theatre count? What about other types of performing gigs?

When we're looking at a new performer, in general, we're not looking for specific criteria, but attempting to get to know or familiarize ourselves with, this new talent; we're taking stock. In an attempt to get a clearer picture of who the performer is, when reviewing a CV, we check the vital statistics (height, etc.), what type of training they have had (graduate program, workshops), whether they have done theatre (what kind of roles they have had, what theatre companies they have performed with), and if they have any film or TV experience (independent, large network or studio, which directors have they worked with).

We're hoping to find talent who is serious about their craft. Performers who have done professional theatre programs are the most encouraging, but pursuing various workshops can also contribute to the creation of a very qualified performer. It is ideal if a performer has participated in a professional theatre, television, or film production, with a known theatre company, network, or studio, as it acts as somewhat of an endorsement. However, having any experience is a plus. When we're searching for an actor for a specific role, obviously, we're looking to match up many qualities, including required experience and training level, perhaps physical demands, and, at times, their physical skills and abilities.

Any and all experience is valuable: student films, web series, university theatre plays, improv shows, professional theatre, film, and television. The experience tells us that the performer is familiar with the environment, the inner-workings and required skills of the medium, and the professionalism required to do the job; this is reassuring to any employer (producer, director, assistant director, casting director).

How crucial is an agent in the casting process? Does a performer really need representation to get an audition?

A talent agent is an asset to a performer and to the casting director. It is possible to get an audition without an agent, but it is less likely. On a daily basis, the established talent agent receives many audition notices (breakdowns) from all of the active casting directors across

Canada, and in some cases from American or European casting directors seeking Canadian performers for their productions that are shooting in Canada.

Due to general time constraints within the film and television industry (delivery of scripts, availability of name talent), and sometimes the very quick required turnaround, casting directors sometimes rely heavily on the submissions of the talent agents and access to interesting new talent suggestions. Casting directors know that the agents are in a position to be most tuned in to the developments of the performers on their roster. In order to meet the requirements of a quick turnaround, the casting director can streamline tasks by contacting one talent agent for several performers, rather than engaging with each performer individually. The agent will work with the performer to prepare them with all of the required materials and information. This is very time consuming, and it's helpful to the process when an agent is involved and part of the performer's team. For an actor, the agent provides access to many more productions than the individual could be aware of on their own.

What preparation should a performer do before attending an audition, beyond knowing the sides? Should they know anything about the casting director or the director?

In preparing for an audition, the performer should educate themselves, as much as possible, about the production: the genre, the director and his or her past productions (type of project, taste of actors' acting style), the script, the audition scenes, the other roles and actors in the scene, and the role itself. It doesn't hurt to be familiar with the casting director so you can maximize the situation: know how the casting director likes to proceed and how available and open they are to providing additional information.

Be sure to understand the significance of all the lines of dialogue and stage directions contained within the audition scenes. It is best not to plan gestures, as they can look rehearsed rather than real and natural. Make choices. Some choices will not be clear or definitive, but make educated choices based on what you have at your disposal. Be ready to change what you've prepared. The director will sometimes have a different vision or ask you to do a variation on the scene in order to test your versatility and work dynamic; you must be able to adjust and adapt. This encounter serves as a sample of the potential working relationship between you and the director, and, hopefully, an indication that you are somebody they would be able to, and would like to, work with.

What strategies can improve an emerging performer's chances of landing a great role?

To improve your potential for success as a performer, it's necessary to continue to train or study, to remain engaged in the process of acting—whether it be personal or professional projects—to continue to care for your instrument (your appearance and fitness), and to be professionally prepared with a talent agent. It is also important to have a current and appropriate CV and headshot. You should also have a well-prepared and professional-looking demo of your best work (not necessarily ALL of your work).

If you approach your career this way, you will be able to focus on the creation of a full life for each of the roles that you present in auditions. All of your work and professional behavior, during auditions and on set, will contribute to the snapshot the casting director has of you. And a good snapshot will improve your potential for landing the next amazing role. Make certain to educate your potential employers (like casting directors) about your noteworthy developments or accomplishments; send links to video materials, announcements of appearances on television or in films, and invites to plays.

Can a performer ever get feedback from a casting director if they don't get the role?

It is sometimes helpful to get feedback, but difficult to get, as the casting directors see many actors for many roles, and are sometimes required to work on more than one project at a time; time is at a premium. An agent can help by inquiring on your behalf and finding out whether the casting director has any constructive feedback or if the encounter was typical of the casting process. It is only after a string of unsuccessful auditions that feedback may even be warranted; otherwise, it is natural that the actor does not always get the part.

Is there any way "in" besides the ordinary audition process? How important is networking between casting directors and performers, for instance?

In order to feel in control of your destiny, it's best to remain engaged in the creative community, if not by making your own projects then by consuming and celebrating the creative works of others. That way, you'll maintain a connection to those who are and may be making the productions of tomorrow. Everything counts, everything matters, and all encounters may be just what somebody remembers the next time they, or someone they know, is searching for an actor with your unique qualities, skills, or experience.

There is no secret formula. Stay engaged in your passion on all fronts, continue to learn, create your own work if professional projects are not on the immediate horizon, always do your best no matter the size or budget of the production, apply yourself fully, and be professional at all times.

Enjoy the process, even if the role is only yours for the ten minutes of the audition. Remember to base your self-worth on YOUR assessment of your efforts and attentiveness, NOT on whether or not you get the part. You know that if you have done your best, you have reason to be proud of yourself. This will reverberate into your essence at auditions and serve as a vital part of the presence that supports your goals of being cast!

Andrea Kenyon is president and casting director at Andrea Kenyon & Associates. Celebrating over thirty-five years in casting, she is a member of the Casting Society of America, Casting Directors of Canada, Casting Directors Association of Quebec, the Academy of Television Arts & Sciences, and the Academy of Canadian Cinema and Television.

PHOTOGRAPHERS

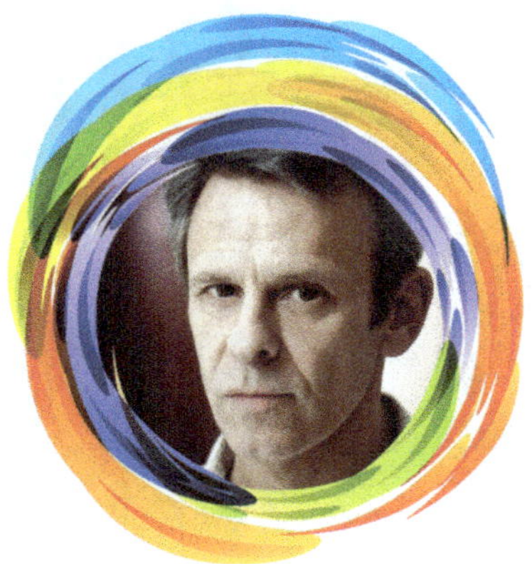

Roger LeMoyne

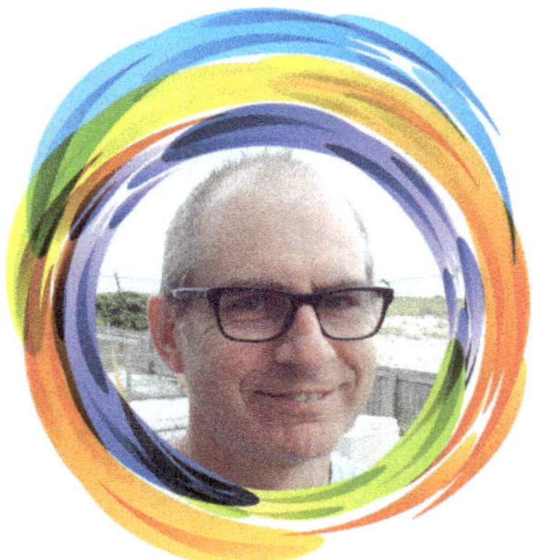

Paul Litherland

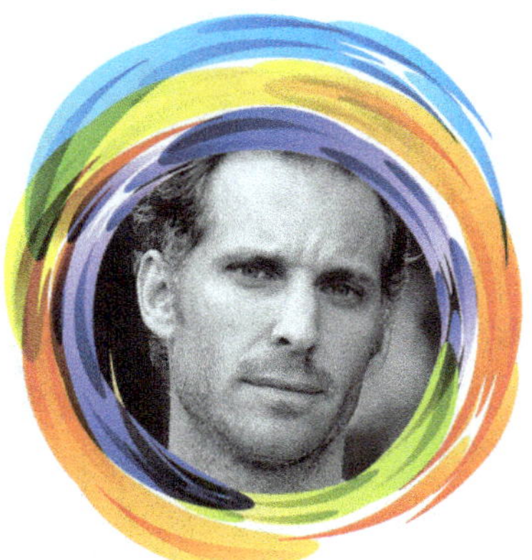

Marcel Mueller

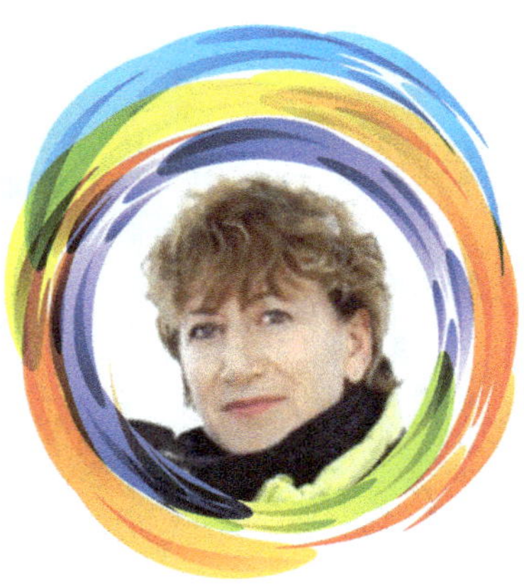

Linda Rutenberg

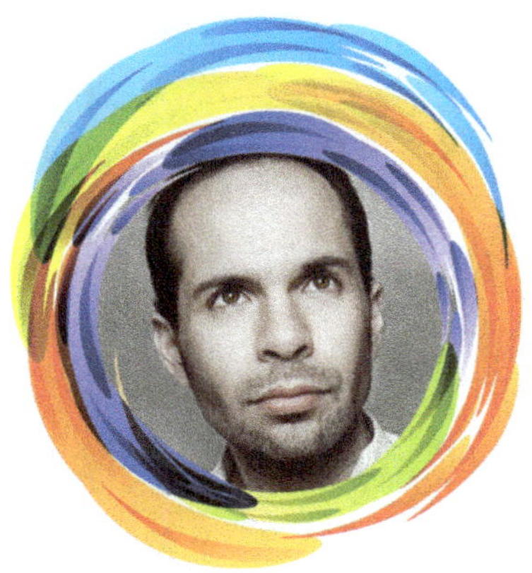

Damian Siqueiros

Having a goal in front of you makes a big difference. The question of where you want to be in five years is always relevant.

- Paul Litherland, fine art photographer

SO YOU WANNA BE A PHOTOGRAPHER?

You've been fascinated by still images your whole life. It continually astounds you how a story can be told through a series of frames. Perhaps photography began as a hobby and then blossomed into a way of life.

Now you plan to embark on a journey, camera in hand, to capture the struggle for democracy in some far-off land. Or perhaps you want to photograph beautiful landscapes closer to home. We're sure you have the skills behind the lens to get your project off the ground, but do you have what it takes to get your work off your hard drive and into the spotlight?

In this chapter, we offer help and advice from professional photographers who all started small but are well known today in their field.

Photographers are employable in a number of areas. If you're unsure where your talents are best put to use, consider the sampling of occupations listed in the National Occupation Classification, published by Employment and Social Development Canada:

> Event photographer

> Editorial photographer

> Evidence photographer

> Fashion photographer

> Finish photographer

> Forensic photographer

> Medical photographer

> Multimedia photographer

> Photojournalist

> Police photographer

> Portrait photographer

> Scientific photographer

> Videographer

> Wildlife photographer

THE EXPERTS

We spoke to the following accomplished photographers for a snapshot of the field today:

Roger LeMoyne studied cinema at Concordia University in Montreal. Since the early 1990s, he has documented conflict, human rights issues, and international aid around the world. His work has appeared in publications such as *Paris Match, Life, Time, Maclean's, Canadian Art, COLORS, Geo,* and Unicef annual reports. His images have garnered more than fifty awards internationally, including the Michener-Deacon Fellowship (2013), Canada Council Grant (2013), CALQ grant (2009), Dorothea Lange Prize (2007), World Understanding Award (POYi, 2006), Prix Bayeux-Calvados (2006), Alexia Grant (2004), and World Press Photo (1999). A freelancer his entire career, his photos are distributed by Getty Images and Redux Pictures. Find Roger's work at http://rogerlemoyne.com.

Paul Litherland is a visual artist/performer living in Montreal. His wide-ranging practice incorporates themes of masquerade, vulnerability, and machismo, explored through photography and multimedia performances. His exhibitions in national and international venues have been reviewed in the *Globe and Mail, Artnews, the New Yorker, the Montreal Gazette, the Hindu* (India), *Diario Monitor* (Mexico). He studied photography and fine art at the Emily Carr College of Art and Design in Vancouver and graduated from the MFA program in photography from Concordia in 1994. For further information about the artist and artwork, please visit the website paullitherland.com.

Linda Rutenberg's one enduring passion has been to create unique photographic images. Her fine art work has been exhibited internationally and can be found in many prestigious collections. Linda has also produced several books: *Mont Royal — A World Apart, The Secret Series* on North American cities (with ECW Press), *The Garden at Night, After Midnight,* and *The English Garden at Night,* a travelling exhibition. Linda's current project is called *The Gaspé Peninsula: Land on the Edge of Time.* It is a three-year photographic exploration of winter that includes a book, a travelling exhibition, workshops, and lectures. Have a look at http://lindarutenberg.com.

Marcel Mueller is an experienced and professional travel photographer, guide, speaker, and mostly world traveller. Through extensive travel in over seventy-five countries, he has given birth to a collection of images dedicated to Asian philosophies, Middle Eastern civilizations, and the hardship and beauty of the African soil. A bank of photographs inspired by *Temba the Tibetan* has become the source of Marcel Mueller Photography, the portal for his images and the trademark of DIRXIONS, the foundation of his work and his vision. Inspire the desire to discover our world. Check it out at www.marcelmuellerphotography.com.

Damian Siqueiros, as a commercial photographer, helps clients find their visual voice and express themselves through compelling imagery that makes a long-lasting impression. As an artist, he is an avid defender of gender equality and the acceptance of diversity. His work has been exhibited in museums and galleries throughout North America, South America, and Europe. Damian has had the opportunity to work with renowned artists such as choreographer Sidi Larbi Cherkaoui and Canadian dance icon Margie Gillis. You can see what Damian is up to at www.damiansiqueiros.com.

Here's what they had to say, photographer to photographer:

WHO NEEDS PHOTOGRAPHY SCHOOL?

Our panel told us that while school isn't a strict requirement, it still provides a stepping stone into the world of professional photography.

According to our experts, studying photography in school gives you the opportunity to master the technical aspects while taking it at your own pace. "When you're working, you don't have as much time to explore your craft," says Linda Rutenberg. "Going to school really gives you the time to research and explore your art. It's also the ideal space for networking with your peers and accomplished professionals." Rutenberg adds, "It permits you to learn about other photographers' ideas and it's a great source of inspiration."

It's all about the KISS principle: Keep It Simple Stupid. Show less and show really strong work.
- Linda Rutenberg, fine art photographer

HOW DO YOU SHOW WHAT YOU'VE GOT?

Besides your actual camera, the most important tool you'll need to start working as a professional photographer is a portfolio. And today that means an eye-catching website. Lucky you're a photographer! It's bound to look amazing. Your site should contain all the reasons why someone should hire you: the perfect combo of arresting photographs, solid credentials, and a sincere artistic vision. Here's what our experts say about putting your best foot forward:

YOUR WEBSITE IS FOR PROMOTION BUT ALSO FOR SELLING

Linda Rutenberg: "Ask yourself who you're trying to attract. Other photographers? No. Your website is there to show your work to curators and clients both for promotion and sales. It is important that it is cohesive. You can show a selection of work; keep it clear and easy to traverse. The worst thing is when websites are all over the place."

TARGET YOUR PORTFOLIO

Damian Siqueiros: "Your portfolio has to be very clean. You have to be very selective of the photos you put in it because those types of photos are the kinds of clients you're going to get. This is especially true for publicity work. There are so many photographers that if you don't have what they're looking for, they'll call someone else. Represent with your images where you want to go."

CRAFT YOUR CV AND BUSINESS CARD

Marcel Mueller: "You need a professional CV and an artistic CV. It's better to distinguish things like where you went to school and your professional jobs from the projects you've worked on independently or shows you've been a part of. And don't forget, you'll need a memorable business card."

My mentors have helped me a lot in becoming business savvy. I met most of them during my studies, but YES was also really important in terms of coaching.

- Damian Siqueiros, fine art photographer

GETTING STARTED

Your friends took you to see a Mapplethorpe exhibit and you didn't blink an eye. You've participated in a number of photo shoots and thought, "Yeah, but wait till they get a load of me." You may be ready to burst into the world of art or commercial photography, but is the world of photography ready for you?

Don't quit your day job just yet. Our experts told us it takes time to develop a name in the industry and cultivate a loyal clientele. That will come with talent, vision, and ongoing efforts to hone your craft as well as your business or practice.

Here, in their own words, is what our experts told us about getting started in photography:

DEFINE WHO YOU ARE AS A PHOTOGRAPHER

Linda Rutenberg: "When I started out, I did freelance work because people needed photographs for all sorts of reasons. I didn't necessarily want to do those jobs, like weddings or catalogue work, but it was a way for me to find what I loved and what I hated."

Damian Siqueiros: "Be true to yourself. Once you know what you want, you can bend enough to make it work without breaking. You'll be faced with a lot of situations, like negotiations, that will ask you to compromise. Find the things that you do like and keep nourishing those things."

SPECIALIZE AND GAIN CREDIBILITY

Paul Litherland: "The more you can specialize in something you're interested in, the better you'll be able to discern a market. If you just say, 'I'm a photographer,' and you take anything that comes, it's too big. People have a much easier time when you say 'I photograph this exact thing really well.'"

DEVELOP YOUR TECHNICAL SKILLS

Damian Siqueiros: "Before becoming a full-time photographer, I was an art assistant at a publicity agency and living off academic and creation grants for my master's degree. Working as an art assistant was mostly tedious Photoshop composite work, but it took my editing skills to the next level."

HAVE CONFIDENCE

Roger LeMoyne: "Your inner dialogue will determine your level of confidence. Learn how to think positive without deluding yourself."

DON'T THINK YOU CAN GO IT ALONE

Linda Rutenberg: "You have to seek out people who can help you; it's impossible for one artist to do everything. You need a group of people around you who can give you advice and want to be part of your experience."

Paul Litherland: "Most people are pretty available. If you say, 'I need help setting up my business and I'd like to know how you've done it,' people have time for that, because they know it was hard for them."

FIND YOUR NETWORK

Marcel Mueller: "Make your LinkedIn profile and find what groups you want to be associated with. Ninety-five percent of the people who will connect with your site will be other photographers. So you're creating a network of photographers. There are also a lot of forums. Google 'forum travel photography' and a bunch of different organizations will pop up. Join the forums and sign up for the newsletters. People will be asking all kinds of questions, ones you want to ask yourself."

GET A BUSINESS COACH

Linda Rutenberg: "What I did, way too late, was take on a business coach. I'd say everyone needs to do that early on. It will really help get your administrative work under control and help figure out exactly what direction you're heading in."

OR TAKE A BUSINESS COURSE

Paul Litherland: "I thought I could wing it, but that wasn't working out. Then I was referred to a business development program. That's where I learned to make a business plan with a three-year outlook and goals to obtain in those three years. That was really a wake-up call. The difference between cash flow and actually making money is huge. Making money is what's left after you've put your cash flow back into your business."

LOOK FOR A MENTOR

Roger LeMoyne: "You need to hang with the right people. Keep your eye out for a mentor and nurture relationships with mentors."

COMBINE PHOTOGRAPHY WITH OTHER SKILLS AND INTERESTS

Marcel Mueller: "I tell my photography students to make sure they attach their other skills and interests to their work. For instance, when I was starting out, I collected all the photos I'd accumulated over ten years of being a travel guide. I began showing them in galleries. It gave me an edge to be showing images from Yemen and other places that other people didn't even know about. If you don't blend together different interests, you won't be successful as a photographer."

As soon as you have something publishable, work hard at getting it published. Have a relentless presence in the marketplace, in every medium possible. Publishing is the best form, of course. Publish or perish.

- Roger LeMoyne, photojournalist

TAKING IT TO THE NEXT LEVEL

Great, you landed a gig as a photography assistant to the city's premier wedding photographer. You learned as much about portraiture and proper lighting in those years as you did about networking and managing raging brides. You've got a pretty good sense of what it takes to be self-employed in the arts.

Now, you're ready for your journey. You have the technical know-how to pull it off, combined with confidence in your creative vision and a strong belief in the value of your work.

We've asked our panel of experts to share their thoughts on making it as a professional photographer. They had loads of advice on the photography business today, financing your projects, and getting noticed in the field. Have a look:

I. THE PHOTOGRAPHY BUSINESS

SCOUT OUT THE MARKET
Roger LeMoyne: "[In photojournalism], photography jobs are typically doled out by photo editors. Study the market of your choice. Find out who the real buyer is in that area. Offer them free services for a while, recognizing that this is a learning experience for you and therefore a fair exchange. But don't work for free for very long. You will either become useful and therefore worth paying, or not. You need to build their confidence in your abilities."

PITCH WRITTEN CONTENT WITH PHOTOS
Marcel Mueller: "First you find out which magazines talk about the type of photography you're doing, and which are in your area. For instance, I would propose a story on an adventure that I've done in my travels. I'll pitch a story with photographs, and that's where I've got an advantage. And I can write in English and in French. You won't get huge amounts of money for it, but you'll get a good credit for your portfolio."

PRICING JOBS REQUIRES RESEARCH
Damian Siqueiros: "Never give a price when you first talk with a client, and never give a price without considering your needs first. Unless you've done something similar a thousand times, you need to do your research."

RESPECTABLE PRICES GARNER RESPECT

Paul Litherland: "I started off with a very limited number of clients and I didn't know how to really run a business. I thought price was everything, but that wasn't working. Eventually, I ended up doubling my rates. That got rid of all the clients who complained! When you charge more for your service, you want to deliver a better product. Your clients expect more, but have more confidence in you. It goes both ways."

SHARPEN YOUR NEGOTIATION SKILLS

Damian Siqueiros: "Work on your negotiating skills; be firm and comfortable with silences. Make sure to write down everything you'll need before starting any discussions. And you should be the one making the contract. You can create a standard one that sets out what you're giving the client. This gives you the upper-hand. Whatever you do, don't be intimidated by your clients. Remember that this might be the first step of a lasting business relationship. You should start by establishing a cordial, respectful, and balanced one."

GET PROFESSIONAL HELP

Marcel Mueller: "I'm not a business-savvy person. I could do the accounting, but I'm not good at it. I learned quickly that I would save time by getting an accountant. I know how to use a lightroom and I have other technical photography skills, but I don't know how to use Photoshop. I hire people for that."

OR INVEST IN ACCOUNTING SOFTWARE

Paul Litherland: "There's software that you can buy that will allow you to do a pretty good job with accounting and tax calculations."

CONSIDER BARTERING

Linda Rutenberg: "The nice part about photography is that everybody needs photographs of themselves or their business for the Internet. I found an accountant who loved photography, so I was able to trade my photographic services for accounting services."

II. FINANCING AND MAKING MONEY

PREPARE TO SPEND YOUR OWN MONEY

Paul Litherland: "To start a business, you need at least a year's income somewhere. If you only have enough for the next month, you won't be able to relax."

Linda Rutenberg: "If I'm looking for something very specific, like plane fare to Israel, I would look for some sort of funding that supports relationships between Canada and Israel. I put the money up front, then hopefully get reimbursed. I've gone into debt many times because of that. But I was very determined to do my project."

Marcel Mueller: "In photography, you have a huge initiation fee for your equipment, your cameras, your software. The first type of financing is love-money from your parents and family."

DON'T OVEREXTEND YOURSELF

Paul Litherland: "Don't try to go too big too soon. People can get themselves into trouble if they buy a lot of equipment and get themselves into debt. If you are overextended financially, you won't make it through a slow period, especially at the beginning."

APPLY FOR GRANTS, BUT DON'T DEPEND ON THEM

Damian Siqueiros: "Grants aren't a lottery, but they feel like it. You need to have everything right, and there are so many artists applying at the same time. Grants are important to give credibility to an artist's career, so you should apply, but don't make them your only option for financing. When it comes to funding, I rely more heavily on building a successful art business than getting a grant."

GET HELP WITH YOUR PROPOSALS

Linda Rutenberg: "Try to get help from senior artists and have a look at how people write grant proposals. There's a certain way to do it. You have to show the historical context, the continuity between what you're doing now and what you want to do."

SEEK SPONSORSHIPS

Linda Rutenberg: "It's all about sponsorship for me. I get individuals and companies to sponsor me in return for some of my work. For my Gaspé project the sponsors are Gaspé companies who would like a little publicity. You don't need to get a lot of money from each company, because it adds up very quickly. I'm having a show in a museum in the Gaspé and it's an opportunity for them to have their name plastered on things, and that's what they want, PR."

REQUEST DOWN-PAYMENTS WHEN YOU CAN

Roger LeMoyne: "I always need financing because I almost always shoot foreign stories. The money comes from magazines, the UN, foundations, grants, unpredictable sources like selling stills for inclusion in films, museums, agency sales, and book covers."

TRY CROWDFUNDING

Linda Rutenberg: "Kickstarter and Indiegogo are two new ways of crowdfunding, but if I looked at the people who contributed to my funding campaign, it's about 90 percent from my list and 10 percent via Kickstarter. You don't just put it out there and hope unknown people will support it. You have to work at it with your own contacts."

Damian Siqueiros: "Crowdfunding is really relevant nowadays, but it's a lot of work. It's very difficult for me because I'm not that sociable, and it requires that you send personal emails asking for money. A good crowdfunding campaign mixes social media promotion with consistent human personal interaction. Indiegogo is the one I've used. The first time I used it, it was good. The second time, someone else managed it and it was an all or nothing campaign. We ended up with nothing."

III. GETTING VISIBILITY

These days everybody's a photographer, right? After all, with an iPhone in hand and a bit of drama on the street, your protest photo could go viral on five continents in twenty-four hours. But, wait a minute, a few viral images doesn't make a professional photographer. You have to be recognized as the real deal.

Here are some tips to enhance your online presence:

CREATE AN IMPRESSIVE WEBSITE

Marcel Mueller: "The website was the main way to get visibility. It took a lot of time, but I made it with advice from people who are in web design."

ON SOCIAL MEDIA YOU'RE THE STORY

Linda Rutenberg: "For me, what's important when using social media is that it's human. It's really important to express what you're passionate about. You don't want dry communication. That's boring. When I do my blog, it has to sound like I'm speaking. Ultimately, they want to know Linda. It's not about photography, it's about my story, my hard work, my vision, how I do it. A lot of people don't have time to have their own adventures, so they live vicariously through mine and that's what intrigues them. People want to be entertained and engaged in your project."

BALANCE PERSONAL AND PROFESSIONAL

Damian Siqueiros: "You have to be slightly personal, without putting up a picture of yourself in your pyjamas—unless you're wacky and that's part of your brand or artistic identity. It's good to show that you're human. And part of the human experience is to struggle and commiserate. People trust Trip Advisor because they don't just show the positive reviews; they leave in some of the bad ones."

DON'T TREAT SOCIAL MEDIA AS AD SPACE

Damian Siqueiros: "If you always address people on social media like you are advertising something, it won't work. People go on social media for leisure. They're there for the show, not the commercial. Give them interesting content, not only about your work, but also about what you are passionate about, things that interest you, helpful tips within your expertise. This will make you a well-rounded person in your followers' eyes."

TRY OLD-FASHIONED EMAIL

Marcel Mueller: "I find sending out a regular email newsletter is better for me than social media. My list has been built over the years. I find it's more personal. I don't want to be out there too much, harassing people."

MANAGE YOUR ONLINE TIME

Linda Rutenberg: "You shouldn't be looking at your email more than twice a day, fifteen minutes each time. You don't want to become a slave to your email. It will take you away from the things you need to do."

And here are their tips for getting the attention of traditional media:

HAVE A GOOD PRESS RELEASE AND A COMPELLING STORY

Damian Siqueiros: "Having a good press release is very important. It requires a lot of work, so it's only for specific projects. You have to be able to express what your project is about very articulately, make it compelling, and show why you're passionate about it. Most written media will print your press release instead of creating original content about it. Make sure that your text is accurate, well written, and easy to read. I just finished a project called From Russia with Love, which spoke about sexual diversity rights in Russia. It ended up being in a lot of magazines. Be grateful for that exposure and to the journalists who covered it. A little thank you note leaves the door open for the next time."

STAND OUT FROM THE CROWD

Linda Rutenberg: "Journalists receive hundreds of packets every day. So how are you going to stand out? For instance, if I'm about to go on television in the middle of summer to promote my book that takes place in the winter, I'll show up with my winter clothes on. I'll make people laugh. People will remember the project and the crazy woman with the red hat and the orange coat."

BE TOPICAL

Roger LeMoyne: Re: photojournalism: "You've got to do things that connect with leading stories. You don't have to do it when it is dangerous, you just need to follow important stories, their ebb and flow."

And here is their general marketing advice:

DEVELOP A STRONG BRAND/ARTISTIC IDENTITY

Damian Siqueiros: "Having a strong brand doesn't mean you're being pigeon-holed. A strong brand or identity can be broad enough to include different kinds of work. People need to know that you can be versatile within your artistic identity and that there's a coherency to your vision. Artists with a strong brand, those are the people who get the biggest jobs and they're the ones who go down in history. Being eclectic without any stylistic coherence, you might have more day-to-day work, but you will never have a recognizable body of work. It might be tougher at the beginning, having a specific style, but it will bear more fruit in the end."

USE AN IDENTIFIABLE LOGO

Linda Rutenberg: "I have a logo and the logo goes on everything that I do. It's on my website, it's on my business card. I think it's important. My teaching, lectures, private lessons, sales, exhibitions, and books all fall under my branding as a fine art photographer.

MARKETING IS CREATIVE; TRY DOING IT YOURSELF

Marcel Mueller: "I did pay someone to take a look at the branding and marketing side of it, but in the end it was a lot of blah-blah. Getting hooked by a company that promises to take care of your branding… It becomes very expensive for something you can do mostly yourself."

DO A SURVEY

Paul Litherland: "The most successful promotion I ever did was the survey for my business plan. I asked questions to potential clients like what price they expected to pay for my services. I wasn't really telling them to use my service, I was just asking them what they wanted. Inevitably, halfway through the interview, they'd ask for my phone number. Because I wasn't putting pressure on them to become a client, by the end of my market survey process I had a pile of clients."

SET ASIDE TIME FOR PROMOTION

Damian Siqueiros: "I set aside part of my time for promotion and part of my time for creation. I think that promotion is half the success of your work. You can have great work, but if nobody sees it…"

NURTURE PERSONAL CLIENT RELATIONSHIPS

Linda Rutenberg: "You have to contact people individually and personally. Sometimes it's a question of having a list and going and taking someone out for a coffee, asking them 'what do you need?' The bottom line is, as a service, what can you do to make someone else's job easy? There's a saying that 20 percent of your clients make up 80 percent of your business and it's true."

WORD OF MOUTH WORKS BEST

Paul Litherland: "Word of mouth is really the [networking tool] that works the best. You do a good job for someone and they like working with you, they will work with you again and recommend you to someone else. Happy clients are going to give you more happy clients. I used to advertise in the classifieds. That brought me difficult clients because they didn't know or trust me. With word of mouth, the level of trust is already established. When you start from zero, the clients are much harder to please and they're always suspicious that you're trying to rip them off."

BE PERSISTENT

Damian Siqueiros: "It's very important that you promote yourself. If you want someone specific to be your client, you have to send them an email. If they don't answer, send a follow up. One of my personal heroes, the choreographer Sidi Larbi Cherkaoui, was going to come to Montreal to perform in 2012 for a dance festival. I tried to approach him through all the formal ways and I wasn't getting though. So I decided to find his Facebook and send him a personal message. In the end he responded and was incredibly nice. He gave me four hours of his time at my studio and I got photos of him."

KEEP IN TOUCH WITH YOUR BEST CLIENTS

Paul Litherland: "The clients that I really like working with, I make sure to contact them every few months just to say hello, inquire about what's coming up for them. It doesn't necessarily precipitate work right then, but it lets them know I'm still interested."

EXPAND YOUR NETWORK BEYOND PHOTOGRAPHY

Linda Rutenberg: "I belong to a women's networking group that has been extremely helpful and supportive; they all have lots of contacts. It's about meeting professional women who are well connected and are in the business world, who have enough money to either buy things themselves or can hook you up with people who would be interested in buying things."

REACH FOR THE STARS

Damian Siqueiros: "It's not easy or obvious, but sometimes you just need to go for it and send your portfolio out for something unattainable. A lot of the fears that other people will warn you of are socially constructed."

I'll be honest: once every few months I wake up and think, 'That's enough. Time to do something else.' The counter-argument is that photography is my passion. How many people look at artists and say, 'I wish I had that freedom?'

- Marcel Mueller, travel photographer

LIVING AS A PHOTOGRAPHER

Living life as a professional photographer these days is tough, no doubt about it. Competition is stiff, technology is constantly changing, and, like any artist, achieving a good work-life balance is challenging. But for those passionate about the craft, there's no life like it. Our experts had lots to say about how to manage the lifestyle and the kinds of skills you'll need to get you over the bumps in the road:

KEEP YOUR BASIC PRIORITIES STRAIGHT

Marcel Mueller: "I'm a bit of a dreamer. You have to be comfortable managing your life day to day if you're like that. You need a roof over your head, three meals a day, and your health. Keeping those very basic needs in mind enables me to find my priorities, both in my work and my life."

FIND A BALANCE FOR PERSONAL AND PROFESSIONAL PROJECTS

Paul Litherland: "I think of it in percentages. For practical reasons, maybe I have to give 60 percent to my photography business, but then I'll make sure I give 40 percent to my personal artistic projects."

BE COMFORTABLE CONNECTING

Marcel Mueller: "I always concentrate on the fact that while I'm shooting someone with the camera, I'm also interacting with them. You need to be aware of the cultural background and the energy. And know how to get out of a delicate situation."

DEVELOP YOUR EMOTIONAL IQ

Roger LeMoyne: "Emotional IQ is what so much of doing business is about. You also need emotional IQ to work with your subjects. In photography, emotional IQ is more important than IQ."

EXPECT TO SOLVE PROBLEMS

Damian Siqueiros: "I don't think you have to have a certain type of personality to be a photographer, but you need to be the one who solves problems instead of making them. If things aren't working, don't be hasty in breaking things off. Don't stomp out of the room. Try to build good relationships with your clients It works much better than being a diva."

BE ORGANIZED IN BUSINESS, IF NOT IN LIFE
Damian Siqueiros: "Artistic types tend to be a bit messy—I know I am. That's fine, but make sure you're organized with your images. Have a system to classify them. Be organized with your accounting and with your time. Make sure you get something done every day."

KEEP A TO-DO LIST
Linda Rutenberg: "You're doing everything yourself, so it's a question of being clear about what direction you're going in. Every day you need to make a to-do list and you need to know what your priorities are—with dates accompanying them when things need to get accomplished. A to-do list for today, this week, this month, and long-term goals. It gives you a sense of accomplishment, crossing things off your list."

MAKE SURE YOUR LOVED ONES ARE COOL WITH THE LIFESTYLE
Damian Siqueiros: "Being a freelancer is very different from working nine to five. People might think you're working less; they might think your life is great. But when I have an idea, it doesn't matter what time it is. I need to deal with it right away. Your partner should know your schedule will be all over the place. My husband knows that my art is a priority. He knows that I work a lot, and it doesn't mean that I don't love him."

GET COMFORTABLE WITH FINANCIAL UPS AND DOWNS
Marcel Mueller: "One month you'll have nothing, the next month you'll be fine. The financial insecurity is huge. It's not just when you're twenty-two and right out of school. At forty-six, I still have that. You have to be comfortable living that type of life."

FINAL THOUGHTS

Finally, some parting words based on what our experts might have done a tad differently if they had to do all over again:

GET SOME BUSINESS TRAINING
Linda Rutenberg: "If I had to redo things, I would take on a business coach much earlier in my career. A lot of artists don't want to think about the business side of things; they think it interferes with the creative process. But the bottom line is if you don't have money, you can't do your projects. Artists need to change their attitudes. One day a week you should spend with your organization/marketing hat on, then the rest of the week you can spend on your art. For me, that was a mistake."

DON'T "JUST SAY NO"
Roger LeMoyne: "If you want to keep a client, then you can't cherry pick the jobs that client offers. Turning down jobs is really un-cool. You don't have to do any job. I don't do weddings, for example, even when people offer good rates. But if you want to keep a particular client, you should do any job for them that's reasonable."

SILENCE YOUR INNER PERFECTIONIST

Marcel Mueller: "I'm a perfectionist. I've wasted a lot of time worrying about where that dot is going, or whether or not something is the exact right thing to put out there. But if it isn't out there, no one will ever see it! I regret not getting some of my older projects out there. I don't want to count how many hours I wasted making my website. Two years it took me!"

KEEP YOUR CAREER FRUSTRATIONS TO YOURSELF

Paul Litherland: "The absolute biggest mistake I ever made was telling a client that I was thinking of doing something else. She transmitted that message to a pile of different people. That cost me everything. I saw my business fade. The message was out that I was getting fed up, so they found someone else. I made sure to look after my main regular clients, so they would see me still working and I managed to survive that period. But if you need someone to commiserate with, it shouldn't be a client."

VISUAL ARTISTS

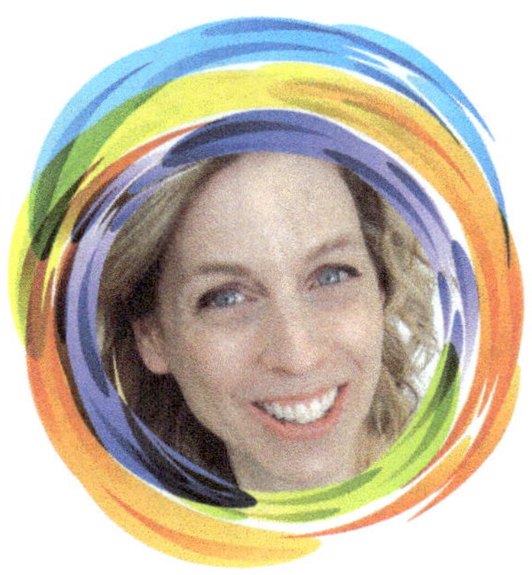

Nathalie Dion

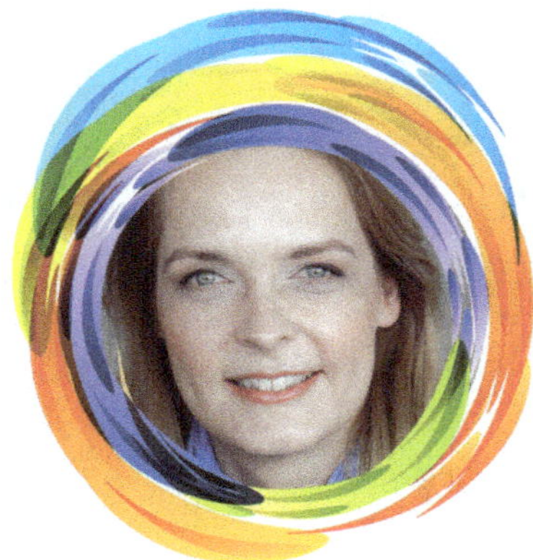

Bettina Forget

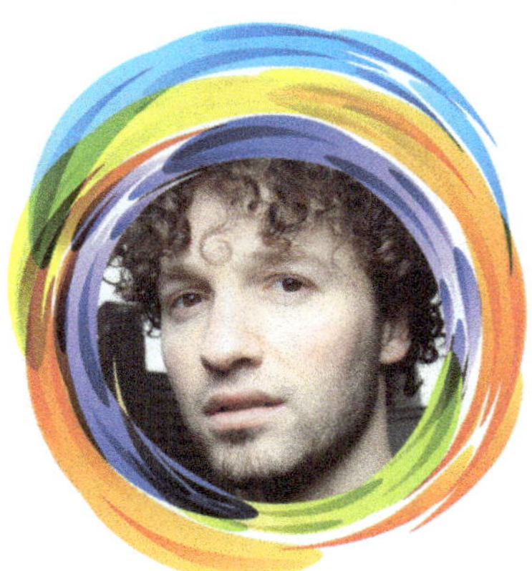

Adad Hannah

G. Scott MacLeod

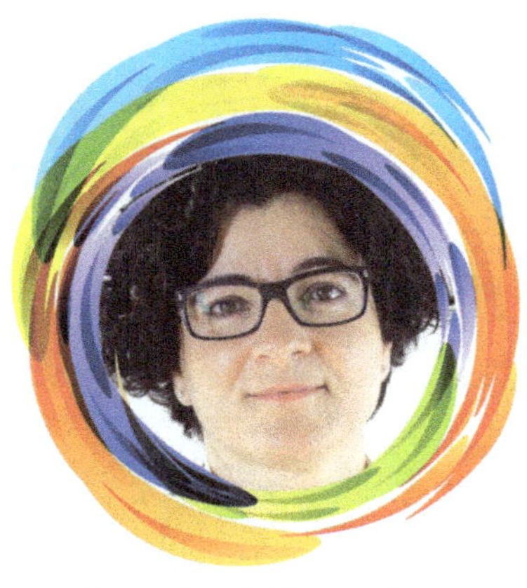

Rachel Stephan

I'm a little jealous of people who work nine to five. They get home, they drink a beer, and they're not thinking about work at all. Whereas, I always have a to-do list that I know will never get done.

- Adad Hannah, visual artist

SO YOU WANNA BE A VISUAL ARTIST?

Remember how much fun you had the first time you experimented with a finger-painting kit? Remember how you used your stubby little fingers to draw all over the brown paper laid down for you on the kitchen table?

If you still enjoy the thrill of dragging your paint brush through a glob of paint, pressing down on an empty canvas, and creating your own little world, or if you crave expressing yourself with chalk, pencil, or anything else you'd find at an art supply store, then this chapter is for you.

In this section, we offer help and advice from several visual artists making a living—and headlines—with their work.

Finding a steady source of income as an artist isn't always easy. You may want to consider supplementing the revenue from your fine art projects with other work. As a highly creative individual, you likely have a series of transferable skills that can be put to use in many occupations like those listed in the National Occupation Classification, published by Employment and Social Development Canada:

> 3D animation artist

> Advertising designer

> Animator

> Art teacher

> Cartoonist

> Commercial artist

> Fine artist

> Graphic artist

> Illustrator

> Layout designer

> Medical or scientific illustrator

> Multimedia designer

> Printmaker

> Video artist

THE EXPERTS

We spoke with the following accomplished visual artists to get a view of the landscape:

Nathalie Dion's talent flourished in the textile and fashion industry after graduating from Concordia University in design arts. It was during this period, in 1995, that she crossed paths with Anna Goodson, who soon became her agent. Nathalie specialized in creating settings where elegance and humour intertwined. She has collaborated with a number of publications including *Elle Québec, Coup de Pouce, the Los Angeles Times, the Wall Street Journal, the Boston Globe, Chatelaine, Modern Brides, Health, Best Health, Redbook, Red, Simon & Schuster*, and *Random House*. See Nathalie's work at www.agoodson.com/portfolio/nathalie-dion/.

Bettina Forget is the owner and director of Visual Voice Gallery, Visual Voice Lab, and Visual Voice Collections. All three enterprises are aimed at introducing contemporary art to a wider audience. Bettina also produces and edits the online art magazine the *Belgo Report* and serves on the board of the English-Language Arts Network (ELAN) as vice-president and representative for visual arts. Born in Germany, Bettina has studied at Central St-Martins School of Art in London, England, at Curtin University in Perth, Australia, and Nanyang Academy of Fine Arts in Singapore. She now lives and works in Montreal. Find out more about Bettina at www.bettinaforget.com.

Adad Hannah has produced commissioned projects for museums around the world and been exhibited and collected widely. He has been awarded numerous grants and prizes. His work can be found in the permanent collections of many institutions including the Musée d'art contemporain de Montréal, National Gallery of Canada, Montreal Museum of Fine Arts, Museo Tamayo (Mexico City), Samsung LEEUM Museum (Seoul), Zacheta National Gallery of Art (Warsaw), La collection Prêt d'œuvres d'art du Musée national des beaux-arts du Québec, and the Canada Council Art Bank / La Banque d'oeuvres d'art du Conseil des Arts du Canada. He is represented by Pierre-François Ouellette Art Contemporain and Equinox Gallery. Check out his work at www.adadhannah.com.

G. Scott MacLeod received a D.E.C. in fine arts at John Abbott College, a BFA and MA from Concordia University, attended the Banff Centre on the Tevie and Arliss Miller scholarship, and studied master works at the Uffizi Gallery in Florence on the Elizabeth T. Greenshields Scholarship. Scott is a fellow at the Helene Wurlitzer Foundation of New Mexico and a recipient of the William Blair Bruce European Travel Fine Arts Scholarship, and an affiliate at the COHDS at Concordia University. His work has been collected by corporations and museums, and he continues to consult and lecture on better business and creative art practices. See his work at www.macleod9.com.

Rachel Stephan is president of sensov/event marketing, a boutique agency helping small to large associations promote their national and international meetings and events through 360/5 inbound and outbound marketing campaigns. Rachel has over eighteen years of event marketing experience. She is a prominent speaker in marketing and business circles, including engagements with Marketing Professionals International (MPI) and the Professional Convention Management Association (PCMA). Rachel is fluent in three languages and holds a master's degree in advertising and graphic arts. See more about the agency at www.sensov.com.

Here's what they had to say, artist to artist:

WHO NEEDS ART SCHOOL?

While true artistic talent and vision can be developed outside of an academic environment, most of our experts noted the benefits of a good art education. Acclaimed visual artist Adad Hannah told us, "These days, it seems school is becoming more and more necessary for artists." He also spoke about the important contacts an artist can make at school that can last a lifetime. "When you do a bachelor's degree, you're a young cohort and everything is fast and fun. Then for your master's, things slow down and get more serious. I would say a lot of my [current networks] came out of those experiences."

Creative director Rachel Stephan concurred. In her field, a formal education is a definite plus. "People tend to take you more seriously when you have a formal education. Although I find that what you learn in school is way off from what happens in the real world. In school you learn theory and structure, which are key. But when you face a real deadline or a real client's objection, it's a real shock. I believe schools have a huge responsibility to upgrade their programs to reflect today's reality."

Rachel also said she learned two important skills at school that allowed her to make her mark in the business world: working within a structure and working within guidelines. "The rest I learned on my own with actual projects and clients. I take each project as a learning experience and try to find a way to innovate and bring something new."

But whether you've racked up the degrees or are completely self-taught, our experts had loads of advice on making it as a professional visual artist.

I worked with good graphic designers for my print media, invitations cards, posters, and catalogues. My personal and company image was important enough to hire professionals.
- G. Scott MacLeod, fine artist

HOW DO YOU SHOW WHAT YOU'VE GOT?

In our interviews, we were told that your success in this field depends on your reputation, and that starts with building your portfolio and presenting your work. Here are our experts' tips on how to put your best foot forward to show what you've got.

WHAT EVERY VISUAL ARTIST NEEDS
G. Scott MacLeod recommends:

> A good portfolio.

> A good website.

> Good-quality photos of your work.

> Well-written bio and artist statements.

> Well-designed art catalogues, invitations, and business cards. I printed mine with www.lulu.com and my business cards with www.moo.com.

> A short promotional video on your website.

> A thorough press kit chronicling your art career.

SHOW YOUR BEST WORK
Rachel Stephan: "You're a designer; if your CV and website don't reflect how good you are, you won't get the job."

ALWAYS DOCUMENT YOUR WORK
Bettina Forget: "Some people do a lot of really interesting installation pieces and performance art. If you do, don't forget to get some really good photographs of those, because later on you'll need them for your website."

BUILD YOUR PORTFOLIO WITH VOLUNTEER WORK
Rachel Stephan: "People in a position to hire young graphic designers will only look briefly at work produced in school. When you're just getting started, consider volunteering your services. This will help you build your portfolio by giving you projects from the real world."

BE SELECTIVE IN WHAT YOU PRESENT
Rachel Stephan: "[In graphic design] you cannot just have one portfolio and use it at every interview or for every pitch you make. Your portfolio has to be tailored to and personalized for each company you approach."

Adad Hannah: "I had one gallery tell me that I was showing too much to them and I should show less. That was a valuable lesson. If you've made a hundred paintings, only show five of your best work."

SAVE THE BEST FOR FIRST AND LAST
Rachel Stephan: "You need to get their attention from the outset, like you would with a title. And you need to finish off with a bang. First impressions are important, and the last thing they see is what they'll remember the most vividly."

LET YOUR WEBSITE SHOW YOU OFF
Bettina Forget: "Right now, a good, clean website is the basis for everything. The first thing every potential employer will do is Google you and check out your website. What will they find? If it looks professional and well put together, you're 50 percent there. It helps if your website is clean and streamlined. Artists send me websites sometimes with virtual reality walk-throughs and stuff that takes forever to load. It's very hard to see the actual art. Just show me the art!"

POLISH YOUR ARTIST STATEMENT AND CV
Bettina Forget: "Artist statements are very important. They determine if your work is doing what you say you want to be doing. The CV is important too. Indicate where you've shown before, mention any article where you've been interviewed, point out if you shoot videos. Make it the complete package."

Choosing the visual arts has to be a visceral choice. If it is, you'll have the perseverance needed and desire to always evolve. And that's what it takes.

- Nathalie Dion, illustrator

GETTING STARTED

If you are reading this, you're closer to reaching your goal than you think. You probably have more artistic talent than 95 percent of people on the planet. You've got stacks of paintings or illustrations under your belt, and maybe even an MFA degree. But what do you need to do to make the shift from part-time painter or illustrator to genuine artiste?
Our experts say that you need to start with a vision. Ask yourself where you want to be in one year. Write your goals down and, in a year, pull out the piece of paper. See if you have achieved your objectives, and re-adjust your career plans accordingly.

Here is what else our experts had to say about starting out as a professional visual artist:

FIND YOUR VOICE
Bettina Forget: "Decide what kind of art you want to be making and think about why you want to make it. That doesn't mean that you have to have a gimmick, but you do need to have a direction. Are you all about First Nations culture, or astronomy, or animal rights, or something more abstract? Knowing that will be your compass throughout your career."

FIND YOUR NICHE
Rachel Stephan: "You can't be Jane-of-all-trades; you won't please everyone. Pick something you love and do it very well. I picked event marketing and fourteen years later I still get excited to go to work every day."

TRY WORKING FOR AN ESTABLISHED ARTIST
Adad Hannah: "Working on your own art is important, but working for another artist is a great way to get established. You'll pick up on how things work. I worked for several artists as a video editor and it kept me in the field. Those people are usually generous and make good contacts for later."

BE WILLING TO PAY YOUR DUES
Rachel Stephan: "Some people aren't willing to climb the ladder. They want to start at the top. You have to be willing to start small. Whatever it is, it's a foot in the door. From there, show them what you can do. If you're good, you'll move up very quickly."

CONSIDER WORKING IN RELATED FIELDS
G. Scott MacLeod: "In the first ten to fifteen years of my art career, I also worked in other art-related industries like freelance photojournalism and illustration, music production, and art education."

STEP OUT AS AN ARTIST

Bettina Forget: "Get out and meet people, including gallery owners. When I was starting out as an artist, I went to all the symposiums, fairs, and exhibitions that I could. You want to be out in front of people. When you get to these places, get people's contact details and start building your email list. "

DON'T STAY IN YOUR COMFORT ZONE

Rachel Stephan: "Always push yourself out of your comfort zone. Mine was public speaking. One year I made it my business New Year's resolution to do more public speaking. That year I spoke at six conferences, the largest one was to 150 CEOs from across North America. Not bad for an introvert, right? Point is, if I can do it, you can too."

DON'T DO IT ON YOUR OWN

Adad Hannah: "Bounce ideas off of people. If you have an exhibition somewhere, talk to people about your ideas for the exhibition. It's not a magic show; you don't need to hide anything. It's important to show people what you're doing."

JOIN AN ARTIST COLLECTIVE

Bettina Forget: "Artist collectives are important. You can organize group shows with them. These kinds of shows got me noticed, especially with my astronomical art. After that, I got invited to speak at events. It grew from there."

STAGE YOUR OWN SHOW

Adad Hannah: "In Quebec there are lots of artist-run centers and people organizing their own exhibitions in abandoned buildings, or putting together one-month projects. So, if you haven't shown much before, try to get in on one of those. If you don't know anyone who's doing it, put it together yourself. Get five to six artists, find a space, and put on a show. It's not as hard as you think. Invite everyone you know, and invite the press, and see what happens!"

GETTING NOTICED TAKES TIME AND PERSISTENCE

Adad Hannah: "The thing about art is it's not like other stuff. If you're a shoe company, you can put up some posters and the visibility for your product goes up. As an artist it's different; it's hard. You just have to keep showing and hope that people will come see your stuff. I keep sending invites to people for my shows who don't come. I aim high, and mostly they don't show up, but one day they do and then something good comes of it."

SENIOR ARTISTS CAN HELP

G. Scott MacLeod: "Find a mentor or senior artist for advice and encouragement. A handful of teachers I met during my years at art school took the time to invest in me and my work. Without this long list of people, I never would have made a living as an artist."

FIND AN INTERNSHIP

Rachel Stephan: "Interning gives emerging graphic designers a chance to see if they like a certain company or a specific job. It also allows them to learn and grow without the pressure of being an employee; it is understood that interns are there to learn. I got my first job after an internship at an advertising agency."

MAKE TIME FOR YOUR ART

Bettina Forget: "Other things will encroach on your creative time, and they might seem more important than your art. Art doesn't really have a deadline unless you have a show, so always allow a large enough block of time to create art. When you hit a creative plateau, it's very tempting to say, 'Well I'm going to do something else now.' But don't do that. Stay in the studio. Set aside an entire day and say, 'I know my work sucks today but I'm staying.'"

PERSEVERANCE PAYS OFF

Nathalie Dion: "At the beginning, my career was really s-l-o-w! After studying in design arts at Concordia University, I had a few mind-numbing 'artistic' jobs such as colour separator for a textile company. Actually, I'd have preferred to have a waitress job (and kept my artistic energy intact). I did this for ten years! Ten years of portfolio updating and going around visiting art directors. My perseverance finally paid off though. I've now been working as an illustrator full-time for over fifteen years.

The instability of not having a steady income can be scary. You really have to be able to plan ahead for when times are a little slow.

- Rachel Stephan, creative director

TAKING IT TO THE NEXT LEVEL

You know everything possible about mixing colours. You have all the technical abilities. You think your paintings are better than most stuff you see in gallery windows. Maybe young painters are now coming to you for advice.

Things are looking great. You are on the right track. But how can you continue to grow as an artist? What is the next step? How can you use your talents and experience to generate more income?

We've asked our panel of experts to share their thoughts about making a sustainable career as a visual artist:

I. THE VISUAL AND FINE ARTS BUSINESS

HAVE A PLAN
Bettina Forget: "You're self-employed, so you have to set your own goals. Decide where you want to go with your work. What festivals, what curators, what art directors interest you? Your goals can't be so specific as selling ten works of art in a year, but it's important to know what your creative goals are. What do you want to achieve with your art?"

GET HELP WITH YOUR BUSINESS PLAN
G. Scott MacLeod: "Make a business plan to understand how to run your art business. You can learn how from artists who have had successful art careers."

STAY AHEAD OF THE TECHNOLOGICAL CURVE
Rachel Stephan: "Stay current. Graphic design is a very fast-paced business and you always need to be learning more about your craft."

STAY DISCIPLINED IN ART AND IN BUSINESS
G. Scott MacLeod: "You've got to develop a disciplined studio practice and a disciplined business practice, and then find a balance between the two."

TAKE ORGANIZATION AND SCHEDULING SERIOUSLY
Nathalie Dion: "Make yourself a personalized, visual calendar and be very organized time-wise. It will give you peace of mind. And even though you're an artist, clients will appreciate you being on time and professional about the schedule."

MAP OUT YOUR SCHEDULE

Bettina Forget: "I make a list of all my activities, then I make a diagram. I'm a visual thinker, so a diagram is very useful for me. Then I make a timetable. Monday might be a creative day, Tuesday might be a business day. If someone wants to meet with me on my creative day, I reschedule. If you tell everybody that, 'I can't meet you today because Monday is my creative day,' after a while they won't even ask you. The more you stick to your schedule, the more everyone else will stick to your schedule."

YOU DON'T HAVE TO DO EVERYTHING YOURSELF

Nathalie Dion: "Thinking about the business side of my work makes me want to take a power nap. So I have an accountant who takes care of my GST/QST and income tax. For legal stuff, I'm a member of Regroupement des artistes en arts visuels (RAAV) and Illustration Québec (IQ); they have tons of legal-type contracts that really help. And I'm represented by Anna Goodson for management. It is much easier to negotiate a contract when there's someone between you and the client."

G. Scott MacLeod: "Early in my career, I got an accountant and a lawyer. That helped me understand how to become a registered business, file my taxes, write off business expenses, get tax receipts through donations of artwork, and use the cultural properties tax credit for the years that I did make money. My lawyer helped me write up contracts for galleries and commissioned work. In the beginning I bartered for their services with my paintings."

KNOW WHEN TO MOVE ON

Rachel Stephan: "I started as a contract worker, then got a permanent job, and finally became head of a department. That gave me a lot of experience and prepared me for the next step. When I reached the point where I wasn't learning anything new anymore, I decided to take the leap into self-employment. Fourteen years later, I haven't looked back. I employ five people, promoting national and international events.

II. FINANCING AND MAKING MONEY

Surprise surprise! No one we interviewed became a visual artist for the money, but that doesn't mean it isn't on their minds. Getting the cash to live and work as an artist can be hard-going, but all our experts have somehow found solutions—often creative ones—to this persistent concern.

GRANTS ARE AVAILABLE

Adad Hannah: "[For financing projects] the Conseil des arts et des lettres du Québec and Canada Council for the Arts are great; they both have grants for emerging artists. It's not as hard to apply for those as people seem to think; it's all online. A lot of artists don't send out anything, or they send out a hundred packages to everywhere. It's important to find the grants that apply to you, then only apply to those ones."

DON'T BE INTIMIDATED TO APPLY FOR GRANTS

Adad Hannah: "Artists often think they're going to have to use 'art-speak' in a grant application. That's really not true. Have a clear idea, clear images; show a clear path between your existing work and what you want to do. It's not rocket science, but it is a bit of a crapshoot. It depends on whoever the jury is. A lot of grants will give you the opportunity to ask them for feedback. Wait a few weeks until you're clear-headed and then approach them."

POLISH YOUR PROPOSAL

G. Scott MacLeod: "If you are asking for money, learn how to write clear and realistic proposals and budgets, and practise pitching your project. I've gotten funding from Canada Council for the Arts, the Conseil des arts et des lettres du Québec, Indiegogo, and the private sector."

KNOW WHAT YOU HAVE TO OFFER

G. Scott MacLeod: "If you're approaching corporations or organizations for sponsorship, target those that may have a vested interest in your project or work. Meet with company owners, if possible, and offer something in return for their support. You can put their logo on your printed materials and website or donate a work of art for their collection."

But don't depend on grants alone!

DIVERSIFY YOUR INCOME STREAMS

Bettina Forget: "My grandfather once told me that every good business stands on two legs. It's also true for artists; don't just do one thing. Do two things, so that if one aspect is slow, you can balance it with another. [My two things] are teaching and fine arts. Over the years I've grown a couple more legs too! In the arts, the income is so unpredictable, one show will do spectacularly well, but it has no bearing on your next show. I try to make all my extra-curricular work as relevant to my creative work as possible. Thankfully, I've never had to deliver pizza!"

TRY BARTERING

Adad Hannah: "A barter economy with friends is always a big help. I've had people help me with my projects and then I'll help them with theirs. With film and video, you often need an extra set of hands. I used to trade art for dentistry, a long time ago. That also had the added benefit of getting my art out there."

III. GETTING VISIBILITY

Making it as an artist is about getting seen—obviously. Our experts suggest a host of ways to get you and your creative endeavours out there, starting with exposure in your own artistic community. From that base, they suggest you launch into social and traditional media, making a name for yourself that people won't soon forget. Here are their concrete tips on making it happen:

IT'S UP TO YOU

Bettina Forget: "You're your own agent, so you need to be good at research and making yourself aware of opportunities and deadlines. Make sure you're on several email lists for calls for submissions."

G. Scott MacLeod: "Cultivate your own client base; don't rely solely on galleries to sell your work. [I've had success] meeting people at functions and in private settings, asking them for their business cards, putting them on my mailing list, inviting them to my exhibitions, and cultivating long-term relationships with them. Follow-up is important."

STEP BY STEP WILL GET YOU THERE

Nathalie Dion: "I personally worked hard to get my first client, making phone calls and appointments with artistic directors to show my portfolio. But then that first client led to another and another until I was contacted by [agent] Anna Goodson. Now, being part of an agency brings a whole new network of clients, colleagues, and friends!"

NETWORK THROUGH YOUR ARTISTS' ASSOCIATION

Rachel Stephan: "Joining a specific association was part of my marketing strategy. I wanted to meet people and create personal contacts. Becoming a member of industry associations is a good way to do this. It's also important to be active within those associations. For example, I often sponsor events that my association runs or I sit on committees. This way, my company logo is everywhere."

FIND YOUR SPECIFIC COMMUNITY

Bettina Forget: "I do astronomical art, so what helped me was the International Association for Astronomical Artists. Yes, that exists! If you look around, there will be artists and organizations in your field. There are groups that can help you in your specific area, and you get more bang for your buck going to more targeted places."

BE OF SERVICE TO YOUR NETWORK

Bettina Forget: "Your attitude shouldn't be: How can all these organizations help me? Instead, ask how you can help them. Go to them and say, 'You don't have a website. Can I help you build it?' or 'Can I lend a hand in your gallery?' You will be the only person who isn't asking them for stuff, and they'll remember you."

GIVE AND GET BACK

G. Scott MacLeod: "I've done many community outreach projects in service of various causes. These 'feel good' stories stand out. They're noble and will interest the public and media, given the many negative stories that journalists and the public are exposed to every day."

DON'T FORGET YOUR THANK YOUS

Adad Hannah: "You can get busy sometimes and move on to other projects, but you have to thank the people who helped you with the last one. To that end, it's good to keep a list of names of who's working on each project when you start. People end up helping you in so many different ways. And later you can add that same list to your mailing list."

FACEBOOK TRUMPS A WEBSITE FOR VISIBILITY

G. Scott MacLeod: "I have had the most success with Facebook because I transferred my email list there. I find that it's often more effective than a website. There's lots of day-to-day traffic and it's an inviting platform. It's easy to post photos of new work and events there. My website acts more as an archive. I can direct people there if they want to see more of what I do."

Rachel Stephan: "Facebook is a good way for people to get to know the team and what we do at the office. It adds that human dimension."

CREATE A SOCIAL MEDIA STRATEGY THAT SUITS YOU

Bettina Forget: "It's not enough to create a Facebook event and invite your friends; that's not a marketing strategy. Look at the kind of content you're creating and figure out which platform is best suited to you. If you're a visual artist, then Facebook and Pinterest are good. Find out where your voice is best suited."

DON'T SPREAD YOURSELF TOO THIN

Bettina Forget: "Don't have fifteen platforms and only be posting three things. No one will follow you. And don't just promote yourself. People will hide you from their news feed faster than you know. The percent should be 80 percent interesting content and 20 percent promotion."

Adad Hannah: "Facebook is the one I'm using. Part of the success is to not overdo it. I'm not on it often. There's so much of it, and I think it's easy to get fatigued. If I could do it again, I'd probably do a personal one and one for work. People invite me to parties on Facebook and I never see them because I'm getting everything on the same account and I never check it."

SCHEDULE YOUR SOCIAL MEDIA TIME

Bettina Forget: "Have a schedule, every day, half an hour to an hour; find an article that is interesting and related to the work you're doing. Publish that on the social media platforms that you've selected. When people come to your shows, they'll appreciate your content and they'll know to expect interesting things from you."

MAKE IT EASY FOR JOURNALISTS TO COVER YOU

G. Scott MacLeod: "I have a lot of success in cultivating good relationships within the media because I've made it as easy as possible for journalists by taking the time to write good press releases, designing nice graphics, giving them taglines, photos, etc. Remember that journalists are bombarded every day with projects and events just like yours. So you have to offer them something that will set you apart from the ordinary. You have to be strategic and make an effort to be reviewed."

Bettina Forget: "The secret of a good press release is to put yourself in the shoes of the reporter or editor and think about why your story is interesting to them. For instance, when it's International Astronomy Day, I'll send them a note saying, 'Did you know it's International Astronomy Day? By the way, here's some of my astrological art you might be interested in.' You're helping them tell a story. Find which outlet is best for the kind of work you're doing and pitch it."

PROVIDING VISUALS HELPS GET YOU IN PRINT
Adad Hannah: "There's always an arts section in every little newspaper, and the person who's doing it is usually a volunteer, or just [there] part-time. They can't always send a photographer to every event. If you have good photos, ready to go, that's easier for them. I used to get a lot of coverage when I had little shows just by getting in touch with journalists and giving them good images."

DON'T OVERBURDEN YOUR MEDIA CONTACTS
Bettina Forget: "My friend at the Gazette knows about all my shows, but I'll send him a personal email when I think something is relevant to him specifically. You don't want to carpet-bomb your journalists. You should know them well enough to know what they're likely to write about."

DOES STRONG BRANDING HELP WITH VISIBILITY?
Our experts had different opinions on this question. Not surprisingly, in the more commercial sectors of the field, branding is a bigger preoccupation.
Nathalie Dion: "I think cohesive branding is somehow inherent to a 'successful' illustrator. Even though my style has evolved over time, clients come to me for a particular style. So I have to work with that."

G. Scott MacLeod: "Branding one style of art has worked for many artists. I however have worked by developing multiple series over the years. In the long-term, it opened my work to a broader clientele. I chose to be more diverse, which enabled me to attain a broader market."

Bettina Forget: I don't think your brand should become a straitjacket. Brand is something that develops over time, and it will develop better if you know who you are and why you're making your art."

FIND UNIQUE DISPLAY AND SALES VENUES
Bettina Forget: "I had a kiosk at a convention for hard-core astronomers. I got into lots of conversations with people there and sold my astrological paintings to many attendees. They were there to network and to talk about Mars rovers, but they also walked away with my paintings!"

Adad Hannah: "We're sitting here in this café, and I'm looking at the walls with nothing on them. I could go up to the manager and ask to put my paintings up. When I was younger, I had shows in cafes and it was a lot of fun."

HAVING AN AGENT CAN EXTEND YOUR REACH
Nathalie Dion: "Having a good rep really helps. My agency, Anna Goodson Management, is really active on social media, taking ads on illustration-related web sites. And once a year they send printed postal promos."

BE DOWN TO EARTH AND ACCESSIBLE
G. Scott MacLeod: "You need to be able to talk to your client base and the public about your work in a coherent fashion, and forego any pretense and elitist views of yourself in the art industry. Be interested in what other people do and say, and show humility."

LEARN HOW TO EXPLAIN YOUR ART TO THE PUBLIC
Bettina Forget: "In your show text, where you're talking to the general public, you need to be able to explain your work clearly. It's sometimes harder to write that kind of text. Test it on your grandmother."

I find I become a workaholic if I work from home. I never leave and I never stop.
- Bettina Forget, visual artist and gallery owner

LIVING AS A VISUAL ARTIST

You're in your basement studio touching up that final coat of paint. Well, you think it's the final coat, but you said that an hour ago, and it's 2:00 a.m. and you haven't had anything to eat since lunch, and you can't remember if you put the kids to bed yet…

It's not for everyone, this artists' life. Our experts weigh in on how to navigate the ups and downs of this pothole-ridden path you've chosen. And please listen to them; they've been on this road a while.

GROW A TOUGH SKIN

Adad Hannah: "I know people who get a rejection from the Canada Council for the Arts and that's it, they never apply again. You have to have a tough skin, to pick yourself up and get back out there. My trick was to always have something out there while I was waiting to hear back on those applications. You'll always have hope, but you have to be ready to get maybe ten pieces of bad news in a row. You need to believe in what you're doing, but not so much so that you don't question why you're getting ten rejections in a row."

KNOW WHEN TO STAY CONNECTED AND WHEN TO DISCONNECT

Nathalie Dion: "It is good to be aware of what is happening in your field but don't overdo it. It can be discouraging, time consuming, and overwhelming, especially these days with the Internet and social media. Disconnect now and then just to focus on your art."

STAY IN THE PRESENT

Nathalie Dion: "Practice Zen and the 'power of now' as much as possible. You have no idea how much you will need it when it takes six months to be paid after the completion of a project and bills are piling up."

BALANCE FAMILY AND WORK

Rachel Stephan: "When I first started, my days and nights blended together. Today, I can say that I truly enjoy the balance between work and home. I learned to delegate and empower my team."

Adad Hannah: "I work until 6:00 p.m., take a break to put the kids to sleep, then I work another couple of hours. When I finally go to bed, I feel good because I've done what I wanted to do."

YOU MAY NEED A SEPARATE WORKSPACE

Bettina Forget: "It's important to have a place of work and a place to go back home. If you can get a studio space, you'll probably have other artists working around you. Personally, I like that. It creates an ephemeral artistic buzz that's beneficial to everybody."

Rachel Stephan: "I moved out to an office space after six years working from home. I enjoy walking to work and having it separate from home."

ENGAGE WITH OTHERS
Bettina Forget: "It's not enough to be alone in your studio. I've noticed over the years that visual artists tend to be more introverted. They aren't the product, their art is the product, so they take themselves out of the limelight a little bit. That's fine, but you still need to be able to connect to others. That's an important life skill."

FINAL THOUGHTS

What might our visual artists have done differently if starting over today? Just a few things. Here's their parting advice to help you avoid a pitfall or two along the way:

WORK WITHIN YOUR COMFORT ZONE
Nathalie Dion: "Once, at the beginning of my career, I took a contract way outside my comfort zone; a huge publicity campaign on billboards involving architectural illustration. I almost lost my health, and all for a poor end result. Since then, I don't accept contracts that I don't feel I'm suited for—even if the client thinks I am. It's good to be challenged, but not to your point of incompetence! Know yourself and know where you can be flexible with your style. It'll help avoid professional failure and a breakdown of self-confidence."

DON'T GO IT ALONE
Adad Hannah: "I used to think that solo shows were the big thing that everyone should go for, but in retrospect I think that group shows are much more useful because you build a group of peers. Solo shows are a lot of work. You have to organize everything yourself. It's nicer to do things with other people and have that community. And you become part of something that's bigger than yourself."

FIND SECURE STUDIO SPACE
G. Scott MacLeod: "I've made the mistake of establishing my studios in industrial buildings that were potentially slated for condo projects. I once moved three times in a twelve-month period because of this."

TAKE A BUSINESS COURSE
Bettina Forget: "The first time I sent out an invoice to a client, it was a disaster! No date, no client number... He sent it back to me asking if I wanted to try again. He realized he was dealing with a recent graduate and was good-humoured about it. Then I took an evening course for small-business owners, and that was really useful for doing market research and accounting. That course, like a lot of learning, came from making mistakes."

BUILDING YOUR ETSY EMPIRE IS ABOUT BEING SOCIAL
An interview with Norma Andreu, Owner/Operator of Cara Carmina.

We sat down with Norma Andreu, the social media maven and entrepreneurial artist behind the enterprise Cara Carmina. Norma has loads of experience on Etsy and other online sales platforms. From her humble beginnings, making Frida Kahlo–inspired dolls for craft fairs, Norma's now selling her designs and products around the world. And she owes it all (or lots of it) to her mastery of social media. Here's her advice on how you can do it too:

What are your top pieces of advice for visual artists who want to sell online?

Number one: Use social media properly. A lot of people think having a Facebook page or a website is enough, but you need to learn how to use the web properly and invest time into it. It's your most useful resource, and it's free! I spend around four hours a day on my social media, but that's because it's my principle means of attracting clientele. I don't think everyone needs to rely on it that much. You can spend one hour in the morning and one at night on it. I put in the time because I'm using several social media sites (Facebook, Twitter, Pinterest, Flickr, Instagram). I also have a website and a blog. But not everyone needs all that. I'd suggest you pick the best ones for you and then really dedicate your time to them.

Number two: You have to get out into the real world; don't just stay online or in your studio. Even though you may eventually sell your work online, you first have to build a local following. It's no good being on social media if no one's interested in you, and you have to start somewhere. There are so many venues to get the word out: craft markets, art shows, conferences, public interest talks, whatever works for you. All those little events in the community will help you get in contact with your colleagues and your clientele. Don't forget, your first and best merchandising tool is yourself.

What type of platforms are best for selling online?

A lot of people create a website shop and expect they'll make all their sales through that. But unless you're already really well known, it's very difficult. Starting a web store doesn't equal sales. Personally, my main source of income is Etsy, because it's a huge community of handmade goods with millions of accounts, and it's a great social network. I've tried other platforms, especially print on demand (POD) sites where you submit your art and they have a whole structure to make prints, cushions, phone cases, etc. with your designs. With these sites you don't have to worry about producing the items yourself. The catch is that sometimes they'll take more than 90% of the profits. Using them is actually more like a licensing deal. So unless you have a lot of sales, you'll make nothing. Some POD sites are better than others, but the margin of profit is usually very low for the artist. I used them in the beginning, but now I just use Etsy.

How does an artist stand out in the on-line community?

Photographs of your work are super important. You have to make them appealing for people, because they can't touch or experience your work like they can in a store. You have to attract customers visually and you only have a split second to do it, because people are browsing everywhere and you only have their attention for a brief moment. If they don't click on your image in the first three seconds, they'll move on.

For instance, I started printing my designs on leggings for adults and kids and needed to get pictures of them for the site. I took a couple of photos of them flat, and the reaction was fine, but I wanted something more dynamic. So I gave a bunch of leggings to a friend for her very cute daughter. She took some amazing photos of her daughter wearing them, and as soon as I put them online, my shop started going crazy—just because people were seeing them on a cute little girl. That effect was fantastic. And that's a very good example of how people can have a much stronger reaction to compelling photos.

Besides good pictures, you also need a good write-up, or "story" for each item. Be specific and very descriptive. There are a lot of sites that will give you ideas on how to write these descriptions.

How much time do you have to dedicate to online activities?

I'm online all the time, because I always have my cell phone with me and that's a great resource. I'm following up with comments and questions and emails all the time. I answer everything personally. I have templates for some replies but I try to make it all as personal as possible. If you're selling online, you have to be available for much of the day, at least once you really get going. If you're just setting up your store, it'll start slowly. You'll spend most of your time just building your site and designing your posts. Everything has to be done step by step. To have the structure I have now has taken me about four years.

How social do you really need to get on social media?

I have a profile on Facebook for personal use and a Facebook page where I talk about my work. It's better if you don't mix the two. I had a couple of guys hit on me back when I was married—and my status was clearly married! So I exposed them, posting publicly what they'd sent me, tagging them in it. You should be clear about your intentions over the Internet. If someone misunderstands or crosses the line, you need to set them straight right away. If they persist, don't engage them, just block them. Don't waste energy on it. And be smart with what you post as well. If you're respectful in your posts, it will go a long way. When I got divorced, some people noticed differences in the way I was posting, and they asked me questions. I didn't want to get personal, so I just posted something very metaphorical about the changes in my life and people appreciated that I'd somehow clued them in. You can be honest in a way that's discreet.

What misconceptions do artists have about using social media?

A lot of artists just don't think social media is worth doing. Either they think it's too much work or it doesn't do their art justice. But I'm astounded when someone tells me they're an artist and they don't have a Facebook page. Having a website is more time-consuming than opening a Facebook page. And most people agree you need a website. But social media sites are great tools that you can use for free. And I find they're much more useful than buying ads. With social media it's more about creating awareness and then letting word of mouth naturally take its course. Your social network isn't for selling; it's for meeting people and telling them about yourself and your work. If you're just posting your work with price tags, people aren't going to be interested. But if you tell them about yourself, your process and your challenges, and then show a bit of your work, you'll engage them.

Besides selling directly to the public, how can artists get larger wholesale customers online?

Etsy has another site now which is Etsy Wholesale. You open another store in the back-end of your current Etsy store, which has a wholesale function. On this wholesale site they have everything from big retailers to smaller buyers. You have to go through a screening process with the Etsy administration to make sure all your manufacturing is in order and your business practices are ethical. Wholesale buyers have to do the same. Etsy then puts you in contact with the potential buyers who can order thousands of your items directly. It saves you a lot of time. So far I've made four wholesale sales though Etsy Wholesale; they're independent libraries from the United States and Canada, including the Yukon! It's been really interesting for me because it's expanded my network and the way I sell.

Are there any sales mistakes you've made that you could help other artists avoid?

One of the first things I did when I arrived in Montreal was go to the museum, and I loved the boutique. I said, "I'm going to sell here one day," so I asked for the manager's card. I sent her my work and she was interested! We met a while later and she ordered a lot of dolls, which are very time consuming to make. A doll can take me up to ten hours. I couldn't sell them for very much because I wasn't known. But at the beginning I just wanted the exposure. And getting shown in a museum boutique is prestigious.

When I brought in the dolls, the manager explained my payment plan options: She could pay me in full after thirty days if she purchased them wholesale. Or she could take them on consignment, and I would get paid as soon as any sales were made. I didn't know anything about business, so I thought waiting thirty days was a long time to get paid! I don't think she was a very nice person, because she convinced me to sell them on consignment. It ended up taking a whole year for all my dolls to sell and for me to make the money. That was a very bad decision and I regretted it. I've since learned better and actually took some coaching from YES, which helped a lot.

Any parting words?

The Internet is so crowded that, no matter what platform you're on, there's already a big community of people selling. You're never going to be the only one selling jewellery or prints or cushions. So I'd suggest focusing more on your work than on the specific platform, because if your work has no value you won't sell it anywhere. In the end, it's the quality of your work that's most important; after that you can worry about the quality of your online sales strategy.

Norma Andreu is the artist entrepreneur behind Cara Carmina. Check out Norma's creations at www.caracarmina.com.

WRITERS

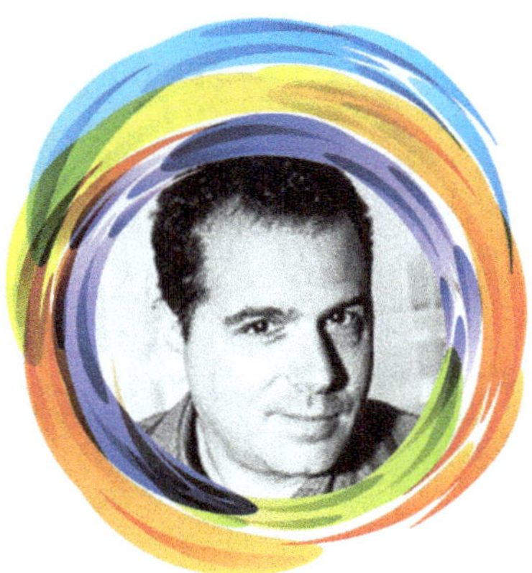

Steve Galluccio

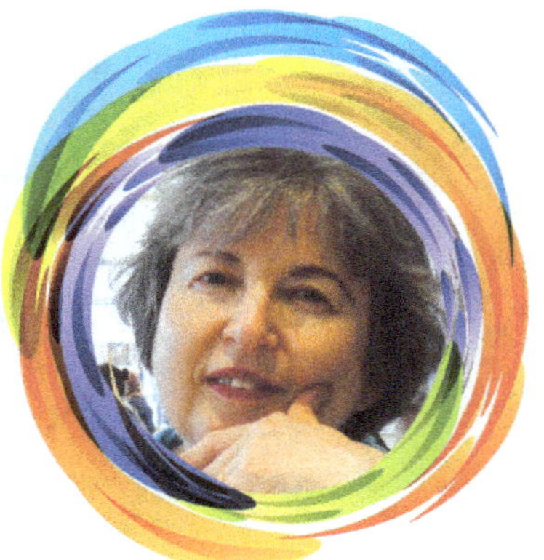

Elaine Kalman Naves

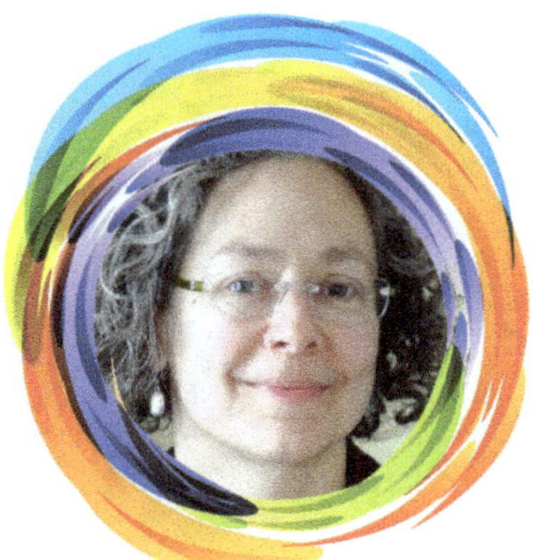

Elise Moser

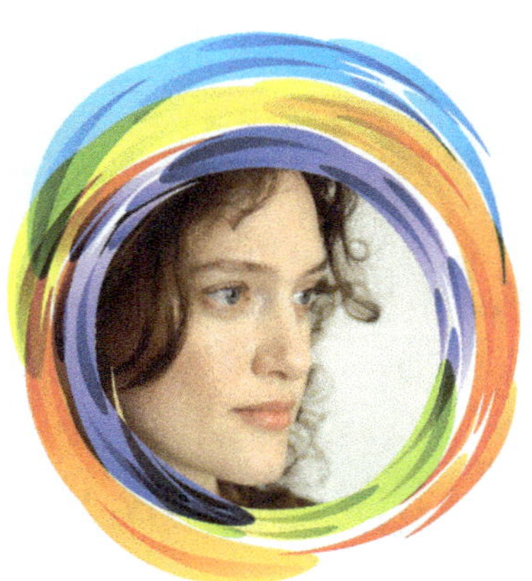

Heather O'Neill

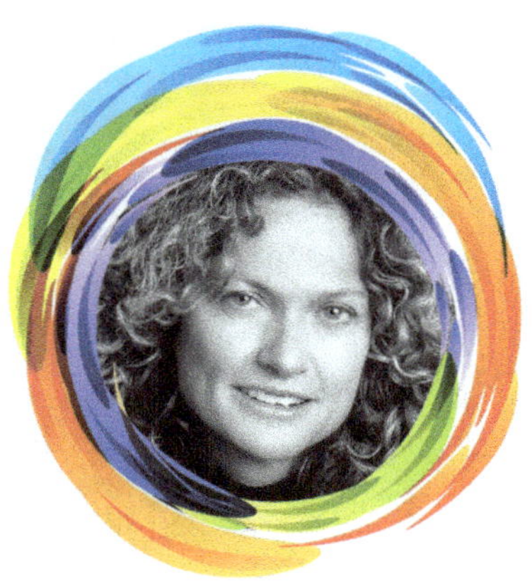

Monique Polak

It's important to put in the time. You have to write all the bloody time, even when you don't feel like it.

- Monique Polak, young adult novelist

SO YOU WANNA BE A WRITER?

Ahhh, the lonely, tormented life of the writer... Late nights spent hunched over a sticky keyboard in a dimly lit room, coffee stains on every printed page, demons and muses locked in a bloody battle to be heard through your words.

Well, that's the way your concerned friends and family may have envisioned it for you. Thankfully, this bleak picture needn't be a portal into your future. In fact, the writing scene is alive and thriving in Canada, and the wordly wise have myriad opportunities to put their talent to work for them.

In this section, we feature the advice of several Quebecers who all write to live and live to write. Keep in mind that our panel represents only a small sampling of the many career paths a writer can walk. If our expert advice piques your interest in writing, you may want to further investigate the following occupations listed in the National Occupation Classification, published by Employment and Social Development Canada:

> Advertising copywriter

> Blogger

> Book reviewer

> Copy editor

> Editor

> Essayist

> Novelist

> Interactive media writer

> Journalist

> Playwright

> Poet

> Speech writer

> Screenwriter

> Technical writer

THE EXPERTS

We spoke with the following accomplished writers for a look under the covers of the writing life:

Steve Galluccio burst into the mainstream theatre scene with *Mambo Italiano*, one of the most successful plays in Canadian theatre history. The play was made into a movie that became an international hit. Galluccio followed *Mambo* with the Gemini-award-winning TV series *Ciao Bella*. Galluccio's second feature film, *Surviving My Mother*, won the audience favourite award at the Montreal Film Festival. Galluccio's third feature was the bilingual *Funkytown*. In 2012, Galluccio released his first book, *Montréal à la Galluccio*, a whimsical guide of his beloved Montreal. Steve's new play, *The St Leonard Chronicles*, opened in 2013 and sold out before its run. See more about Steve's screenwriting work at www.imdb.com/name/nm1241330/.

Elaine Kalman Naves is a writer, journalist, and broadcaster. She worked for many years as a literary columnist for the *Montreal Gazette*, and is the author of seven books, among them the award-winning memoirs *Journey to Vaja* and *Shoshanna's Story*. A frequent contributor to CBC's *Ideas*, Elaine lectures widely about her own books, the literature of Montreal, and noteworthy new titles. Elaine's honours include a Canadian Literary Award for Personal Essay, two Quebec Writers' Federation prizes for non-fiction, and two Jewish Book Awards for Holocaust Literature. Her newest book is *Portrait of a Scandal: The Abortion Trial of Robert Notman*. For more, check out www.ElaineKalmanNaves.com.

Elise Moser is a writer and editor. She has published about thirty short stories, a novel for adults called *Because I Have Loved and Hidden It*, and a YA novel, *Lily and Taylor*, that was named to the American Library Association's list of Best Books for Young Adults 2014. She also edited *Salut King Kong: New English Writing from Quebec*, the anthology of Quebec Writing Competition–winning stories. She has been a mentor and led short story workshops for the Quebec Writers' Federation, and served on their board for five years, three as president. She joined the board of PEN Canada in June 2014. Check out Elise's latest book at http://houseofanansi.com/products/lily-and-taylor.

Heather O'Neill's first novel, *Lullabies for Little Criminals*, was an international bestseller, the winner of CBC's Canada Reads and the Hugh MacLennan Prize for Fiction. It was also a finalist for six other awards including the Governor General's Award for Fiction and the Orange Prize. She is a regular contributor to CBC, NPR, the *New York Times Magazine*, *ELLE* magazine and the *Walrus*. Her latest novel, *The Girl Who Was Saturday Night*, was published to rave reviews and shortlisted for the 2014 Scotiabank Giller Prize. Read more at www.harpercollins.ca/authors/30326/Heather_ONeill.

Monique Polak is the author of sixteen novels for young adults, the most recent of which, *Hate Mail*, won the 2014 Quebec Writers' Federation Prize for Children's and YA Literature. Her historical novel, *What World is Left*, won the 2009 Quebec Writers' Federation Prize for Children's and YA Literature. Monique's next YA novel, *Learning the Ropes*, will be released by Orca Books in spring 2015. Monique is a frequent contributor to the *Montreal Gazette* and to Postmedia publications across the country. She is also a columnist on ICI Radio-Canada's *Plus on est de fous, plus on lit!* Monique has taught English and humanities at Marianopolis College for thirty years. Learn more about Monique at www.moniquepolak.com.

And here's what our experts had to say, writer to writer:

WHO NEEDS A UNIVERSITY DEGREE?

The first thing a writer needs is an impeccable grasp of the language. Hopefully you paid attention in high school the day they taught subject-verb agreement, and while you may not be able to tell us what a dangling modifier is, we hope that doesn't mean you're using them. You'll also need a strong vocabulary and a well-developed critical thinking process.

These abilities may come from reading books, and certainly reading helps keep the mind in top writing form, but they are also important skills that are learned and improved upon by studies at the university level. A university degree, particularly at the graduate level, also allows you to develop expertise and informed opinions about particular areas of interest. Award-winning author Heather O'Neill puts it this way, "I did English literature as a degree at McGill and took some creative writing classes. I didn't get an [MFA], but if you have the opportunity and the money to do it, why not!"

According to the National Occupation Survey and a cursory glance at job ads for professional writers, a bachelor's degree or college diploma in fields like journalism, English, or communication studies is frequently a requirement.

Heather goes on to say, "One of the advantages of doing an MFA program is you get to meet teachers and professionals, and if one of them takes a liking to you and decides to mentor you, that's the sun shining on you. If they like your work, then they're able to get it shown around and read immediately."

So while a university degree, especially in writing, isn't essential, it can sure help to jumpstart your career.

It doesn't matter if your published work is paid or unpaid, it matters that you're out there and that [people] can read what you've written.

- Elaine Kalman Naves, writer and journalist

HOW DO YOU SHOW WHAT YOU'VE GOT?

No magazine editor or PR executive or film director is going to hire you to write for them because you say you can. You need a portfolio to show them that you're serious, smart, and able to communicate.

If you have never been published, don't worry. While published pieces lend credibility to a writer, editors and publishers know that everyone has to start somewhere. You can start your portfolio by writing about what you know: a travel article about a place you've visited, a road trip you've taken, or the neighbourhood you live in now. Write a restaurant review, movie review, or product review. Published or not, if it's well written, editors and publishers will see that you are a talented writer. Here's what our experts advise:

GET SOME WRITING CREDITS

Elaine Kalman Naves: "The hardest thing of all is to get some kind of writing credits, especially when you're young and all you have on your CV is your schooling. So try writing for the school newspaper or an actual newspaper, or have a blog. Your credits are really important. Keep a log of all your writing."

"AUDITION" WITH UNPAID PUBLISHED WORK

Heather O'Neill: "When I started writing I never got paid. The beginning places are like auditions almost, and they lead to a lot of stuff. One of the first places I published was for a website which didn't pay me. But the publisher at the website ended up working at the New York Times Magazine and ended up hiring me there. You have to establish your relationships with editors. Through that connection I got a New York agent and a book deal!"

PAY ATTENTION TO DETAIL

Elaine Kalman Naves: "Write clean copy. Don't send in stuff with mistakes. Edit yourself before you have an editor."

GUMPTION CAN GET YOUR FOOT IN THE DOOR

Monique Polak: "What you need is gumption. Years ago I wrote my first book review for a newspaper. I was stupid enough to write it for a three-year-old book! It was a beautiful review and the books editor wrote me back and said, "Interesting review but it has to be a new book." Which is so obvious! But it got me a contact. I sent him another book review and he used it."

KEEP PITCHING

Heather O'Neill: "It is really hard to get in. Before I published Lullabies, I would pitch to places and never hear back. It is really hard to break in, and very hard to get people to respond to you. You just have to keep going."

FIND THE BEST WAY TO SHOWCASE YOUR WORK

Heather O'Neill: "Everything's online now. Whoever you're pitching to, you can say, 'I've written for such and such a place' and they can always Google it."

Elise Moser: "Each writer has to find the [best way to showcase her talent] that works for her art, temperament, and circumstances. Some people swear by Twitter and Facebook and their websites."

PUBLISH WHEREVER YOU CAN

Heather O'Neill: "When you publish something and make it available for an audience, your growth is exponential. If you stay at home and work at crafting it, you will develop, but as soon as you put it out there, even if you get humiliated and rejected, your learning process is huge. Don't worry what the venue is, publish and show your work where you can. Everyone pays their dues. No one starts out by writing for the New York Times, they just don't."

My top top five pieces of advice? #1: Never give up. #2: Never give up. #3: Never give up. #4: Never give up. And finally #5: Never give up.

- Steve Galluccio, playwright and screenwriter

GETTING STARTED

It's perhaps too pat to say that to be a writer you first have to write. But that simple stumbling block has tripped up many an aspiring author. Our experts are all people who write well—obviously—and they also write often. In fact, they write all the time, and that appears to be an essential ingredient to their success. But take heart, even if you have a day job you can still pursue your inner Hemingway. Just listen to their advice on getting started in the writer's life.

STEP #1: HONE YOUR CRAFT

Monique Polak: "You need to work on your craft before starting to worry about how much money you're going to make. Put in your time in the writing. It's hard and slow. Even after the number of years I've been writing and the number of books I've published, I still find it hard and rough-going a lot of the time. You shouldn't think that it'll fall into place right away."

FIND YOUR IDENTITY AS A WRITER

Heather O'Neill: "When you start off, you have to think about what your themes are going to be and develop your identity as an author. If you look, most authors will have a central theme to all of their books. If you look at your life and find what's authentic to you, you'll find what you want to say. If you want to talk about race, or gender, and you have that in your mind before you start writing, it will make your stuff that much more interesting."

DISCOVER YOUR AUDIENCE AND YOUR VOICE

Heather O'Neill: "While I was developing as a writer, I would do a lot of readings. I would notice what made people laugh and what didn't, and I would scratch out the stuff that didn't work. I was unconsciously developing a persona based on what people liked, using the audience and readers like a mirror to figure out what about myself was the most interesting."

FIT WRITING INTO YOUR LIFE

Elise Moser: "You can do an awful lot of writing if you spend a couple of hours in the evenings or a Sunday afternoon every single week, or put aside two weeks or a month in the summer. Almost no writer in the world does nothing but write. I still definitely juggle my artistic career with the reality of making a living, but I have always done work that feeds my writing life in some way beyond the financial."

PERSISTENCE PAYS

Elaine Kalman Naves: "Write even when you have nothing to say. Make a point, especially when you're starting out, to sit down, even if it's just for an hour a day, a half hour a day. Even if you have nothing to say, something will come to you if you do it over and over again."

Elise Moser: "Revise and send your work out even when you feel like an imposter or a failure. Acting like a writer is the only way to get to be one, whether you feel like one or not. Persistence does pay."

DON'T EDIT YOURSELF TOO SOON

Elaine Kalman Naves: "Trust in your talent and your vision. Don't second guess yourself. There will come a time when you'll have to edit your work [before you submit it for publication], but believe that what you're doing is worthwhile."

WRITE FOR YOURSELF FIRST

Monique Polak: "I started writing because I love telling stories. I love teaching, but I sometimes get the feeling that I'm just helping other people, like a nurse. The students are wonderful but sometimes the nurse wants to be taken care of too. The writing was just a thing for me. I never meant it to be a money-making thing so that's been kind of a pleasant surprise."

SEEK OUT A WRITING COMMUNITY

Elise Moser: "Join a writing group, take workshops, go to events, read journals and magazines that publish the kind of writing that interests you. Meeting people will help you develop your sense of yourself as a writer and will link you to resources and information."

TAKE WRITING COURSES

Monique Polak: "Taking a course is a really good way to do the writing; you're forced to write. And it's said that you learn the most when it's someone else's work being critiqued, because you're so sensitive when it's your own work that it's difficult to take the critique in. When it's someone else's critique, you internalize it better."

LOOK FOR A MENTOR

Heather O'Neill: "What you're looking for when you're younger is an older writer who will shine their light on you. I never had a mentor, but people who do are so lucky. The first person who helped me was the editor of Open Letters. He did some favours for me because he really liked my writing. He put it in the hands of important people, and all it takes is one person to do that."

JOIN WRITERS' ORGANIZATIONS

Elise Moser: "The Quebec Writers' Federation (QWF) was essential to my development as a writer. I took workshops from them that gave me a ton of good training as well as a community of peers and mentors. I did a mentorship through them that gave me a more experienced writer to work with on my novel."

Monique Polak: "CANSCAIP (for children's writers) has been amazing. When I was first starting out, they had really practical tips."

EAGER BEAVERS GET THE WORK
Monique Polak: "Let people know that you're eager for the work. My father gave me this advice as a freelancer: 'Whatever they pay you, tell them you'll take $50 less but you want another assignment.' My newspaper editor didn't accept that, but he did give me another assignment!"

KEEP KNOCKING UNTIL THEY OPEN
Steve Galluccio: "Don't be afraid to knock on doors. Keep your eyes and ears wide open for any opportunity."

Monique Polak: "There's nothing wrong with being nervous about making the call or sending the email to a publisher or editor. Just do it! Every time you do it, it gets a little easier."

My new philosophy is, when you're 90 percent done, you're done. The last 10 percent is just self-doubt. Once it's at 90 percent, I'm done and it's out. I'll never get to 100 percent. Nothing is perfect, everything is flawed.

- Heather O'Neill, novelist and essayist

TAKING IT TO THE NEXT LEVEL

If spending quiet evenings alone with your private diary or laptop is your idea of the writer's life, think hard as you read this section. Many people can't foresee a future without a steady-paying job so choose to satisfy their creative urges by writing as a hobby, sharing their creations with family and friends, and maybe going so far as participating in public readings every now and again.

But if you're like Steve Galluccio, author of the award-winning play Mambo Italiano, and you can't imagine a full-time career that isn't writing, read on for some tips about jump-starting an emotionally and financially rewarding career.

I. THE BUSINESS OF BEING A WRITER

MAKE WRITING YOUR JOB
Steve Galluccio: "Write everyday if you're serious about writing. Make it your full-time job, and if you already have a job, use it and write about it. Everyone is a character and everyone has a story to tell—do a little embellishing, change the names, and you have yourself a script. Oh, and if you want to make it, get ready to fight. Only fighters succeed. The rest, no matter how talented, will fail.

WRITING IS A BUSINESS; BE PROFESSIONAL
Elise Moser: "As in any business, being organized helps a lot. Being professional—meeting deadlines, polishing your skills, preparing for readings and workshops, following through when you say you'll do something. It sounds obvious, but people fail to do these basic things all the time —and believe me, it will be noticed."

RESEARCH THE MARKET
Monique Polak: "Do your research before you get serious about a project and then again when you start submitting it. Is there a need for it? Think about where you'll place it, who will be interested in it. A good place for me to research is Babar Books, a great children's book store [in Montreal]."

EXERCISE YOUR DISCIPLINE MUSCLE

Heather O'Neill: "Discipline is something that develops. When I first started writing in my early twenties, I would write a couple of hours a day and that was exhausting. But you build up that muscle. Now I can write twelve hours a day and it's pleasurable. Your skill isn't in demand, so if you don't have that self-discipline, nobody cares."

KEEP EXCELLENT RECORDS

Monique Polak: "I really like that I'm running a small business. I started keeping records as a very young writer, keeping a little log of everything I sent out: the date of sending, the response. That's actually been very helpful to have. Every time I get a cheque I'll put it in the system and it feels great!"

COMBINE THE WRITING LIFE WITH YOUR "REGULAR" LIFE

Elaine Kalman Naves: "I mentor, I edit, I do translation work. They're all modest paying but they all take me to places where I can find inspiration for a book idea. They become related. You have to look around you and find out what's interesting to you. If it's interesting to you, it will be interesting to other people. A set of columns that I did many years ago became my book, The Writers of Montreal."

Monique Polak: "I have a teaching job at Marianopolis College in literature and humanities. I also write for the Gazette and other publications. What's good about that is it feeds into the fiction. If you're going to write fiction you need to get out of the house and have a story to tell. You need to be filling up with experience and ideas, and meeting people."

GET PROFESSIONAL HELP WHEN NECESSARY

Elaine Kalman Naves: "Sometimes you can't do everything yourself. I had a legal problem once, and the Writers' Union of Canada helped me grieve."

Elise Moser: "I have an accountant who specializes in working with artists who prepares my taxes. Apart from that, I issue my own invoices and such."

NURTURE YOUR WORKING RELATIONSHIPS

Elaine Kalman Naves: "Listen to your editors once you're lucky enough to have them. They're a sensible lot and they give good advice. You'll write better and you'll be better off."

Elise Moser: "Behave in a respectful and generous way with the people who publish you, hire you, host you, or read your writing. That's a skill and you may have to work on it."

KEEP TRACK OF YOUR CONTACTS

Monique Polak: "I still keep track of every [editor] I speak to. People shift from one publishing house to another. If you want to keep track of who's working where, pay attention to the acknowledgements page in the books you read. There's a lot you can learn from that. You'll learn that so-and-so is now working at such-and-such. That's helpful."

II. FINANCING AND MAKING MONEY

Being a writer doesn't take loads of cash, but you may need a of couple different income streams to make ends meet. And sometimes you'll need financing for a larger writing project that involves research or travel. Grants are a possible source of funding if you've already published. And, luckily, you're a writer, so that grant application shouldn't be too excruciating. But you should expect most of your projects to be self-financed—another reason you might need to keep your day job for awhile. And remember, there are always ways to extend your published work into other paid gigs like speaking engagements. Here's our writers' two cents on the subject:

LIVE WITHIN YOUR MEANS
Elise Moser: "Constantly stressing about money sucks up a lot of energy. Keep your expenses down. If you don't need a car and a warm vacation and fancy shoes, you can work less (or retire sooner) and have more writing time instead."

BE PREPARED TO SELF-FINANCE
Elaine Kalman Naves: "A lot of my projects have been self-financed. I received a very generous grant for Portrait of a Scandal but I didn't apply for a travel component and ended up financing my research trip to Scotland myself."

CHECK OUT AVAILABLE GRANTS
Heather O'Neill: "Canada Council grants aren't a lot of money but they're validation. To apply you need a certain number of publications."

Monique Polak: "My tip for grant writing would be to write with passion and show that you really care about a project. I think I was successful with my grant applications because they could tell that I really cared about the subjects."

LOOK FOR OFFBEAT FUNDING SOURCES
Elaine Kalman Naves: "There are some offbeat places where you can find funding. If you're doing something on Italy, maybe there's something in the Italian community that can help you. When I was writing about immigrant writers, I applied for a grant with the Secretary of State. Heritage Canada also gave me some funding when I went for a talk in the United States."

And for advice on how to get remunerated for what you write:

KNOW WHEN TO NEGOTIATE WITH PUBLISHERS

Elaine Kalman Naves: "I have an agent. Agents can help you land and negotiate contracts. But sometimes smaller publishers are scared by an agent, so you might be better off negotiating yourself once the contract arrives."

Monique Polak: "In the children's industry, there's not that much leeway for negotiation. A big negotiation might get me ten more free copies of my book. I know from talking to writer friends and other people in CANSCAIP that having an agent doesn't make a huge difference unless you're looking at foreign [rights] or something."

SUPPLEMENT YOUR WRITING WITH SPEAKING ENGAGEMENTS

Monique Polak: "One of the reasons I do school visits is for the money. A lot of writers will make their living from the writing and from school visits. They might be doing hundreds of visits a year. I couldn't do that many, but it's a way to get readers and I think it helps."

III. GETTING VISIBILITY

When asked about how to get visibility as a writer, our experts stressed the importance of staying connected with the local writing community. They pointed out that the more you work in the literary business, in any capacity, the higher your name recognition. And cultivating strong media contacts and an online presence can be crucial for when you've got a project worth crowing about. Here's their specific advice:

KEEP YOUR NAME IN THE PUBLIC EYE

Heather O'Neill: "To keep my visibility up, I'll do a lot of freelance stuff for magazines. It keeps my name out there. It's fun and it keeps me visible. People have to see your name a bunch of times before it clicks in their heads. I think it's something like five times before they recognize you."

WORKING IN THE INDUSTRY EXPANDS YOUR NETWORK

Elise Moser: "I had a jumpstart on visibility in the industry because, through my jobs as a bookseller and a sales rep, I knew a lot of people in publishing and in bookstores. That was a great help. And through my volunteer work with QWF my name became visible in a way it wouldn't have otherwise."

Elaine Kalman Naves: "I made a reputation by being the books columnist for the Gazette. When I was a book columnist, I wasn't just writing book reviews, I went to conferences and festivals, and interviewed everybody under the sun. And those interviews ran in the paper with my byline."

CULTIVATE YOUR MEDIA CONTACTS

Steve Galluccio: "I'm very hands on. I know most reporters in Montreal and some in Toronto as well, so I get in touch with them personally (yes I do have their numbers and/or emails) and ask if they want an interview."

Monique Polak: "My personal style is a little apologetic. I'll tell my media contacts, 'I don't want to be a bug, but in case you could use this, what do you think…?' I say I don't want to be a bug, and then I'm a bit of a bug."

BE PREPARED TO DO YOUR OWN PUBLICITY

Monique Polak: "More and more we have to do our own legwork for the promotion. My publisher sends out advanced reading copies and that leads to a lot of reviews, but in terms of extra stuff, I have to drum up quite a bit myself. It's time consuming, time I'd rather spend writing, but I realize that it's a big part of the work."

SELF-PROMOTION IS KEY

Steve Galluccio: "When I started out (at the Fringe Festival), I had to learn how to sell my shows, so I did my homework, found out who was writing for what paper, sent out press releases, invitations, did everything short of waiting in front of their houses to hand them a flyer. This was pre-Internet; I imagine it is easier now. Now I have people who do the work for me, but I still do plenty of self-promotion on Facebook and especially Twitter."

HAVE A VIRTUAL PRESENCE

Monique Polak: "I have a website that I value, and I write a blog. I don't do it a lot, but when I was on my book tour I was doing it every day for ten days. Usually I do it once a week. I've found that Facebook is good for book launches, because people show up when I never thought they would."

Elise Moser: "When I published my first novel, my publisher encouraged me to get a Facebook account, which I'd been avoiding. Now that I have one I find it a tremendous way to be in touch with a very large community and integrate my writing world with the rest of my life. My 'secret' to Facebook is be honest, be present, be generous."

TWEETING IS THE PERFECT WRITER'S MEDIUM

Heather O'Neill: "I've only just recently started to use Twitter. The funny thing about using Twitter as a writer is that your tweets are like little poems, you're tweeting in your medium—versus if you're an actor. But [on the downside] there may be higher expectations about what you'll tweet."

WRITERS OFTEN HELP FELLOW WRITERS

Steve Galluccio: "Once, I saw an ad in the Mirror. It was for a screenwriter looking for a translator for a script he had written in French. I just called this guy up, and he happened to be Émile Gaudreault. He had written Louis XIX, le roi des ondes and was looking to have it translated. Immediately, we started working together; he is the one who opened the door for me on the French side. Émile later went on to direct Mambo Italiano."

REACH OUT TO THE COMMUNITIES YOU WRITE ABOUT

Steve Galluccio: "When I was doing my stuff independently, I'd look at the play I was doing and if it had gay themes or women's themes, then I'd approach associations actively involved with those groups for sponsorship. For instance, when I did Peter and Paul Get Married, I went to Divers/Cité and told them I'd donate all of the box office profits for one night to their organization if they could totally fill the theatre. I did this because I knew that through word of mouth the news would spread and people would come see my show."

I waited a long time before I had the courage to start writing. Don't wait. Write.

- Elise Moser, writer and editor

LIVING AS A WRITER

The writers' life isn't for everyone. You need to balance the drive to write with the discipline to stop and smell the roses (especially if you want to write about them). Here's how our writers explain it:

LIVE LIFE! IT GIVES YOU SOMETHING TO WRITE ABOUT

Elaine Kalman Naves: "You have to work out your own balance. If you have time only for writing, you won't have that much to write about. You have to live. You need to have a life in order to have material to write about."

TAKE CARE OF YOURSELF AND OTHERS AROUND YOU

Elise Moser: "Be good to yourself and to the people around you; a nourishing life nourishes your art. A wild life is not very sustainable—hard on the organism and hard on relationships. You might only write on Sundays, but on Sundays you will absolutely write. Or maybe you'll take two years off to do a degree or have a baby, and then go back to your art, feeling refreshed and eager and full of new knowledge about life and about yourself."

BALANCE THE SOCIAL WITH THE STUDIOUS

Monique Polak: "I'm quite sociable. It's hard to find a balance between working and seeing everybody. I don't end up seeing anyone until I've had a full day of writing. But if I didn't have any of the social stuff going on I think I'd get lonely. I'm a runner, and when I'm running I often think about my story. Find what works for you."

COMPARTMENTALIZE YOUR DIVERGING PRIORITIES

Heather O'Neill: "You have to be very compartmentalized with all your jobs and do them one at a time. I find having a kid was the one thing that I prioritized over writing. I never skimped on time with my kid. After you learn how to balance work with having a kid, then everything is cake."

SET WRITING GOALS

Monique Polak: "The more time I have, the more time I waste. I need to be tough with myself. I give myself a word-count goal for the day. If my next project is thirty thousand words, I figure out how many words I have to write a day. Usually I beat the daily goal. In the summer I don't write on weekends, but during the year I do. I'm not the most fun to be around; my husband will sometimes say that my balance is off. But I have to work. The discipline part is about 95 percent of it. I don't know if I have more talent than another person. What I do have is discipline."

PUT THE WORK FIRST

Elise Moser: "Put the work first. Don't let your ego stop you from taking criticism, don't let resentment stop you from celebrating the successes of others in your community, and don't let the rest of your life get in the way of spending time with your writing, whatever form that takes (sometimes thinking is the best use of your writing time)."

Steve Galluccio: "Never lose focus and always remember that you are married to your work. Your work must give you the greatest satisfaction. Your work is your mistress."

BUT KNOW WHEN TO TAKE A BREAK

Heather O'Neill: "I find a lot of writers are really obsessive-compulsive workaholics. They actually need discipline to tear them away from writing."

BE STUBBORN EVEN IN THE FACE OF REJECTION

Elaine Kalman Naves: "You have to be stubborn. You have to be obsessed. You can't give up. Maybe you will for a while, but you need to stick with it. You need to be able to accept rejection, while still being sensitive enough to write perceptive and empathic pieces. I don't have a tough hide when it comes to rejection; it's a blow. But you have to be able to accept it and move forward."

FINAL THOUGHTS

When asked what they might have done a tad differently if they were starting out today, our writers had some wise words to share. Luckily, you're getting this advice now, so you can make your own totally unique mistakes. Just don't make theirs!

STICK TO IT

Monique Polak: "I really only figured out the stick-to-it-iveness in my thirties. In my twenties there were no computers, and I remember typing a little bit, wadding up the paper, and throwing it in the trash. I found it so depressing. All these years later, I'm up there in my office working on draft eighteen and there's no garbage can full of paper, but I've spent most of my time doing just that same thing; one step forward and another step back. Most of the time I feel grumpy and miserable, but I know I'll reach the goal by the end of the day.

If someone had said that to me in my twenties, I wouldn't have waited until I was in my thirties to really get serious about writing. I would have used that time to really push through those miserable feelings. Pushing through those miserable times is what it means to be a writer. I don't think it's a negative, I just think it's true. I guess I thought being a writer would mean loving every sentence and being a genius. It isn't! And I'm still doing it. The more you work at it the better it gets; eventually you read it over and it looks good."

DON'T FEAR REJECTION

Heather O'Neill: "When I was younger I would get really nervous and insecure. I'm not sure why. I should have just gone for it and not been so afraid. I think what holds writers back is thinking that they can't handle the rejection. But rejection is just part of life. One year my New Year's resolution was to get rejected! So I kept doing things that were out of my league and I would convince myself to go for crazy stuff. It was fantastic! I did get rejected for a bunch of things, but I also ended up with a few amazing things too. I heard a writer say once, 'Let other people reject you, don't reject yourself.' And I agree. Don't reject your own story!"

THERE ARE NO MISTAKES

Steve Galluccio: "First off: There are absolutely no mistakes, only lessons. Second: What should you avoid? No one should avoid anything. Listen, [this business] is like jumping off a series of mountains without a parachute. If you're not willing to do that, you need to be doing something else."

A PUBLISHER'S PERSPECTIVE
By Simon Dardick, Co-Publisher of Véhicule Press

Before a book can be published there has to be a manuscript!

Writers work in many different ways—some idiosyncratic, some totally formal—to arrive at a finished manuscript. There is no "right" way to create a work. However, when submitting work for publication, the type of work (i.e. non-fiction, fiction, graphic novels, poetry) sometimes necessitates different approaches.

THE BASIC WRITING GENRES

Non-Fiction: The subject of a non-fiction book usually arises out of a writer's personal experience or professional interest (e.g. a collection of essays on nature subjects, history, biography), but the designation "non-fiction" can get a bit complicated. In the last several years writers and publishers have used the term "creative non-fiction." Creative non-fiction is a hybrid of literature and non-fiction—facts presented within the context of fiction.

Poetry: A collection including new poems and/or poems which may have been previously published.

Fiction: Novels, novellas, and short stories (which may have been published).

Graphic Novels: Some say it's a term created by comic book pioneer Will Eisner. This genre is a self-contained comic book (fiction or non-fiction) in book format with high-quality storyline and artwork.

WHAT DO PUBLISHERS WANT TO RECEIVE?

Depending on the kind of work you're submitting, you'll want to send publishers a selection of the items listed below:

Correspondence: For non-fiction, send a simple and clear email that includes a brief description of the book project.

Your credentials: Include a short bio and/or CV that includes anything you may have published—student publications, online journals, etc.

A project sample: Send fiction publishers two chapters and poetry publishers no more than fifteen poems. Fantasy fiction publishers want to see a synopsis before inviting the manuscript to be sent. A synopsis can be sent to fiction publishers too, but what they really want to see is a sample of the writing. For non-fiction, the publisher can pretty well tell from a description of the project whether it interests them or not.

Images: Include a good sampling of images if submitting a graphic novel, plus a synopsis.

GET THE BASICS RIGHT

Don't be sloppy: You are a professional writer, so write a professional email! Spell-check exists for a reason!

Check the publisher's guidelines: Many publishers will not accept multiple submissions. Check their website to ascertain their policy.

Use correct formatting: Most prose should be double-spaced using a practical typestyle like Times New Roman (11 pt), with 1.5 inch margins all around.

FIND THE BEST PUBLISHER FOR YOUR WORK

In the beginning, your submission options may seem overwhelming. And you will get overwhelmed if you don't narrow down the number of publishers you target.

Try online publications: Online journals (such as the Quebec Writers' Federation's *Carte Blanche*: http://archive.carte-blanche.org/) plus web versions of actual magazines are a good place for first-time authors to get work published. Online publication is definitely an option.

Do your research: You can go to bookstores to find publishers with work that is simpatico with yours, or check out the reference section of a library for *Literary Market Place* (United States) and *The Book Trade in Canada*—the bibles of the book trade that include information on publishers and agents. However, it is easier to go directly to publishers' websites, which can be found through their association websites. You will find information that includes the genres they publish, manuscript submitting procedures, the names of the editors, and other useful information. It's always better to send an email to a specific person.

CHECK OUT PUBLISHERS' WEBSITES

For the most current and comprehensive information it's best to check out each publisher's website before submitting. Most can be found through the association websites below:

Association of Canadian Publishers: www.publishers.ca
Literary Press Group: www.lpg.ca
Association national des éditeurs des livres: www.anel.qc.ca
Magazines Canada: www.cmpa.ca

SUBMIT TO WRITING COMPETITIONS

Don't overlook writing competitions that are available from literary journals such as *Vallum* (http://www.vallummag.com/) and the *Malahat Review* (http://web.uvic.ca/malahat/). Check out the journals listed above with Magazines Canada. The annual Quebec Writing Competition provides an opportunity for writers to get short prose pieces published and read on CBC Radio (http://www.cbc.ca/montreal/features/writingcompetition/).

NETWORK WITH OTHER WRITERS

Emerging writers should join groups like the Quebec Writers' Federation (http://www.qwf.org/) where writers exchange valuable information in a collegial manner at their various events. In addition, the association offers workshops and mentorship programs. It is not expensive to join.

HOW PUBLISHERS DEAL WITH MANUSCRIPTS

Most large publishers will not accept unsolicited manuscripts. The good news is that books do get published. For first books it's usually smaller and medium-size publishers who will look at a submission and take a chance. Editors sometimes approach writers whose work they have seen in other publications.

It takes just a few minutes for an editor to know whether the manuscript is good writing and appropriate for the publishing house. If you are fortunate, what you have submitted excites the editor and you will get an immediate response to send the full manuscript. But publishers can take up to three months to respond. Many, regrettably, take longer. After two months it is okay to make an enquiry.

DO YOU NEED AN AGENT?

Literary agents are listed in *Literary Market Place* and *The Book Trade in Canada*. It is important to note that a legitimate agent never charges a fee for evaluating a manuscript. And it's worth noting that it can be just as difficult to find an agent as it is to find a publisher—maybe more so! Before an agent takes on an author they assess the market potential of the manuscript to determine if they think it's saleable. Only then will they take an author on.

So what can a genuine agent do for you?

Agents sometimes provide editorial comments for authors they take on, but their principle role is in finding a publisher and negotiating advantageous contractual terms. Though they may negotiate on your behalf, they will never make a deal without your approval. Agents are paid by charging a commission on all revenues from the book sale. They also collect monies owing from the publisher and other licensees, and they protect the author's copyright.

What's the sign of a good agent? Even if a sale is not made, if your agent gets your manuscript read by reputable editors, they've done their job. The rest is up to you, or more precisely, your work.

Simon Dardick is the Co-Publisher of Véhicule Press.

RESOURCES

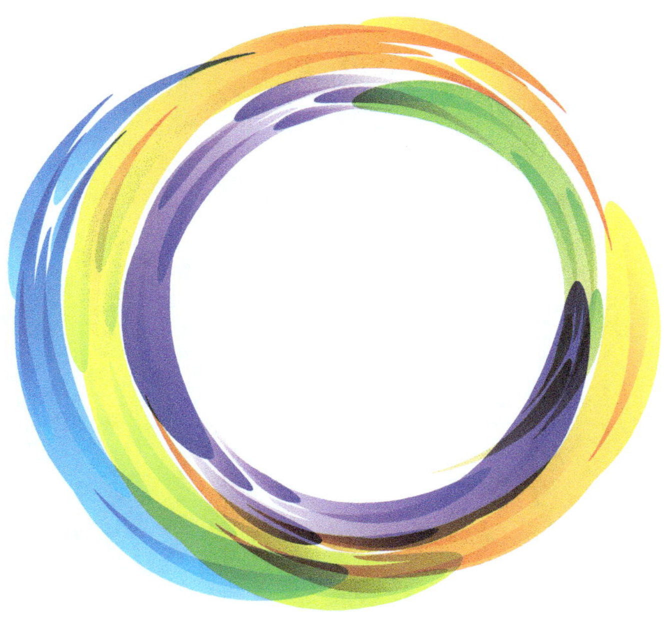

Here you will find a list of resources that can help you establish and fund your business, promote your work and defend your interests. Visit the **www.yesmontreal.ca** website for additional video content from some of the contributors.

Please note: We have endeavoured to make our resource information as accurate, complete and up-to-date as possible. Nevertheless, this is not a complete listing of every organization serving artists, and the information listed below is subject to change.

FILM AND TELEVISION

THE ACADEMY OF CANADIAN CINEMA & TELEVISION
416-366-2227
www.academy.ca

The Academy's Mandate is to honour outstanding achievements in Canadian film, television & digital media; heighten public awareness and increase audience attendance, viewership, and appreciation of Canadian screen productions through awards shows, social media channels and activities; provide a wide range of industry-related professional development events; preserve and promote Canada's film, television and digital media legacy.

ALLIANCE OF CANADIAN CINEMA, TELEVISION AND RADIO ARTISTS (ACTRA)
514-844-3318
www.actra.ca

The Mission of ACTRA has always been to negotiate, safeguard and promote the professional rights of performers working in The English-language recorded media: Film, Television, Video and all other recorded media.

ASSOCIATION DES CINÉMAS PARALLÈLES DU QUÉBEC (ACPQ)
514-252-3021
www.cinemasparalleles.qc.ca

ACPQ's mission is to promote the independent Quebec film culture as a high-quality and diverse form of entertainment.

ASSOCIATION DES RÉALISATEURS ET RÉALISATRICES DU QUÉBEC (ARRQ)
514-842-7373
www.arrq.qc.ca

ARRQ is a professional association committed to the advocacy and professional, economic, cultural, social, development of directors in Quebec, primarily in the French fields of cinema, television and the web.

ASSOCIATION QUÉBÉCOISE DE LA PRODUCTION MÉDIATIQUE (AQPM)
514-397-8600
www.aqpm.ca

The APFTQ represents the vast majority of independent film and television production companies in Quebec.

CANADIAN ASSOCIATION OF FILM DISTRIBUTORS AND EXPORTERS (CAFDE)
613-238-3557
www.cafde.ca

CAFDE serves to represent the Canadian film distribution industry and its members on matters of national interest.

CANADIAN FILM CENTRE
416-445-1446
www.cfccreates.com

The Canadian Film Centre (CFC) is a leader in mentoring content creators and entrepreneurs in the entertainment and digital media landscapes. With over 100 participants in more than a dozen programs each year, our mandate is to promote and invest in original projects, encourage commercial opportunities and build collaborative relationships between our alumni and media companies.

CANADIAN MEDIA PRODUCTION ASSOCIATION (CPMA)
1-800-656-7440
www.cmpa.ca

The Canadian Media Production Association (CMPA) is Canada's leading trade association for independent producers. The CMPA works on behalf of members to promote and stimulate the Canadian production industry.

DOCUMENTARY ORGANIZATION OF CANADA/DOCUMENTARISTES DU CANADA (DOC)
416-599-3844
1 877-467-4485
www.docorg.ca

The Documentary Organization of Canada (DOC) is the collective voice of independent documentary makers across Canada. DOC helps Canadian documentary-makers get their work made and seen. DOC offers top-notch professional development and networking opportunities through our workshops, master classes, mentorship programs, services and benefits.

FEMMES DU CINÉMA DE LA TÉLÉVISION ET DES NOUVEAUX MÉDIAS (FCTNM)
514-285-1840 ext. 250
www.fctnm.org

FCTNM is a non-profit association representing all women in the film industry, television and new media.

MAIN FILM
(514) 845-7442
www.mainfilm.qc.ca

Main Film's mandate is to facilitate, stimulate and promote independent filmmaking by providing filmmakers with production equipment and post-production facilities.

MONTREAL FILM AND TV COMMISSION
(514) 872-2883
www.montrealfilm.com

The Montreal Film and Television Commission coordinates all of the logistical aspects of film and television shoots on its territory and promotes Montreal to foreign producers.

MONTREAL FILM GROUP (MFG)
www.montrealfilmgroup.com

The Montreal Film Group's mission is to bring together like-minded film and TV industry folks who are eager to be part of a thriving - and growing - community.

NATIONAL FILM BOARD OF CANADA (NFB)
1-800-267-7710
www.onf-nfb.gc.ca

Canada's public film producer and distributor, the National Film Board of Canada creates social-issue documentaries, auteur animation, alternative drama and digital content that provide the world with a unique Canadian perspective.

NATIONAL SCREEN INSTITUTE (NSI)
204-956-7800
www.nsi-canada.ca

The National Screen Institute is the leader in developing the careers and projects of Canadian writers, producers and directors by delivering professional, market-driven and innovative training that gets results.

RÉGIE DU CINÉMA QUÉBEC
1-800-463-2463
www.rcq.gouv.qc.ca

La Régie du cinéma's mandate consists of monitoring and controlling the exhibition of cinematographic works in Québec.

SOCIÉTÉ DES AUTEURS DE RADIO, TÉLÉVISION ET CINÉMA (SARTEC)
(514) 526-9196
www.sartec.qc.ca

Unite and represent authors working in French in Canada in radio, television, film and audiovisual arts. The objective of the organization is the study, protection and development of the economic, social and ethical interests of its members.

WOMEN IN THE DIRECTOR'S CHAIR (WIDC)
604-987-0747
1-877-913-0747
www.widc.ca

The Women In the Director's Chair (WIDC) is an intensive, hands-on mentorship program providing professional and creative development to mid-career Canadian women directors of screen-based fiction.

WRITERS GUILD OF CANADA
1-800-567-9974
www.wgc.ca

The Writers Guild of Canada represents screenwriters working in television, film, radio and new media and negotiates on behalf of its members on matters concerning pay rates, contracts and working conditions for English-language productions in Canada.

DANCE

CANADIAN ALLIANCE OF DANCE ARTISTS, ONTARIO CHAPTER (CADA-ON)
416-657-2276
www.cadaontario.camp8.org

CADA-ON is a professional association for dance artists founded and run by dance artists that works to empower and educate members towards self-representation.

REGROUPEMENT QUÉBÉCOIS DE LA DANSE (RQD)
514-849-4003
www.quebecdanse.org

The Regroupement québécois de la danse (RQD) is a non-profit association, active at the municipal, provincial and federal levels, that represents and defends the interests of over 500 dance professionals.

FASHION

APPAREL QUÉBEC / VÊTEMENT QUÉBEC
514-382-3846
www.vetementquebec.com

Apparel Quebec (AQ) is a non-profit organization that supports and promotes the fashion industry throughout the Province. Apparel Quebec is committed to raise the growth of the fashion industry and to promote it on the national and international level.

MONTREAL FASHION BUREAU
311 (In Montreal)
514-872-0311 (Outside Montreal)
http://ville.montreal.qc.ca/portal/page?_pageid=6257,50563615&_dad=portal&_schema=PORTAL

The role of the Montréal Fashion Bureau (MFB) is to promote Montréal fashion by working with the industry's leading stakeholders, resulting in value-added activities that help give Montréal its distinctive identity.

MONTREAL FASHION MART
514-381-5921
www.montrealfashionmart.com

The largest fashion marketing center in Canada, Montreal's Fashion Mart houses the greatest concentration of fashion collections and resources in the country. The Montreal's Fashion Mart offers a constantly changing environment, mixing showrooms, offices, marketing agencies, design, innovation and distribution centers, this space is at the service of renowned and emerging designers, sales agencies and many buyers from across the country.

TORONTO FASHION INCUBATOR (TFI)
416-971-7117
www.fashionincubator.com

The Toronto Fashion Incubator (TFI) is an award-winning and highly-acclaimed non-profit organization dedicated to supporting and nurturing Canadian fashion designers and entrepreneurs.

GRAPHIC DESIGN & ILLUSTRATION

SOCIÉTÉ DES DESIGNERS GRAPHIQUES DU QUÉBEC (SDGQ)
514-842-3960
1-866-842-3960
www.sdgq.ca

SDGQ is a professional association where graphic designers from all backgrounds in Quebec can share and network.

ILLUSTRATION QUEBEC
514-522-2040
www.illustrationquebec.com

Illustration Quebec is a nonprofit organization whose mission is to consolidate and sustain illustrators as well as promotes and distributes the artwork.

MEDIA ARTS

ALLIANCE QUÉBÉCOISE DES TECHNICIENS DE L'IMAGE ET DU SON (AQTIS)
1 888 647-0681
www.aqtis.qc.ca

AQTIS is the representative of some 4,500 artisans and freelancers in over 126 jobs related to audiovisual and sound design, planning, and implementation.

CONSEIL QUÉBÉCOIS DES ARTS MÉDIATIQUES (CQAM)
514-527-5116
1-888-527-5116
www.cqam.org

CQAM is the only media arts advocacy organization in Quebec welcoming professional independent artists, cultural workers, emerging artists and artist-run centres devoted to media arts as members.

INDEPENDENT MEDIA ARTS ALLIANCE (IMAA)
514-522-8240
www.imaa.ca

The IMAA is a national arts service organization that advances the interests of the media arts community in Canada.

MUSIC

ALLIANCE NATIONALE DE L'INDUSTRIE MUSICAL (ANIM)
613-298-1380
www.anim.ca

ANIM'S mission is to contribute to the consolidation and growth of the French-Canadian music industry by supporting the efforts of its members in achieving their individual and collective goals.

ASSOCIATION DE L'INDUSTRIE DU DISQUE, DU SPECTACLE ET DE LA VIDÉO (ADISQ)
514-842-5147
www.adisq.com

A non-profit organization that defends the interests of its members and helps develop the Quebec music industry.

CANADIAN AMATEUR MUSICIANS / MUSICIENS AMATEURS DU CANADA (CAMMAC)
1-888-622-8755
www.cammac.ca

At CAMMAC, you can make music in a relaxed and non-competitive atmosphere, make new friends with similar interests, learn from passionate teachers and discover new repertoire both in class and in concert.

CANADIAN INDEPENDENT MUSIC ASSOCIATION (CIMA)
416-485-3152
www.cimamusic.ca

CIMA is the not-for-profit national trade association representing the English-language, Canadian-owned sector of the music industry.

CANADIAN INDEPENDENT RECORDING ARTISTS' ASSOCIATION
416-203-1011
1-866-482-4722
http://ciraa.ca/

CIRAA helps to empower Canada's Independent recording artists. Their programming is designed to improve Canada's independent artist development system through education, opportunity and support. Membership is free and gives you full access to The New Indie, The CIRAA Mentorship Program and The CIRAA Groundbreaker Grant.

CANADIAN MUSIC CENTRE
416-961-6601
www.musiccentre.ca

The Canadian Music Centre exists to stimulate the awareness, appreciation and performance of Canadian new music by making the music of its Associate Composers available through the Centre's collection.

CANADIAN MUSICAL REPRODUCTION RIGHTS AGENCY LTD. (CMRRA)
416-926-1966
www.cmrra.ca

The Canadian Musical Reproduction Rights Agency Ltd is a music licensing collective representing music rights holders who range in size from large multinational music publishers to individual songwriters.

CANADIAN SOCIETY FOR TRADITIONAL MUSIC
416-736-2100
www.yorku.ca/cstm/home.htm

The Canadian Society for Traditional Music is dedicated to the study and promotion of musical traditions of all communities and cultures, in all their aspects.

CODES D'ACCÈS
514-879-9676
www.codesdacces.org

Codes d'accès is an organization that is dedicated entirely to the promotion of young talent in new music, including composers, performers and arts administrators who wish to make their debut in the industry.

CONSEIL QUÉBÉCOIS DE LA MUSIQUE (CQM)
514-524-1310
www.cqm.qc.ca

The Conseil québécois de la musique (CQM) is a non-profit organization. Its mandate is to bring together professional organizations and individuals working in the field of concert music.

MUSIC CANADA
416-967-7272
musiccanada.com

Music Canada's members are engaged in all aspects of the recording industry, including the manufacture, production, promotion and distribution of music.

ORCHESTRAS/ORCHESTRES CANADA

416-366-8834

www.orchestrascanada.org

Orchestras Canada is the united national voice of Canadian orchestras: a focal point for industry intelligence and collective action.

POP MONTREAL SYMPOSIUM

514-842-1919

http://popmontreal.com/symposium-about/

The POP Montreal Symposium is a conference focusing on the relationships between music, art, culture, and creativity. The Symposium includes workshops, conversations with icons new and old, panels and round table discussions.

QUEBEC MUSICIANS' GUILD/GUILDE DES MUSICIENS DU QUÉBEC

1-800-363-6688

www.gmmq.com

The mission of the GMMQ is to represent and defend the moral, social and economic, social interests of professional musicians, to ensure that their contribution to the community is duly recognized.

SOCIÉTÉ DE MUSIQUE CONTEMPORAINE DU QUÉBEC (SMCQ)

514-843-9305

www.smcq.qc.ca

The SMCQ is an institution that has been at the heart of musical creativity for almost 50 years whose mandate is to promote contemporary music from both Canada and abroad.

SOCIÉTÉ PROFESSIONNELLE DES AUTEURS ET DES COMPOSITEURS DU QUÉBEC (SPACQ)

514-845-3739

1-866-445-3739

www.spacq.qc.ca

SPACQ is an association that represents the moral, economic and professional interests of Quebec composers as well as all music composers across Canada.

SOCIETY OF COMPOSERS, AUTHORS AND MUSIC PUBLISHERS OF CANADA (SOCAN)

1-800-55-SOCAN (7-6226)

www.socan.ca

SOCAN is a not-for-profit organization that represents the Canadian performing rights of millions of Canadian and international music creators and publishers.

SONGWRITERS ASSOCIATION OF CANADA (SAC)

1-866-456-7664

www.songwriters.ca

The S.A.C. exists to nurture, develop and protect the creative, business, and legal interests of music creators in Canada and around the world.

SOUND EXCHANGE

202-640-5858

www.soundexchange.com

SoundExchange helps the music and creative community thrive in the digital age. SoundExchange is the independent nonprofit performance rights organization that collects and distributes digital performance royalties to featured artists and copyright holders.

NEW MEDIA

INTERNATIONAL GAME DEVELOPERS ASSOCIATION (IGDA)

www.igda.org

The IDGA's mission is to advance the careers and enhance the lives of game developers by connecting members with their peers, promoting professional development, and advocating on issues that affect the developer community.

OBORO

514-844-3250

www.oboro.net

Montreal-based artist-run centre dedicated to production and presentation of art, contemporary practices and new media through services, workshops and some grant opportunities.

WOMEN IN GAMES INTERNATIONAL (WIGI)

www.womeningamesinternational.org

Women In Games International stands as strong advocates for issues crucial to the success of women and men in the games industry, including a better work/life balance, healthy working conditions, increased opportunities for success and resources for career support.

PERFORMING ARTS

ASSOCIATION DES PROFESSIONNELS DE L'INDUSTRIE DE L'HUMOUR (APIH)
514-527-8300
www.apih.ca

APIH is a non-profit organization that oversees the development and promotion of comedians.

CANADIAN ACTOR ONLINE INC.
www.canadianactor.com

Canadian Actor Online Inc is a national, online education and information resource for actors.

CANADIAN ACTORS' EQUITY ASSOCIATION (CAEA)
416-867-9165
www.caea.com

Canadian Actors' Equity Association represents professional artists including performers (actors, singers, dancers), directors, choreographers, fight directors and stage managers, engaged in theatre, opera and dance in English Canada.

CONNECTING THE CANADIAN LIVE PERFORMANCE COMMUNITY (CITT/ICTS)
613-482-1165
1-888-271-3383
www.citt.org

CITT is a national arts service organization that actively promotes the professional development of its members and works for the betterment of the Canadian live performance community.

UNION DES ARTISTS (UDA)
514-288-6682
www.uniondesartistes.com

The Union des artistes (UDA) is a professional union representing artists working in French in Quebec and Canada, and all artists working in a language other than French and English in Quebec.

PHOTOGRAPHY

CANADIAN ASSOCIATION FOR PHOTOGRAPHIC ART (CAPA)
604-855-4848
www.capacanada.ca

CAPA promotes art and science of photography in all its forms throughout Canada and the world and provides useful information to photographers.

CANADIAN ASSOCIATION OF PROFESSIONAL IMAGE CREATORS
1-888-252-2742
www.capic.org

As a professional association, CAPIC's mission is to promote quality and creativity among professional photographers, illustrators and digital artists in Canada as well as good business practices.

DAZIBAO
514-845-0063
www.dazibao-photo.org

Dazibao is a centre dedicated to the dissemination of contemporary image practices—photography, multimedia, video and film and is a springboard for young and established artists, an ideal space for developing projects of an experimental nature.

PHOTOGRAPHES PROFESSIONELS DU QUÉBEC (PPDQ)
438-397-8182
www.ppdq.ca

PPQD is a non-profit organization whose mandate is the advancement of professional photography while ensuring consumer protection and a high level of quality.

PROFESSIONAL PHOTOGRAPHERS OF CANADA (PPOC)
1-888-643-7762
www.ppoc.ca

The Professional Photographers of Canada's mission is to qualify and support photographers to become industry leaders and to inform the public of the value in hiring an accredited professional photographer.

THEATRE

ASSOCIATION DES COMPAGNIES DE THÉÂTRE ASSOCIATION (ACT)
1-866-348-8960
www.act-theatre.ca

ACT is a non-profit organization that supports French-language theatre producers in Canada.

ASSOCIATION DES PROFESSIONELS DES ARTS DE LA SCÈNE DU QUÉBEC (APASQ)
514-523-4221
1-877-523-4221
www.apasq.org

APASQ is an association that represents lighting, costume, décor and sound designers and artists in the performing, recording and cinema industries.

CONSEIL QUÉBÉCOIS DU THÉÂTRE (CQT)
1-866-954-0270
www.cqt.ca

The mission of the Conseil québécois du théâtre (CQT) is to gather and represent the professional theater community in Quebec and provide support to lever for development in the service of theatre in province.

FÉDÉRATION QUÉBÉCOISE DU THÉÂTRE AMATEUR (FQTA)
819-752-2501
www.fqta.ca

The mandate of the FQTA is to bring together individuals and theater groups, to promote the development of amateur theater thus contributing to the aesthetic, artistic and social education of the population.

NATIONAL ARTS CENTRE/CENTRE NATIONAL DES ARTS
1-866-850-2787
info@nac-cna.ca

The National Arts Centre collaborates with artists and arts organizations across Canada to help create a national stage for the performing arts, and acts as a catalyst for performance, creation and learning across the country.

PLAYWRIGHTS GUILD OF CANADA (PGC)
416-703-0201
www.playwrightsguild.ca

PGC is a registered national arts service association mandated to advance the creative rights and interests of professional Canadian playwrights, promote Canadian plays nationally and internationally, and foster an active, evolving community of writers for the stage.

PLAYWRIGHTS' WORKSHOP MONTREAL (PWM)/ATELIER DE RAMATURGIE DE MONTRÉAL
514-843-3685
www.playwrights.ca

Playwrights' Workshop Montréal (PWM) is a national new play development centre established to support the development of playwrights and contemporary work for the stage.

QUEBEC DRAMA FEDERATION (QDF)
514-875-8698
www.quebecdrama.org

Through a combination of education, communications, professional training and networking initiatives, the Québec Drama Federation sustains and supports the development of English-language theatre in Québec.

VISUAL ARTS

ARPRIM
514-525-2621
www.arprim.org

Arprim strives to increase the visibility of emerging practices in print art by presenting exhibitions, events and meetings.

ARTICULE
514-842-9686
www.articule.org

Articule is an open-access artist-run centre dedicated to the presentation of a broad range of contemporary art practices.

ASSOCIATION DES GALERIES D'ART CONTEMPORAIN (AGAC)
514-798-5010
www.agac.qc.ca

AGAC is a not-for-profit organization whose primary mandate is to further develop the recognition and prosperity of the contemporary art market in Canada.

CANADIAN ARTISTS' REPRESENTATION / LE FRONT DES ARTISTES CANADIENS (CARFAC)
1-866-344-6161
www.carfac.ca

CARFAC's mandate is to promote the visual arts in Canada, to promote a socio-economic climate that is conducive to the production of visual arts in Canada, and to conduct research and engage in public education for these purposes.

CENTRE CLARK

514-288-4972

www.centreclark.com

The Centre CLARK is an artist-run centre dedicated to the presentation and production of contemporary art in addition to housing a library, as well as offering a residency program and several off-site projects and partnerships.

CONSEIL DES MÉTIERS D'ART DU QUEBEC (CMAQ)

1-855-515-2787

www.metiers-d-art.qc.ca

As a professional corporation of artists and artisans in the crafts, the Council of the Quebec Craft (CMAQ) is the main lever for development of Quebec crafts and their national and international marketing.

COOP ST-LAURENT DES ARTS

514-289-1009

514-985-5319

www.coopstlaurent.com

Coop St-Laurent des Arts is dedicated to creating and maintaining an urban space devoted to artistic development in Montreal. It operates an art supply store and low-rent art studios, and offers art classes.

DARE-DARE

514-849-DARE (3273)

www.dare-dare.org

As an artist-run center DARE-DARE supports research and valorises emerging practices and is a flexible, open space devoted to research, experimentation, risk and critical inquiry.

FEDERATION OF CANADIAN ARTISTS (FCA)

604-681-2744

www.artists.ca

The mission of the FCA is to advance the knowledge and appreciation of art and culture to all Canadians, offering education, exhibition and communication in the Visual Arts, and to support and promote emerging to professional member artists.

REGROUPEMENT DES ARTISTES EN ARTS VISUELS DU QUÉBEC (RAAV)

514-866-7101

www.raav.org

The mission of RAAV is working to improve the living conditions and professional practice of artists who wish to pursue a career in the visual arts in Quebec.

SCULPTORS SOCIETY OF CANADA (SSC)

647-435-5858

www.cansculpt.org

The Sculptors Society of Canada promotes Canadian sculpture and sculptors nationally and internationally, and nurtures young talent, including graduating students and emerging sculptors.

SOCIÉTÉ DES MUSÉES QUÉBÉCOIS (SMQ)

514-987-3264

www.smq.qc.ca

The Société des musées québécois (SMQ) is an umbrella group representing museums and similar institutions (exhibition centres and interpretation sites) and museology professionals in Quebec.

SOCIETY OF CANADIAN ARTISTS

www.societyofcanadianartists.com

The Society of Canadian Artists is the young, national, non-profit artists' organization born to foster and celebrate the visual arts in Canada.

WRITING & PUBLISHING

ASSOCIATION DES ÉCRIVAINS QUÉBÉCOIS POUR LA JEUNESSE (AEQJ)

www.aeqj.com

The Association of Quebec writers for Youth was founded to promote youth literature and its creators and represent its members to the public, government, media and all stakeholders in the publishing world.

ASSOCIATION FOR CANADIAN AND QUÉBEC LITERATURES (AQCL)/ASSOCIATION DES LITTÉRATURES CANADIENNES ET QUÉBÉCOISE

www.alcq-acql.ca

The Association for Canadian and Québec Literatures is a learned society that promotes research, pedagogies, new knowledge, literary criticism and theory about the diverse literatures of Canada and Québec.

ASSOCIATION OF CANADIAN PUBLISHERS (ACP)

416-487-6116

www.publishers.ca

The ACP assists Canadian-owned publishers in promoting the excellence of Canadian books, in bringing more Canadian books to more readers in Canada, and in expanding Canadian-owned publishers' domestic and international market share.

ASSOCIATION OF ENGLISH-LANGUAGE PUBLISHERS OF QUÉBEC (AELAQ)

514-932-5633

www.aelag.org

The Association of English-language Publishers of Quebec advances the publication, distribution, and promotion of English-language books from Quebec.

BLUE METROPOLIS FOUNDATION

514-932-1112

www.bluemetropolis.org

The Blue Metropolis Foundation brings together people from different cultures to share the pleasure of reading and writing, and encourages creativity and intercultural understanding.

CANADIAN AUTHORS ASSOCIATION

705-325-3926

www.canadianauthors.org

The Canadian Authors Association provides writers with a wide variety of programs, services and resources to help them develop their skills in both the craft and the business of writing, enhance their ability to earn a living as a writer, and have access to a Canada-wide network of writers and publishing industry professionals.

CANADIAN BOOKSELLERS ASSOCIATION

1-888-373-8245

www.retailcouncil.org/mystore/booksellers

The communities that form around independent bookstores are a unique intersection of art, business, community and self-improvement, and independent bookstores are a key element to maintaining a thriving and developing book industry in Canada.

CANSCAIP

416-515-1559

www.canscaip.org

The Canadian Society of Children's Authors, Illustrators and Performers (CANSCAIP) is a group of professionals in the field of children's culture with members from all parts of Canada.

CENTRE DES AUTEURS DRAMATIQUES (CEAD)

514-288-3384

www.cead.qc.ca

An association of playwrights at the playwrights' service, the CEAD provides support for playwriting development and promotes Canadian Francophone plays and playwrights.

COPIBEC
1-800-717-2022
www.copibec.qc.ca

Copibec's mission is to act on behalf of copyright owners, i.e. Quebec authors and publishers who have given Copibec authority to manage the reproduction rights for their printed works (books, newspapers and periodicals).

EDITORS' ASSOCIATION OF CANADA
1-866-226-3348
www.editors.ca

The Editors' Association of Canada promotes professional editing as key in producing effective communication and offers training opportunities and resources to editors; while providing access to a network of editors, clients and employers in Canada.

FÉDÉRATION PROFESSIONNELLE DES JOURNALISTES DU QUEBEC
514-522-6142
www.fpjq.org

The Fédération professionnelle des journalistes du Québec defends freedom of the press and the public right to information.

L'ASSOCIATION QUÉBÉCOISE DES AUTEURS DRAMATIQUES (AQAD)
514-596-3705
www.aqad.qc.ca

AQAD's mission is to defend the social, economic, professional and moral rights of professional playwrights, librettists and French translators in Quebec and Canada.

LEAGUE OF CANADIAN POETS
416-504-1657
www.poets.ca
www.youngpoets.ca

The League of Canadian Poets is the professional organization for established and emerging Canadian poets.

LITERARY PRESS GROUP OF CANADA (LPG)
416-483-1321
www.lpg.ca

The Literary Press Group of Canada (LPG) is a not-for-profit association that helps member publishers sell, distribute, and market their books to booksellers, libraries, institutions, as well as directly to readers.

LITERARY TRANSLATORS' ASSOCIATION OF CANADA (LTAC)
514-848-2424 ext. 8702
www.attlc-ltac.org

The mandate of the Literary Translators' Association of Canada is to promote the art of literary translation and advance the interests of literary translators in Canada.

PROFESSIONAL WRITERS ASSOCIATION OF CANADA (PWAC)
416-504-1645
www.pwac.ca

PWAC serves Canadian non-fiction freelance writers across the country. As a not-for-profit, PWAC reflects your broader professional interests and advocate for Canadian writers to receive fair pay, contracts and treatment.

QUEBEC WRITERS' FEDERATION (QWF)
514-933-0878
www.qwf.org

The QWF's purpose is to provide community support for the promotion and encouragement of Québec's English-language literary arts and to undertake activities which will increase public awareness of the English-language literary arts and literary institutions.

SOCIÉTÉ DE DÉVELOPPMENT DES PÉRIODIQUES CULTURELS QUÉBÉCOIS (SODEP)
514-397-8669
www.sodep.qc.ca

SODEP is a non-profit organization whose mission is to represent publishers of Quebec cultural magazines and provide them with administrative support.

SOCIÉTÉ DES AUTEURS ET COMPOSITEURS DRAMATIQUES (SACD)
514-738-8877
www.sacd.ca

SACD is an Authors' Society which protects the rights of its members and collects royalties for the use of their work.

UNION DES ÉCRIVAINES ET ÉCRIVAINS QUÉBÉCOIS
1-888-849-8540
www.uneq.qc.ca

UNEQ's mission is to support the promotion and dissemination of Quebec literature, Quebec, Canada and abroad, as well as the defense of socio-economic rights of authors.

WRITERS' UNION OF CANADA
416-703-8982
www.writersunion.ca

The Writers' Union of Canada advocates on behalf of all writers for a stronger literary culture — one that treats artists fairly and with respect, and makes it possible for our nation's stories to continue to be told.

MISCELLANEOUS ORGANIZATIONS

ASSOCIATION DES JURISTES POUR L'AVANCEMENT DE LA VIE ARTISTIQUE
514-954-3471
www.ajava.ca

AJAVA is an association of Quebec lawyers practicing entertainment law, either in private practice or in a business or corporation, and catering to artists and professionals from different cultural industries.

ART CONSULTANTS CANADA/CONSULTANTS CANADIENS EN ARTS (ACCA)
416-921-0208
www.artsconsultants.ca

Arts Consultants Canada is a professional association of consultants who provide services to clients in the arts and cultural sector in Canada. ACCA's members work to improve the health, effectiveness and sustainability of the arts.

ARTÈRE (POUR LA RELÈVE ARTISTIQUE MONTRÉALAISE)
www.artere.qc.ca

An initiative of the Montreal Arts Council, ARTÈRE is an online portal which aims to centralize necessary information to the professional development of emerging artists. (In French only)

ARTEXTE INFORMATION CENTRE
www.artexte.ca

The Artexte Information Centre offers reference and research support for students, artists, curators and other arts professionals.

ARTISTS U
www.artistsu.org

Artists U is a grassroots, artist-run platform for changing the working conditions of artists that pushes artists to build lives that are balanced, productive, and sustainable.

BUSINESS FOR THE ARTS (BFTA)

416-869-3016

www.businessforthearts.org

Business for the Arts aims to strengthen arts and culture in Canada by connecting arts organizations to business patrons and by stimulating investment in the arts through matching incentives and sponsorship.

CANADA ARTS CONNECT

www.canadaartsconnect.com

CAC allows its members (Canadian Artists) to connect with its community while benefiting from its resources and promoting themselves and their work.

CANADIAN CONFERENCE OF THE ARTS (CCA)

613-238-3561

ccarts.ca

The CCA is a not-for-profit, non-partisan member-based organization that represents the interests of over 400,000 artists, cultural professionals from all disciplines of the nation's vast arts, culture and heritage community.

CANADIAN INTELLECTUAL PROPERTY OFFICE (CIPO)

1-866-997-1936

www.cipo.ic.gc.ca

Intellectual property refers to creations of the mind, such as inventions; literary and artistic works; designs; and symbols, names and images used in commerce. CIPO administers and promotes the intellectual property systems in Canada and property interests worldwide.

CANADIAN PRIVACY COMMISSION

819-994-5444

1-800-282-1376

www.privcom.gc.ca

The mandate of the Office of the Privacy Commissioner of Canada (OPC) is overseeing compliance with both the Privacy Act, which covers the personal information-handling practices of federal government departments and agencies, and the Personal Information Protection and Electronic Documents Act (PIPEDA), Canada's private sector privacy law.

CANADIAN SOCIETY OF CHILDREN'S AUTHORS, ILLUSTRATORS AND PERFORMERS (CANSCAIP)
416-515-1559
www.canscaip.org

The Canadian Society of Children's Authors, Illustrators and Performers (CANSCAIP) is a group of professionals in the field of children's culture with members from all parts of Canada. As a National Arts Service Organization, CANSCAIP supports and promotes children's literature through online forums, newsletters, workshops, meetings and other information programs for authors, illustrators, performers, parents, teachers, librarians, publishers and others.

CLINIQUE JURIDIQUE DES ARTISTS DE MONTRÉAL (CJAM)
www.cjam.info

The Clinique Juridique des Artistes de Montreal (CJAM) is a non-profit organization dedicated to offer multiple services and legal information to artists.

COMPÉTENCE CULTURE
514-499-3456
1-877-475-6287
www.competenceculture.ca

Compétence Culture's mission is to contribute to the development and implementation of strategies dedicated to the recognition of the professionalism and development of human resources with cultural sector professionals.

COPYRIGHT BOARD OF CANADA
613-952-8628
www.cb-cda.gc.ca

The Board is an economic regulatory body empowered to establish, either mandatorily or at the request of an interested party, the royalties to be paid for the use of copyrighted works.

CREATIVE BLUEPRINT
416-938-1229
www.creativeblueprint.ca

Creative Blueprint operates on the belief that emerging artists and entrepreneurs must be valued encouraged and recognized in the markets and the communities they contribute so vibrantly to. It establishes empowering venues, collaborative facilities and supportive resources to encourage independent and sustainable growth in the arts community.

CULTURAL HUMAN RESOURCES COUNCIL (CHRC)/CONSEIL DES RESSOURCES HUMAINES DU SECTEUR CULTUREL (CRHSC)
1-866-562 1535
www.culturalhrc.ca

CHRC brings together representatives of arts disciplines and cultural industries to address the training and career development needs of employers and cultural workers including artists, technical staff, managers and all others engaged professionally in the sector.

CULTURE MONTRÉAL
514-845-0303
culturemontreal.ca

Culture Montréal's mission is to assert the central role of the arts and culture in all areas of Montreal's development while encouraging cultural diversity, emerging artists and practices and public art.

DIAGONALE
514-524-6645
www.artdiagonale.org

Diagonale is an artist-run centre dedicated to contemporary art that favours proposals from artists and curators that incorporate the medium of fibres as a material or concept.

DIVERSITÉ ARTISTIQUE MONTRÉAL (DAM)
514-280-3581
www.diversiteartistique.org

DAM's mission is to promote the artists and arts organizations centered around cultural diversity in the Montreal art scene and provides services to empower them so that they realize their artistic projects and / or business.

ÉDUCALOI
1-800-NOTAIRE (668-2473)
www.educaloi.qc.ca/en

Éducaloi is a non-profit organization whose mission is to inform Quebecers of their rights and responsibilities by providing legal information in everyday language.

ENGLISH LANGUAGE ARTS NETWORK (ELAN)
514-935-3312
www.quebec-elan.org

ELAN provides advocacy, support, services and networking opportunities to English-speaking artists of all disciplines in all regions of Quebec.

FOLKLORE CANADA INTERNATIONAL

514-524-8552

www.reelmacadam.com/fci

Folklore Canada helps to arrange performance tours, support and orchestrate the arrival of foreign cultural groups to Canada as well as facilitate the participation of Canadian cultural groups in worldwide activities and performance tours abroad.

QUEBEC COLLECTIVE SOCIETY FOR THE RIGHTS OF MAKERS OF SOUND AND VIDEO RECORDINGS (SOPROQ)

514-842-5147

www.soproq.org

The SOPROQ is a non-profit organization that exists to administer the maker's royalties and to ensure that the makers of sound and video recordings benefit fully from certain rights to which they are entitled.

REGROUPEMENT DES ARTS INTERDISCIPLINAIRES DU QUÉBEC (RAIQ)

514-380-3093

www.raiq.ca

RAIQ is a non-profit organization that represents artists, collectives, companies, and presenters working in interdisciplinary arts practices in Quebec. Their mandate is to defend the interests of arts professionals and to improve the socio-economic conditions of its members.

REGROUPEMENT DES CENTRES D'ARTISTES AUTOGÉRÉS DU QUÉBEC (RCAAQ)

514-842-3984

www.rcaaq.org

RCAAQ is a network of artist-run centres and cultural organizations in Quebec; offers continuing professional education, training, and resources to contemporary artists and cultural workers.

SOCIÉTÉ CIVILE DES AUTEURS MULTIMÉDIA

514-738-8877

www.scam.ca

SCAM's mandate is to negotiate, collect and distribute the royalties of its members whose work consists mostly of audiovisual works, documentaries, radio and literary works.

SOCIETY FOR REPRODUCTION RIGHTS OF AUTHORS, COMPOSERS AND PUBLISHERS IN CANADA

1-888-876-3722

www.sodrac.ca

SODRAC negotiates collective and individual agreements with users of their works, collects royalties and redistributes them to the rights holders it represents, and controls all reproduction of its members' works on any type of audio, audiovisual, visual or digital media, as well as the use of recordings on these media.

THE BANFF CENTRE
1-800-884-7574
www.banffcentre.ca

As the largest arts and creativity incubator on the planet, The Banff Centre provides artists from around the world with the support they need to create, to develop solutions, and to make the impossible possible.

YES (YOUTH EMPLOYMENT SERVICES)
514-878-9788
www.yesmontreal.ca

As a not-for-profit organization, YES (Youth Employment Services) enriches the community by providing English-language support services to help Quebecers find employment and start and grow businesses.

FUNDING SOURCES & RESOURCES

ACTORS' FUND OF CANADA
416-975-0304
www.acldq.qc.ca

The Actors' Fund is the lifeline for Canada's entertainment industry. Over 10,000 professional members of the industry from all over Canada and in the fields of film & TV, theatre, music and dance have been helped by the Fund, which provides emergency financial aid to assist cultural workers in recovering from an illness, injury or other circumstances causing severe economic and personal hardship.

ARTSVEST
416-869-3016
www.artsvest.com

ArtsVest™ is Business for the Arts' signature matching incentive and sponsorship training program, designed to spark new business sponsorship of arts and culture and to build capacity in Canada's cultural sector.

ASSOCIATION DES CENTRES LOCAUX DE DÉVELOPPMENT DU QUÉBEC ENTREPRENEURS (ACLDQ)
418-524-0893
www.acldq.qc.ca

The ACLDQ supports the local economy and facilitates the development of collective or individual companies in Quebec by providing financial assistance to entrepreneurs.

BELL FUND
514-845-4418
www.bellfund.ca

The Bell Fund encourages and funds the creation and development of excellent Canadian digital/TV multi-platform projects.

BRAVOFACT (FOUNDATION TO ASSIST CANADIAN TALENT)
416-384-2738
www.bravofact.com

BravoFACT continues to provide awards to Canadian producers and directors who seek to create entertaining and engaging short-form content, both scripted and documentary, for Bell Media.

CANADA COUNCIL FOR THE ARTS/CONSEIL DES ARTS DU CANADA
1-800-263-5588
www.canadacouncil.ca

The Canada Council offers a broad range of grants and services to professional Canadian artists and arts organizations in music, theatre, writing and publishing, visual arts, dance, media arts, and integrated and circus arts.

CANADA ECONOMIC DEVELOPMENT FOR QUEBEC REGIONS
514-283-6412
www.dec-ced.gc.ca

At the centre of the economic development of the regions of Quebec, the Agency provides assistance to enterprises, communities and the organizations that support them through its network of business offices located throughout the province.

CANADA FILM CAPITAL
416-927.2228
www.canadafilmcapital.com

Canada Film Capital has been the leading provider of tax incentive administration and financing services to US, foreign and domestic producers.

CANADA MEDIA FUND
1-877-975-0766
www.cmf-fmc.ca

The Canada Media Fund (CMF) fosters, develops, finances and promotes the production of Canadian content and applications for all audiovisual media platforms.

CANADIAN HERITAGE
514-283-5191
www.pch.gc.ca

Canadian Heritage promotes an environment in which all Canadians take full advantage of dynamic cultural experiences, celebrating our history and heritage, and participating in building creative communities by investing in the future by supporting the arts.

CANADIAN HERITAGE - COMMUNITY CULTURAL ACTION FUND (CCAF)
514-283-8712
www.pch.gc.ca/eng/1267800383152

The CCAF aims to support and strengthen the cultural, artistic and heritage actions of official-language minority communities by providing funding to successful applicants in the form of grants or contributions.

CANADIAN INDEPENDENT FILM AND VIDEO FUND (CIFVF)
1-888-386-5555
www.cifvf.ca

A private sector funding body which supports non-theatrical film, videos and new media projects created by Canadian independent producers to enable lifelong learning.

CANADIAN PUBLIC ARTS FUNDERS (CPAF)
1-800-263-5588
cpaf-opsac.org

The mission of CPAF is to foster and support the arts in Canada through cooperation and collaboration of the federal, provincial and territorial arts councils and equivalent public arts funders.

CANADIAN WRITERS' ASSOCIATION
613-256-6937
www.canadianwritersfoundation.org/profile.html

The Canadian Writers' Foundation is the only registered charity that provides continued financial assistance to approved senior Canadian writers in times of extreme financial distress. Pierre Berton—who served on the Foundation's board for more than thirty years—considered it "essential to the literary well-being of Canada.

CONSEIL DES ARTS DE MONTRÉAL
514-280-3780
www.artsmontreal.org

The Conseil des arts de Montréal identifies, supports and recognizes excellence and innovation in the creation, production and dissemination of the arts and offers grant programs and other services for organizations working in visual arts, film and video, dance, literature, music and theatre.

CONSEIL DES ARTS ET DES LETTERS DU QUÉBEC (CALQ)
1-800-608-3350
www.calq.gouv.qc.ca

The Conseil des arts et des lettres du Québec offers provincial funds that support artistic creation, experimentation and production by offering grants and bursaries to artists and arts organizations. (Mostly in French)

DESJARDINS GROUP
http://www.desjardins.com/ca/about-us/social-responsibility-cooperation/cooperative-movement/national-involvement/index.jsp

Desjardins Group is actively involved in the community life of its members and clients by promoting and funding the organization of cultural events to: initiate young people to culture, groom new, upcoming artists and promote creativity.

ELIZABETH GREENSHIELDS FOUNDATION
514-937-9225
www.elizabethgreenshieldsfoundation.org

The Foundation provides financial assistance to artists who work in a representational style of painting, drawing, sculpting or printmaking, are in the early or developmental stage of their career, and demonstrate a commitment to making art a lifetime career.

FIDEC, ENTERTAINMENT INVESTMENT
1-877-613-3312
www.fidecinvest.com

Agency providing funding to help Québec artists penetrate international markets.

FINANCEMENT COMMUNAUTAIRE RESPONSIBLE
514-843-7296
www.acemcreditcommunautaire.qc.ca

ACEM provides accessible credit and technical support to individuals living on a low income and to organizations that do not have access to traditional forms of credit for the start up or expansion of their community or business project.

FONDATION MONTRÉAL INC.
514-872-8401
www.montrealinc.ca

The Fondation Montréal inc. is a non-profit organization with a mission to encourage the success of a new generation of promising Montreal entrepreneurs, in concert with a committed business community by investing in newly created businesses in Montreal through start-up grants and expert advice.

FONDATION SOCAN FOUNDATION

1-800-557-6226

www.fondationsocan.ca

The SOCAN Foundation, is dedicated to fostering Canadian music creation and promoting a better understanding of the role of music creators in today's society and fulfils these objectives by distributing grants and awards.

FONDS D'INVESTISSEMENT DE LA CULTURE ET DES COMMUNICATIONS l.p. (FICC)

514-394-0700

www.ficc.qc.ca

FICC provides financial partnerships to Quebec companies in the field of culture, communications and digital.

FOUNDATION OF GREATER MONTREAL

514-866-0808

www.fgmtl.org

The Community Grants Program supports initiatives that aim to improve the quality of life for individuals, families and the collectivity of the Greater Montreal area through projects in arts and culture, education, environment, health, and social development.

FOUNDATION TO ASSIST CANADIAN TALENT ON RECORDS (FACTOR)

1-877-696-2215

www.factor.ca

FACTOR is dedicated to assisting the growth and development of Canada's independent recording industry by providing funding and support to all areas of the music industry.

FUTURPRENEUR CANADA

514-861-7253 ext. 375

www.sajeenaffaires.org/en/cybf.php

In addition to assistance and resources to help you develop a top-notch business plan, Futurpreneur Canada also offers mentoring, financing and post-start-up services to ensure you and your business achieve long-term success.

GOFUNDME

www.gofundme.com

GoFundMe has quickly become the World's #1 fundraising site for personal causes and life-events and can also help you to raise money to help fund your creative projects: musicians, artists, dancers, and more.

HAROLD GREENBERG FUND/LE FONDS HAROLD GREENBURG
514-939-5000
www.bellmedia.ca/harold-greenberg-fund

The Harold Greenberg Fund/Le Fonds Harold Greenberg is a national funding organization that supports the development of Canadian dramatic feature films.

INDEPENDENT PRODUCTION FUND
514-845-4334
www.ipf.ca

The Independent Production Fund was established to provide financial support for dramatic television series created by Canadian independent producers for Canadian private broadcasters.

INDIEGOGO
www.indiegogo.com

Indiegogo is the world's most established crowdfunding platform.

INDUSTRY CANADA
1-800-328-6189
www.ic.gc.ca

Industry Canada works with Canadians in all areas of the economy and in all parts of the country to improve conditions for investment by providing financing and industry research tools to help businesses develop.

JEUNE CHAMBRE DE COMMERCE DE MONTRÉAL (JCCM)
514-845-4951
www.jccm.org

The JCCM is one of the largest networks of young business people in the world that support the development of the next generation of entrepreneurs by offering resources and funding through their foundation and awards.

KICKSTARTER
www.kickstarter.com

Kickstarter's mission is to help bring creative projects to life through crowd funding.

LIVRES CANADA BOOKS
613-562-2324
www.livrescanadabooks.com

In addition to providing direct financial assistance to publishers, Livres Canada Books has played and continues to play a significant role in advancing international sales and building export expertise among Canadian publishers.

MAXFACT
www.maxfact.org/fr/default.idigit

MaxFACT is a privately funded program that aims to promote the production of Quebec and Canadian French-language music videos and video clips of Quebec artists in languages other than French and English.

MINISTÈRE DE LA CULTURE ET COMMUNICATIONS QUÉBEC
514-873-2255
www.mcc.gouv.qc.ca

The Ministry of Culture and Communications aims to contribute to the development of identity and cultural vitality in Québec by providing funding and awards to various artistic and cultural areas and disciplines.

MINISTRE DE LA CULTURE ET DES COMMUNICATIONS
514-873-2255
www.mcccf.gouv.qc.ca

The Ministre provides funding and grants to support a variety of sectors in the Arts.

MUCHFACT
416-384-5000
www.muchfact.ca

MuchFACT considers applications requesting co-financing for music videos and music related content six times a year. Applications are judged by a committee, and successful applicants receive non-recoupable awards.

MUSICACTION
514-861-8444
www.musicaction.ca

Industry-funded non-profit organizations providing funding to support the Canadian independent recording industry and its various stakeholders.

OPERA.CA
416-591-7222
www.opera.ca

National arts service organization that provides technical and financial support to Opera.ca to the creation and development of new opera and music theatre in Canada.

PRÊT À ENTREPRENDRE
514-496-4636
www.pretaentreprendre.com

Prêt à entreprendre provides financial support and guidance to help entrepreneurs take their business to a higher growth rate.

QUEBECOR FUND
514-842-2497
www.fondsquebecor.ca

Thanks to Videotron, who provides annual contributions of over 8 million dollars on average, through grants from a broadcasting distribution undertaking (BDU), to the Canadian industry, the Quebecor Fund is able to provide support to Canadian producers through financial assistance.

RBC EMERGING ARTISTS PROJECT
www.rbc.com/community-sustainability/community/emerging-artists/index.html

At RBC, support of the arts has been a long-standing priority as we believe arts are the heart and soul of our society.

RBC CANADIAN PAINTING COMPETITION
www.rbc.com/community-sustainability/community/emerging-artists/rbc-painting-competition.html

Established in 1999, the RBC Canadian Painting Competition, with the support of the Canadian Art Foundation, is a unique initiative to help nurture and support promising new artists in the early stages of their careers; a time when they need both recognition and financial support.

ROGERS GROUP OF FUNDS
416-935-2526
www.rogersgroupoffunds.com

The Rogers Group of Funds provides a source of funding for the Canadian television and cinema industry that is informed, reliable and responsive.

SCOTIABANK GILLER PRIZE
416-934-0755
www.scotiabankgillerprize.ca

In 2005, the Giller Prize teamed up with Scotiabank to create the Scotiabank Giller Prize. It is the first-ever co-sponsorship for Canada's richest literary award for fiction. The purse increased from $25,000 to $50,000 and grew again in 2008 to $70,000. In 2014, founder Jack Rabinovitch announced that the prize purse would double, with $100,000 going to the winner and $10,000 to each finalist.

SCOTIABANK PHOTOGRAPHY AWARD
416-866-7684
www.scotiabank.com/photoaward/en/0,,6340,00.html

The Scotiabank Photography Award is a prestigious award that acknowledges the outstanding contribution that our winners have made to contemporary art & photography. These are artists who strive to invent, influence and redefine the reception of art in ways that will endure. The Scotiabank Photography Award winner exhibition is a featured primary exhibition at the Ryerson Image Centre during the Scotiabank CONTACT Photography Festival.

SHAW ROCKET FUND
403-750-4517
www.rocketfund.ca

The Shaw Rocket Fund, working in partnership with youth, is dedicated to investing in the Canadian children's and youth production industry with a broader mission of championing Canadian children's programming in Canada and around the world.

SOCIÉTÉ DE DÉVELOPPEMENT DES ENTREPREISES CULTURELLES (SODEC)
514-841-2200
www.sodec.gouv.qc.ca

SODEC's mandate is to promote and support the establishment and development of cultural enterprises, including the media, in all regions of Quebec.

TELEFILM CANADA
1-800-567-0890
www.telefilm.gc.ca

Federal agency funding and supporting the development of the Canadian audiovisual industry.

THE DANIEL LANGLOIS FOUNDATION FOR ART, SCIENCE AND TECHNOLOGY
514-987-7177
www.fondation-langlois.org

The Foundation is a private, charitable organization that aims to further human knowledge by supporting artistic, scientific and technological research.

VILLE DE MONTRÉAL
www.ville.montreal.qc.ca/culture

To encourage artists, artisans, entrepreneurs, creators and arts and culture organizations within its city limits, Montréal offers a variety of technical and financial resources and awards many prizes and distinctions to showcase the initiatives and key players of the arts and culture scene that have been recognized as being the most distinctive and innovative.

LEGAL WEBSITE RESOURCES

ALLIANCE OF CANADIAN CINEMA, TELEVISION AND RADIO ARTISTS (ACTRA)
www.actra.ca

ASSOCIATION DES PRODUCTEURS DE FILMS ET DE TÉLÉVISION DU QUÉBEC (APFTQ)
www.audiovisuel.com

CANADIAN INTELLECTUAL PROPERTY OFFICE (CIPO)
www.opic.gc.ca

CANADIAN TELEVISION FUND (CTF)
www.fondscanadiendetele.ca

SOCIÉTÉ DES AUTEURS DE RADIO, TÉLÉVISION ET CINÉMA (SARTEC)
www.sartec.qc.ca

CANADIAN SOCIETY OF COMPOSERS, AUTHORS AND MUSIC PUBLISHERS (SOCAN)
www.socan.ca

SOCIÉTÉ DE DÉVELOPPEMENT DES ENTREPRISES CULTURELLES (SODEC)
www.sodec.gouv.qc.ca

CANADIAN SOCIETY OF REPRODUCTION RIGHTS FOR ARTISTIC AND MUSICAL WORKS (SODRAC)
www.sodrac.com

SYNDICAT DES TECHNICIENS DU CINÉMA ET DE LA VIDÉO DU QUÉBEC (STCVQ)
www.stcvq.qc.ca

TELEFILM CANADA (TFC)
www.telefilm.gc.ca

UNION DES ARTISTES (UDA)
www.uniondesartistes.com
WRITER'S GUILD OF AMERICA
www.wga.org

CANADIAN PRIVACY COMMISSION
www.privcom.gc.ca

QUEBEC WRITERS FEDERATION (QWF)
www.qwf.org

ENGLISH LANGUAGE ARTS NETWORK (ELAN)
www.quebec-elan.org

INTERNET CORPORATION FOR ASSIGNED NAMES AND NUMBERS (ICANN)
www.icann.org

CANADIAN INTERNET REGISTRATION AUTHORITY (CIRA)
www.cira.ca

CANADIAN ANTI-SPAM LEGISLATION
www.fightspam.ca

OFFICE OF THE PRIVACY COMMISSIONER OF CANADA
www.priv.gc.ca

ÉDUCALOI PROVIDES LEGAL INFORMATION IN EVERYDAY LANGUAGE
www.educaloi.ca

"An immensely helpful, practical book for a business beginner who needs real 'step-by-step' info."
Hilary Radley
Hilary Radley Design Studio

"In Theatre School they teach you how to sing, dance and use your voice, but not how to take care of your finances and business affairs. Later when that catches up to you these lessons are learned the hard way. I wish I had something like this all those years ago."
Tristan D. Lalla
Award-winning actor

"More than a mere book, consider this to be a chastity belt for your psyche; use it properly and you won't get screwed."
Andy Nulman
President, Just For Laughs

"Looks great! I really liked reading everyone's quotes and found the whole thing so well put together."
Mila Aung-Thwin
EyeSteelFilm

Are you an artist who wants to make a living from your art? Let this book be your guide. Not sure that's the path you want to take? Let the expert advice from our experienced artists help you make that decision.

Updated from the popular 2004 edition, including a brand new resource section and the latest in social media strategies, the Artist's Handbook is the perfect package. It will provide you with basic business skills, keep you creative, and help you realize your dreams.

Generously supported by:

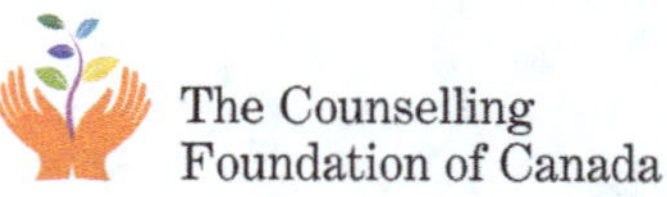